This book is to be returned on or before
the last date stamped below.

SOCIAL INTERACTION AND ETHNIC SEGREGATION

SOCIAL INTERACTION AND ETHNIC SEGREGATION

INSTITUTE OF BRITISH GEOGRAPHERS
SPECIAL PUBLICATION, No. 12

Edited by

PETER JACKSON
Department of Geography,
University College London

SUSAN J. SMITH
Nuffield College, Oxford

1981

ACADEMIC PRESS
A Subsidiary of Harcourt Brace Jovanovich, Publishers
London   New York   Toronto   Sydney   San Francisco

ACADEMIC PRESS INC. (LONDON) LTD.
24/28 Oval Road,
London NW1

United States Edition published by
ACADEMIC PRESS INC.
111 Fifth Avenue
New York, New York 10003

Copyright © 1981 by
INSTITUTE OF BRITISH GEOGRAPHERS

British Library Cataloguing in Publication Data
Social interaction and ethnic segregation.
  1. Sociology, Urban — Congresses
  I. Jackson, P.   II. Smith, S. J.
  307.7′6′0941   HT107

ISBN 0-12-379080-8

LCCN 81-67914

Text set in 11/13 Plantin
by Dobbie Typesetting Service
Printed in Great Britain by
St Edmundsbury Press, Bury St Edmunds

CONTRIBUTORS

ERROL BABOOLAL, Department of Geography, King's College London, The Strand, London, WC2R 2LS, UK

KEVIN BROWN, Centre for Urban and Regional Studies, J. G. Smith Building, University of Birmingham, PO Box 363, Birmingham, B15 2TT, UK

JOHN CATER, Edge Hill College of Higher Education, St Helens Road, Ormskirk, Lancashire, L39 4QP, UK

PETER JACKSON, Department of Geography, University College London, London, WC1H 0AP, UK

R. J. JOHNSTON, Department of Geography, University of Sheffield, Sheffield, S10 2TN, UK

CERI PEACH, St Catherine's College, Oxford, OX1 3UJ, UK

DEBORAH PHILLIPS, Faculty of Social Sciences, The Open University, Walton Hall, Milton Keynes, Bedfordshire, MK7 6AA, UK

VAUGHAN ROBINSON, Nuffield College, Oxford, OX1 1NF, UK

IAN SIMMONS, Jesus College, Oxford, OX1 3DW, UK

RON SIMS, SSRC Research Unit on Ethnic Relations, University of Aston, St Peter's College, College Road, Saltley, Birmingham B8 3TE, UK

SUSAN J. SMITH, Nuffield College, Oxford, OX1 1NF, UK

ACKNOWLEDGEMENTS

We are grateful to the following for permission to reproduce copyright material:

The American Sociological Association for Tables I, II, VII and VIII, Chapter 1, originally published as Tables 4, 6, 7 and 8 in an article by Natalie Rogoff Ramsøy (1966) 'Assortative mating and the structure of cities', *American Sociological Review* **31**, 773-786;

Edward Arnold (Publishers) Ltd for extracts from Manuel Castells' (1977) *The Urban Question: a Marxist approach*, translated by Alan Sheridan, originally published by François Maspero and distributed in the USA by MIT Press;

The Institute of British Geographers for Fig. 1, Chapter 4, originally published as Fig. 6 in an article by P. N. Jones (1978) 'The distribution and diffusion of the coloured population in England and Wales 1961-1971' from the *Transactions, Institute of British Geographers N.S.* **3**, No. 4, 515-533;

Macmillan Publishing Co., Inc. for extracts from Georg Simmel's (1955) *Conflict and the Web of Group Affiliations*, translated by K. H. Wolff and R. Bendix; from R. E. Park's *Race and Culture*, edited by E. C. Hughes (1950); and from R. E. Park's *Human Communities*, edited by E. C. Hughes (1952);

The Editor, *New Community* for an extract from an article by N. Levine and T. Nayar 'Modes of adaptation by Asian immigrants in Slough', **4**, No. 3 (Autumn 1975), 356-365;

Oxford University Press for Fig. 2, Chapter 4, originally published as Fig. 4.2b in J. Shepherd, J. Westaway and T. Lee (1974) *A Social Atlas of London*;

Tavistock Publications Ltd for an extract from Frank Parkin's (1979) *Marxism and Class Theory: a bourgeois critique*, published in the USA by Columbia University Press;

The University of Chicago Press for extracts from R. H. Turner's Introduction to R. E. Park's *On Social Control and Human Behaviour: selected essays*, edited by R. H. Turner (1967); and for extracts from an article by R. E. Park 'The urban community as a spatial pattern and a moral order', reprinted from *The Urban Community*, edited by E. W. Burgess (1926).

PREFACE

These papers have been collected to represent a distinctive geographical perspective on the analysis of social life, stressing the importance of space beyond the mere constraints of distance. According to Park, the city's spatial order reflects its moral or social order, and social distances are accurately reflected in physical distances. In our introduction, we have attempted to elaborate upon this view, offering a broader interpretation of ethnic segregation in terms of social interaction. This perspective also derives ultimately from Park, particularly reflecting Georg Simmel's sociological teaching and the pragmatism of John Dewey and William James. The volume represents various frontiers of research in social geography, combining theoretical insights with empirical evidence and methodological innovation.

The authors include both senior academics and younger research workers, coming in many cases directly from recent experiences 'in the field'. Their work is frequently still in progress, as is reflected in the vitality of their writing which we as editors have sought to retain.

Essays deal with both positive and negative aspects of social interaction, ranging from studies of ethnic intermarriage to studies of intergroup crime. Several others focus on residential segregation as a spatial realization of interaction of various qualities, representing the balance of discriminatory and voluntary tendencies towards clustering or concentration. The interpretation of this balance is controversial and several authors dismiss a simplistic formulation of the issues in terms of the crude concepts of 'choice' or 'constraint'. An alternative formulation emerges which recognizes the crucial role of the state in the city's social geography.

The papers were among those originally presented at a conference on 'Current Research in Social Geography', generously sponsored by the SSRC at the School of Geography, Oxford, in September–October 1980. We are grateful to the SSRC for their financial support; to all who contributed papers or discussion at the conference; to Clyde Mitchell for his characteristically thoughtful comments on an earlier draft of our introduction; and to Academic Press for its encouragement and interest in this project.

August 1981

Peter Jackson
Susan J. Smith

CONTENTS

Introduction

PETER JACKSON

Department of Geography, University College, London, UK

SUSAN J. SMITH

Nuffield College, Oxford, UK

> In society we not only live together, but at the same time we live apart, and human relations can always be reckoned, with more or less accuracy, in terms of distance.
>
> Robert E. Park

One of the most encouraging aspects about collecting these essays together for the present volume has been the growing sense that major issues are being confronted, not avoided. Our two themes of interaction and segregation contain implicit questions about the nature of social structure itself. In response, the authors produce a blend of empirical detail and substantive theory which lays the foundation for more accurate interpretations and adequate theoretical explanations of observed spatial patterns. For example, the balance between voluntary and discriminatory forces in the evolution and maintenance of ethnic segregation has long been a controversial subject among social geographers, and one of the main achievements of this volume is to clarify the issues involved in this debate. This so-called 'choice/constraint' formulation which has characterized much research into Asian segregation in Britain is heavily criticized for its theoretical inadequacy and lack of clarity in previous empirical analyses. A clearer awareness of the extent to which empirical work in British cities has taken for granted the context of advanced capitalism prompts greater consideration of the role of the state, and provides an avenue for *rapprochement* between radical 'Marxist' approaches and more conservative 'bourgeois' positivistic approaches in social geography (see Herbert, 1980). It is our aim in introducing these papers to explore this avenue, focusing on the relationships between social interaction, social structure and spatial segregation.

Appropriately, the opening papers address the theme of social interaction as it has been absorbed by geographers from the work of Robert E. Park and the Chicago school. The centrality and persistent inspiration of Park's work to the development of social geography can scarcely be doubted. The corpus of his work, which includes three volumes of his collected papers (Park, 1950, 1952, 1955) as well as

1

the books which were published during his lifetime, represents a complex accretion of ideas, the interpretation of which is frequently hazardous and always appears to be controversial. Something of that controversy is conveyed in the present volume which presents a variety of interpretations of the social order. Here, however, we are specifically concerned with Park's contribution to an interactionist sociology. His contribution was significant in its time for turning attention away from biological theories of race towards cultural theories: 'instinct' was replaced by 'attitude', a product of contact and communication between groups; the concept of 'race' and 'racial differences' were themselves revealed to be subjective and problematical.

Park himself probably contributed more ideas of lasting value in the field of inter-group relations than in any other area of sociology, and his notion of a relationship between social and physical distance (Park, 1926) has been influential in the development of 'spatial sociology' as represented by the authors whose work was collected in the recent volume by Peach (1975). This body of work, based on the index of dissimilarity—a measure of residential segregation developed by Otis and Beverly Duncan and subsequently applied by many others, including Stanley Lieberson, Karl and Alma Taeuber and Nathan Kantrowitz—has been interpreted as reflecting positivistic philosophies which are increasingly coming under attack. In a recent critique of positivism in human geography, for example, David Ley (1980) quotes Park's early statement on the relationship between social and physical distance as representative of this position:

> Reduce all social relations to relations of space and it would be possible to apply to human relations the fundamental logic of the natural sciences.
>
> Park (cited by Ley, 1980; p.4)

Peach, in the present volume, thus cites this and other quotations from Park's (1926) paper to support his interpretation of Park's ideas as advocating the development of 'social physics'. This approach can be traced back as far as Kant's insistence that the objects of natural science can only be thought of in terms of their space relations, a concept preserved in Simmel's notion of social space and his analogy between human beings and physical atoms. Indeed, Park did examine the positions of people grouped in social space as an expression of the social relations existing between them. That this was not Park's primary concern however, is demonstrated by Entrikin's (1980) recent examination of the supposed positivism of Park's work. He reveals the irony which led human geography to take Park as inspiration for greater quantitative sophistication, when Park himself considered human geography to be a pale idiographic shadow of his own grandiose nomothetic 'human ecology'.

Our own interpretation of Park's ideas is thus much broader. In this we follow Ralph Turner in the introduction to his selection of Park's papers *On Social Control and Collective Behaviour* (Turner, 1967). Although he agrees that Park gave impetus to quantification through his formulation of the idea of social distance as a readily quantifiable phenomenon, he considers the evidence of Park's writings to suggest that he used less and less quantitative material as time went on, such that 'Park is on the side of *verstehen* sociology as opposed to positivistic approaches':

include
anthropology
in lit review

More characteristic, then, than Park's advocacy of a rigorously scientific approach to sociology are his endorsements of the "methods of anthropologists" and his insistence on the crucial place of history.

Turner (1967; p.xx)

A typical statement of the former attitude is contained in Park's essay *The City: suggestions for the investigation of behavior in the urban environment:*

> Anthropology, the science of man, has been mainly concerned up to the present with the study of primitive peoples. But civilized man is quite as interesting an object of investigation, and at the same time his life is more open to observation and study. Urban life and culture are more varied, subtle and complicated, but the fundamental motives are in both instances the same. The same patient methods of observation which anthropologists like Boas and Lowie have expended on the study of life and manners of the North American Indian might be even more fruitfully employed in the investigation of the customs, beliefs, social practices, and general conceptions of life prevalent in Little Italy on the Lower North Side in Chicago, or in recording the more sophisticated folkways of the inhabitants of Greenwich Village and the neighborhood of Washington Square, New York.

Park (1952; p.15)

Hannerz (1980) has also drawn attention to these aspects of Park's work, best illustrated perhaps through his influence on the group of 'Chicago ethnographers' which included Wirth, Zorbaugh, Anderson, Cressey and Thrasher, as well as the collaborative team of Park and Miller themselves. Park in turn recalled that it was James' pragmatism that taught him that

> . . . the real world was the experience of actual men and women and not the abbreviated and shorthand descriptions of it that we call knowledge.

Park (cited by Rock, 1979; p.96)

Representative of his opinions on the importance of history is the following quotation from his essay *The Nature of Race Relations*:

> Looking at race relations in the long historical perspective, this modern world which seems destined to bring persistently all the diverse and distant peoples of the earth together within the limits of a common culture and a common social order, strikes one as something not merely unique, but millennial. Nevertheless, this new civilization is the product of essentially the same historical processes that preceded it. The same forces which brought about the diversity of races will inevitably bring about, in the long run, a diversity in the peoples of the modern world corresponding to that which we have in the old. It is likely, however, that these will be based in the future less on inheritance and race and rather more on culture and occupation. That means that race conflicts in the modern world, which is already or presently will be a single great society, will be more and more in the future confused with, and eventually superseded by, the conflict of classes.

Park (1950; p.116)

Turner's essay also draws attention to the importance of Georg Simmel's influence on Park's work, particularly on the role of conflict in social interaction. It is well known that Park received his only formal instruction in sociology from Simmel while he was studying in Berlin—Park says as much in *An Autobiographical*

Note (Park, 1950). Simmel was a dialectical thinker, concerned with the systematic way in which identities are negotiated, assumed and discarded. It was from him that Park developed his notion of social interaction as involving four basic processes: competition, conflict, accommodation and assimilation. Matthews identifies this as a means by which

> The relations among groups of persons could be classified into a four-stage cycle arranged according to the amount of conscious, willed, symbolic communication which took place during the interaction.
>
> Matthews (1977; p.160-161)

It is not necessary to believe in the completeness of the cycle to appreciate the dynamic regrouping and adjustment it implies. It was developed in Park and Burgess' (1921) *Introduction to the Science of Sociology*—a volume of readings which, incidentally, included ten selections from Simmel (far more than by any other author), and none from Marx or Weber.

As Donald Levine has shown in the introduction to his selection of Simmel's essays *On Individuality and Social Forms*, there are certain ideas which Park appears to have explicitly derived from Simmel, including a view of conflict as "the oscillation between out-group hostilities and in-group morale; the ways in which group antagonisms provide a basis for stabilizing social structure" (Levine 1971; p.1ii). This adds another dimension to a consensualist interpretation of Park as exclusively interested in the study of collective behaviour and concerted action, for Simmel regarded conflict as a necessary integrative force of group life and as a force instrumental to the survival of society:

> A certain amount of discord, inner divergence and outer controversy, is organically tied up with the very elements that ultimately hold the group together; it cannot be separated from the unity of the sociological structure . . .
> Without . . . aversion, we could not imagine what form modern urban life, which every day brings everybody in contact with innumerable others, might possibly take. The whole inner organization of urban interaction is based on an extremely complex hierarchy of sympathies, indifferences, and aversions of both the most short-lived and the most enduring kind . . . antipathy . . . engenders the distances and aversions without which we could not lead the urban life at all. The extent and combination of antipathy, the rhythm of its appearance and disappearance, the forms in which it is satisfied, all these, along with the more literally unifying elements, produce the metropolitan form of life in its irresolvable totality; and what at first glance appears in it as dissociation, actually is one of its elementary forms of sociation.
>
> Simmel (1955; pp.17-20)

Our view, then, of Park's contribution to geography, draws inspiration from those elements of Simmel's formalism which, together with the pragmatism of James and Dewey, were developed in Chicago to portray society as fluid, its 'structure' negotiable, contoured by the flexible boundaries of interpersonal relationships. Simmel, for instance, often chose not to write of society (*Gesellschaft*) but of sociation (*Vergesellschaft*) as continuing collective action. Society was no more than an abstract term summarizing the extent of interaction. Similarly, Dewey observed

> Society is of course but the relations of individuals to one another in this form and that. And all relations are interactions, not fixed moulds . . . I often wonder what meaning is given to 'society' by those who oppose it to the intimacies of personal intercourse such as friendship.
>
> Dewey (1948; p.436)

Envisaging a world of meanings conferred upon people and objects during social interaction, it is hardly surprising that Park should tend to generalize towards process rather than towards social structure. (In fact, no comprehensive theory of social stratification ever emerged from the Chicago school.) Turner's essay illustrates this amply. He suggests that Park's view of the city's moral order might be labelled one of 'dynamic disequilibrium':

> Implicit in his formulations are potential states of equilibrium—the end points of all his idealized natural histories—and the constant pull in the direction of these states keeps the system changing. An idealized state of assimilation stands at the end of conflict; institutionalization is the end product of collective behavior; public opinion process rigidifies into the mores. But either those states are never reached or the approach to one equilibrium creates another disequilibrium that starts a second sequence before the first is finished.
>
> Turner (1967; p.xxii)

Thus, for Park, conflict was technically pre- or extrasocial; a source of disruption or of constructive change in the social order, not constitutive of society as such (Levine, 1971). Much of his work embraces similar seeming dualisms and sets them within a wider social and spatial order. What begins as mere contact or spatial juxtaposition may provoke some form of opposition, competition or conflict but is ultimately accommodated within a new (always provisional) organization (see Matthews, 1977; pp.132-143). In this creative synthesis, differences are resolved but their components retained, not constantly extinguished as an interpretation of Park's work purely in terms of a Darwinian struggle for survival would suggest.

Park and his colleagues at Chicago thus drew together those threads of formalism and pragmatism identified by Rock (1979) as necessary for the development of a somewhat diffuse but influential sociology of symbolic interactionism. The extent of this influence in social geography is apparent in a recent essay by Bobby Wilson (1980). His account reveals how theories of social space deriving from Emile Durkheim and elaborated by French geographers and sociologists such as Chombart de Lauwe and Sorre are directly related to Mead's conceptions of symbolic interaction by way of the Chicago school of human ecology. Turner's denial of Park's economic determinism (a criticism frequently levelled at his ecological analyses) suggests further that his brand of interactionism may not be far removed from that of the Marxian humanists; it may contribute to an exploration of the common ground between humanism and structuralism called for by Brown (see Ch. 9).

> Park reminds us that commercial bargaining is a highly evolved social transaction, and thus different in kind from the biotic competition that underlies social life. Nevertheless, when Park sought to specify just what constitutes the ecological order among

human beings, he sometimes referred to impersonal and utilitarian dealings as contrasted to relationships governed by positive sentiment and obligation. Furthermore the emergence of Marxian class consciousness through a group's discovery of their true interests supplies an excellent instance of the translation of ecological competition into social conflict.

Turner (1967; p.xxx)

Park's notion of social interaction as involving a movement between accommodation and conflict, taken in conjunction with his ideas on social and spatial distance, thus comprise a most appealing theoretical basis for the interests of contemporary social geography. It is a basis which, in seeking to illuminate the dynamic processes underlying ethnic residential segregation, nevertheless requires a clear conception of social *structure*. The fruitful interplay of these two facets of social life is illustrated in the essays collected in the present volume.

Developing his own particular reading of Park, Peach (Ch. 1) accords a central position to the debate over the relative merits of Marxism and 'bourgeois' positivism, and is more sympathetic to the latter than to the former. Characteristically, Peach provides an admirable exposition of the actual mechanics of the methods employed—in this case contingency table analyses. The attractions of empirically testable predictions derived from positivistic analysis are contrasted with the lack of such features in most Marxist analyses. Yet his chapter demonstrates equally well how positivistic social science can mislead, critically re-assessing papers by Kennedy and Ramsøy which had been previously accepted by other social scientists. In this, his critique also represents a vindication of the *spatial* school of urban sociology.

This theme is taken up by Smith (Ch. 2), who explores the contention that 'negative' (low quality) as well as 'positive' (high quality) social interaction arises from spatial propinquity. Her paper emphasizes the advantages to be gained from probing beneath aggregate statistical associations to examine crime as one of several forms of social interaction which vary in quality and quantity. Crime is interpreted as part of a continuum of social interaction from intermarriage at the positive end to sectarian murder at the other. This allows insight to be gleaned from the existing geographical literature on the spatial structure of social relations, specifically linking social and physical distance. However, crime is a type of social interaction even less amenable to the inference of its content and meaning from its 'objective' measurable form than is intermarriage (Peach's measure of social distance). Thus an appeal is made to Park's (and Weber's) *verstehen* sociology, as well as to his positivism, demonstrating one process contributing to the negotiation of ethnic identity, and alluding to a tacit but critical distinction between social structure as an analytic *a priori* and as an emergent product of social interaction (but focusing primarily on the latter).

We would therefore support Peach's suggestion that humanistic and behavioural geographies do not seek to replace positivism. Instead, we argue that, like Marxism in fact, phenomenology and related non-positivistic viewpoints (Mercer and Powell, 1972) provide a critique of conventional positivistic approaches, building upon them rather than representing a complete alternative (see Entrikin, 1976; Tuan, 1976; Smith, 1979). Our interpretation of the core of empirical papers below elucidates this argument.

Baboolal's (Ch. 3) paper is basically a descriptive spatial analysis at the detailed level of small census area data. The paper is not without theoretical interest, however, particularly in the choice of methodology. The familiarity of the index of dissimilarity (ID) obviates the need for much discussion in the paper. An important quality of the index, however, in terms of the conceptualization of segregation and interaction, is its ability to measure the mixing of population subgroups within areal subdivisions, rather than, say, the spatial separation of individuals according to measures of simple physical distance. The existence of the Shankill–Falls divide in Belfast (Boal, 1969, 1970) provides clear evidence of the importance of the distinction between spatial mixing and physical distance. The index of dissimilarity is supplemented in Baboolal's paper by the recently revived P$\star$ 'isolation' index (Lieberson, 1980), which acknowledges the importance in the measurement of social interaction of the relative size of minority groups. It exploits the fact that the probabilities of members of one group interacting with members of another group are not equal if the groups are of different sizes. Although the P$\star$ index conceptualizes segregation in terms of interaction, it differs from the index of dissimilarity in describing (for a specific group in the city) the average probability of interacting with some specified population, based on the distribution of persons by subarea (Lieberson's definition, quoted by Baboolal). Although the P$\star$ index loses some of the immediacy of interpretation characteristic of the index of dissimilarity, it is equally easy to calculate and provides relevant additional information, as witnessed by its increasing use in geographical analyses (see Taeuber, 1980; Robinson, 1980).

Baboolal's focus on the geographical pattern of immigrant concentration in south London is complemented by Robinson's (Ch. 7) process-orientated approach. He employs Monte Carlo simulation to model ethnic residential change in Blackburn. Recognizing the lack of a coherent theoretical basis previously ascribed to the technique in several American studies, Robinson insists that stochastic models of this type are only valid when used as a simple monitoring device. The simulated pattern simply reflects quantitative changes in the initial variables, themselves chosen to reflect apparently relevant social processes. Simmons' (Ch. 4) paper focuses more directly on the theoretical issues involved in accounting for processes of social change. He discusses the residential segregation of Asians in Britain with particular reference to the London Borough of Hounslow and rejects a crude 'choice/constraint' framework in his account of the cultural continuities which migration threatens. His conception of assimilation as a process involving "the transplanting of one social system into another, and the gradual adjustment of each, not necessarily harmoniously, as they mutually interact", relates closely to Park's definition of social interaction discussed above. It alludes particularly to the existence of a 'dynamic disequilibrium', recognizing the possibility of conflict as well as accommodation.

The vocabulary of ethnic relations seems to be fundamentally quixotic. The

Negro ghetto (Morrill, 1965) was transformed a decade later into the black inner city (Ley, 1974), reflecting changes in minority group consciousness rather than any dramatic change in the city's social geography, either here or in the USA. In Britain in the 1960s, policies of dispersal were discussed (Cullingworth, 1969) reflecting a negative evaluation of 'segregation' as inevitably the product of discrimination. Once the term began to lose these exclusively negative connotations, through the recognition that ethnic concentration had at least some advantages for the immigrant groups themselves, the evaluation of 'segregation' began to change. It was eventually realized that in some important respects "segregation just is" (Kantrowitz, 1980).

Thus it can be argued that voluntary segregation (as illustrated by evidence of internal sorting) represents no more than selective interaction by the minority group. In the present volume, Deborah Phillips (Ch. 5) most closely approaches this interpretation. According to her analysis of Asians in Leicester, cultural, religious and linguistic differences "provide a basis for social interaction, community organization and voluntary segregation". The Asians in Leicester are a particularly complex group (not a single community in any sociologically meaningful sense). Earlier immigrants from India and Pakistan were joined by an influx of 20 000 exiles from East Africa between 1968 and 1978. Kenyans, Ugandans and Tanzanians are now the dominant Asian groups. Predominantly Gujarati in origin, the majority are Hindu. Their arrival intensified the process of 'internal sorting'. But this process was not, however, entirely voluntary and represents an interesting example of discriminatory managerialism. Phillips reports instances of active discrimination *within* the Asian population, with East African Hindu vendors in the Belgrave area refusing to sell to Pakistani Muslims, who consequently avoided the area.

The managerialist theme is pursued by Cater (Ch. 8). He alludes to the ecological school's inability to say anything meaningful about the housing market, and thus to account for processes of residential differentiation (the criticism of Bassett and Short, 1980). Cater studies a particular group of 'urban managers' (estate agents) and their effects on patterns of Asian residential segregation in Bradford. His analysis shows the extent to which Asian residents are concentrated both areally and according to housing tenure. He also shows how those estate agents who serve the (predominantly Pakistani) Asian community also operate as 'gatekeepers' to a limited housing market.

Although ecological theory may have little to say concerning 'urban managerialism' in either the public or private sectors, the broader interactionist perspective which we derive from Park provides a context for the interpretation of certain processes and the resulting locational changes observed in Cater's study. He reports a propensity for Asians to buy property at the very bottom of the price range, which can be interpreted either in terms of a return orientation and a lack of commitment to the UK or, in Cater's words, as "a conflict-evading function — a negative reaction to attitudes prevalent in the host society". This is little more than a reformulation of the 'choice/constraint' concept. But another trend — the demand by Asians for property on the fringes of the major immigrant areas — cannot be fully explained in

terms of either choice or constraint, internal sorting or discrimination. Rather, it seems to reflect what Smith (Ch. 2) refers to as the symbolic status meanings attached to space. Some Asians, particularly the relatively less deprived members of the Gujarati community, are willing to pay a premium for residential locations outside the worst areas of the inner city which are already relinquished by Whites for minority group residence, but they are apparently unwilling to lose all touch with their fellow ethnics. The importance of such a process for understanding changes in Asian segregation seems to justify Simmons' plea for a focus on the boundaries to ethnic areas rather than on what those boundaries supposedly enclose—a plea made earlier by Barth (1969) and recently elaborated by Jackson (1980).

From the evidence, it is clear that arguments explaining segregation purely in terms of discrimination cannot be sustained. However, the controversy over the relative strength of 'choice' and 'constraint' has rarely been very enlightening, and the present essays suggest both the theoretical bankruptcy of the concept and the impossibility of reaching any empirically satisfying consensus with the concept as it stands. Partly the problem is one of different conceptualizations of segregation. Peach's (Ch. 1) clear exposition and reconciliation of the apparently basic differences between the positions of Robinson (1979) and Sims (Ch. 6) illustrates this amply. Sims' paper pinpoints the difficulties of inferring social processes directly from spatial patterns despite the apparent simplicity of the index of dissimilarity in verbal, mathematical and logical terms. A more fundamental problem of interpretation derives from cultural differences between Asian groups and the majority British society, influencing the very conception of segregation. In this vein, Simmons (Ch. 4) argues that "free choice is not in the nature of traditional Indian and Pakistani family life". Phillips (Ch. 5) too identifies how traditional Indian and Pakistani lifestyles, presumably reflecting the expression of choice, are based on "intense social interaction within the group and a complex network of kin and friendship links" which might appear to be constraints from the viewpoint of Western independent individualism. Given the degree of internal sorting among diverse Asian subgroups, it is also quite possible for the operation of voluntary segregation by one group to imply some measure of enforced segregation for other groups, as in the previously mentioned case of Leicester's Gujarati East Africans.

Phillips' (Ch. 5) paper also provides one of the best examples of our contention that ethnicity may be interpreted as a matter of negotiable identity, rather than simply as a reflection of innate characteristics. She presents the case of dispersing Asians in Leicester, following a pattern of non-assimilation, who forsake the protection offered by spatial isolation and the positive aspects of clustering. They face increased conflict with the majority white society and may react by giving greater adherence to tradition, with women being confined to the home to avoid 'cultural contamination'. The interplay between social and physical distance can be quite complex and the adequacy of a simple 'choice/constraint' dichotomy in *social* space is therefore questioned.

In pointing to the weaknesses of existing conceptual frameworks, the papers are not merely destructive. Rather, they offer the possibility of a sound theoretical basis for the interpretation of detailed patterns and processes of residential segregation, teased out from a wealth of empirical analyses. Here, Brown's (Ch.9) paper provides an appropriate starting point. Recognizing the central importance of power relationships, he adopts a wholly theoretical Marxist stance. To date, positivistic social science has proved itself unable or unwilling to deal with the challenge which Marxism makes of its basic working assumptions. How can we take as 'given' the social, political and economic context of late twentieth century advanced capitalism, while simultaneously ignoring the progressively growing role of the state? Value-free geography was long ago declared to be a myth (Pahl, 1967; Buttimer, 1974) yet it seems curiously persistent in positivistic social geography.

This is the point of Brown's critique of members of the Chicago school who worked within the 'natural' order of capitalism. Their descriptive analyses relate each part of the city to an essentially simple organic or moral totality. Brown, however, specified a more complex 'whole' and seeks to fill the gaps left by the ecologists' assumptions that "reality is present in appearance". His exploration of the middle ground between Marxian humanism and structuralism provides the basis for his theoretically more sophisticated interpretation of the 'choice/constraint' concept. It also alerts us to the existence and geographical relevance of not one but many established conceptions of Marxism.

Brown adopts a structuralist position to criticize more liberal theories which fail to probe beyond observed measurable facts. However, not least because of the charges of rationalism and functionalism often lodged against structuralism, "the case for a (complementary) lower level of generalization" (the humanists' stress on experience) is also examined.

The distinction between humanism and structuralism in Marxist thought is usually made with reference to the controversial 'epistemological break' identified by Althusser in Marx's own writings. The break occurred about 1845 and, arguably, divides his work into (early) ideological or historicist and (later) scientific theses.

Althusser's structuralism, concerned to develop Marxism as a science, rejects the role of man or free will. It is a basically anti-humanist 'theory without a subject' in which individuals are totally constrained by a set of economic, political and ideological determinants. The notion of structure here does not refer to observed social relations but to a more abstract level of reality which precludes choice and brands even the distinction between voluntary and involuntary segregation as bourgeois and untenable (Shah, 1979; p.364). The very concept of a free thinking individual is the 'ideological effect' of capitalist society. Thus Shah asserts in his detailed Althusserian analysis of Asian residential segregation in London that

> The phenomenon of segregation does not constitute a problem 'to be explained', but is itself the 'explanation' or 'proof' of the interactions and determinations of the economic, political and ideological structures.
>
> Shah (1979; p.357)

Ethnic residential segregation is an integral part of the class position of the minority groups concerned. As people are born into predetermined social structures, their spatial differentiation follows logically.

> The distribution of residential locations follows the general laws of the distribution of products and, consequently, brings about regroupings according to the social capacity of the subjects, that is to say, in the capitalist system, according to their income, their professional status, educational level, ethnic group, age group, etc.
>
> Castells (1977; p.169)

This is the key to Peach's (Ch. 1) dissatisfaction with a Marxist approach which involves the relegation of space to a mere record of social relations and a view of segregation as "the end-point of economic relations rather than the starting point for social analysis".

Althusserianism has been one of the most controversial of the structuralist theories imported from France over the last few years. Until then the characteristic form of British Marxist theory was the study of history, a tradition vigorously reaffirmed by E. P. Thompson, whose writings, spanning more than twenty years and emphasizing the role of man's conscious choice and active will, form an impressive body of socialist-humanist work. His polemical treatise *The Poverty of Theory* (1978) sets his 'culturalism' (see Johnson, 1981) firmly against Althusser's structuralism, raising issues which continue to dominate intellectual debate on the left.

Concerned by the absolutism implied in both the structuralists' and the culturalists' positions, Brown alludes to Gramsci for the common ground between them; between choice and constraint as they are represented not only in locational options, but also in the degrees of freedom or restriction in social, economic and political spheres of life. It is a move endorsed by Hall whose view is that the humanist-structuralist debate

> leaves us with a set of matching sectarianisms — the theoretical absolutism of Althusser's theory, the implicit absolutism of Thompson's "Poverty". Against both we need Gramsci's "pessimism of the intellect, optimism of the will".
>
> Hall (1981; p.385)

Whether Gramsci's Marxism is ideology or science, humanist or structuralist, is open to debate (Hall *et al.*, 1977), for his ideas (written in prison, and therefore sometimes necessarily undeveloped) have been absorbed by both schools of thought, and have attracted a resurgence of interest from political theorists in recent years. By examining ideology at the level of popular knowledge, Gramsci was able to specify its effects on 'common sense' as a means of dealing with everyday life. He thus drew attention to the *non-coercive* aspects of domination through his theory of hegemony, asserting the ability of those holding a monopoly of power to secure the voluntary and spontaneous consent of their subordinates. Racism, an institutionalized ideology, plays a role in the establishment of hegemony, representing "the systematic structural determinant which sets the limits upon the social actions of black people". Within this over-riding constraint, it is through race also that 'class consciousness' may be realized. On the one hand, "particular forms of action are negotiated" in relation to the nature of structural subordination (so that the return migration orientation of Asians in Britain can be interpreted as a negotiated solution to the migrant workers' position in a racist society). On the other hand, forms of resistance or opposition also have to be expressed through race. Brown's emphasis on 'negotiated cultural strategies' and 'dynamic negotiated processes' gives a firmer grounding (in the social structure and the role of the state) to the notion of ethnicity as a negotiable variable (the interpretation we derive from Park).

Like Brown, Johnston (Ch. 10) (from his philosophical position as 'naive realist') finds structuralism attractive, but insufficient to demonstrate the central importance of the state in advanced capitalism and its relevance for social geography. He suggests the distinction that economic geography deals with the sphere of production and distribution while social geography deals with consumption. He argues that most goods are now provided by some combination of private and public sectors, rather than exclusively by either, so that most goods must now be recognized as 'impurely' distributed. Thus his emphasis is on the role of the state, particularly the local state, as it influences the geography of consumption. He illustrates, using specific examples, that instrumentalist, managerialist and pluralist strategies each account for the spatial variations encountered in different sets of circumstances.

Managerialism is a theme whose influence on patterns of ethnic residential segregation is alluded to by Phillips (Ch. 5) and specifically investigated by Cater (Ch. 8). Cater, with Johnston (1980) laments the limited research linking managerialism with spatial pattern and process, and suggests from his own focus on the owner-occupied housing sector that estate agents (Asian and white) are more than the passive intermediaries in the housing market that they claim to be. (We might suggest their role as mediators of the institutionalized racism specified by Brown, Ch. 9.) However, it is in Johnston's examples of instrumentalism and pluralism that a more truly voluntarist notion of class and social structure emerges, tying in closely with the interactionist framework attributed to Park. Instrumentalism implies the 'downwards' use of power whereby (in Johnston's example) high income suburban consumption 'classes' are able to create a separate local government unit and so maintain the exclusive character of their suburb. Pluralism, in contrast, denotes the 'upwards' use of power by local protest movements and neighbourhood organizations vying to influence the activities of the local state (in its role as planning authority).

This aspect of voluntarism in social life is developed in contemporary extentions of the Weberian foundations of action theory (see Binns, 1977). Weber's contribution to the debate on methodology in early twentieth century Germany was an attempt to bridge the rift between hermeneutics (the method of studying culture through interpretation) and more positivistic methods of analysis. He was intimately concerned with the differential distribution of power, and formally excluded social life not orientated towards the negotiation of domination and subordination from his theory. Like Brown's (Ch. 9) contribution to the present volume, he offered the possibility of a theory sensitive to the structural dimensions of society without violating a commitment to the methods of a humanistic *verstehen* sociology. Several essays further a theoretical interpretation of ethnic residential segregation in this vein through their recognition and specification of the patterned exchanges sustaining *observed* structural boundaries.

Like Marx, Weber saw class conflict as an endemic feature of capitalist society. Unlike Marx, he defined classes primarily in relation to the distributive sphere (at the level of market interaction), rather than in terms of access to, or control over, the means of production. His concept of property classes, particularly the housing classes introduced by Rex and Moore (1967) and elaborated upon by Pahl (1972) and by Rex and Tomlinson (1979), is the branch of Weberian theory most developed in social geography. As Rex (1980a) has recently reiterated, in Sparkbrook it was in the sphere of housing that class interests were expressed *through ethnicity*. This can be seen as the explanation for a specific pattern arising from the fundamental constraints of racism pinpointed by Brown. Subsequently, Rex (1980b) identified an inherently spatial dimension to these inner city housing classes, recognizing that the occupants of General Improvement and Housing Action Areas, irrespective of tenure, comprise a new bottom rung to the housing ladder.

Despite the extension and popularity of the housing class formulation, which is discussed critically by both Brown (Ch.9) and Johnston (Ch.10), it is Weber's introduction of the concept of social honour or prestige which has more generally been understood as a successful attempt to improve upon Marx's model of stratification (see Parkin, 1971). Weber's notion of status, "the positive or negative social estimation of honour", has been successfully employed in the analysis of ethnic 'communities' by Neuwirth (1969). Ethnic segregation is here interpreted not simply as the result of economic competition, but also as an outcome of the desire to protect or maintain status. The salience of this interpretation rests in its application specifically to *ethnic* segregation; ethnic 'honour' is the only form of social honour which does not necessarily or typically rest upon an economic hierarchy. The importance of opportunities to accrue symbolic (status) rewards where economic or political power is negligible is also discussed by Smith (Ch.2) who identifies them as a rationale for the adoption of ethnic criteria as a basis upon which to organize the meaning of social action in the inner city. Ethnic status is thus reflected in the symbolic use of territory.

Perhaps the most comprehensive analysis of negotiation and voluntarism within the social structure is offered in Parkin's (1979) extension of Weber's notion of social closure. It is a tacit acknowledgement of flexibility in the use of power to secure both symbolic and material rewards, or, in Weber's terms, to procure goods, gain a position in life and find inner satisfaction (Weber, 1968; p.302). Parkin's thesis stems from a recognition, with Marxists such as Carchedi (1975) and Poulantzas (1975), that the identification of classes at the productive level must be supplemented by analyses taking full account of the symbolic and behavioural determinants of class. Parkin's argument thus crystallizes around the difficulty of identifying behaviourally significant class boundaries within pre-defined Marxian moulds of the social structure Parkin, 1979; pp.11-28). He recognizes the increasing significance of linguistic, religious, racial and cultural cleavages which apparently cut across economic divisions, and asserts that

> distributive arrangements and social formations should not be regarded as side effects of a particular productive system, such that the latter is granted some sort of theoretical primacy over the former.
>
> Parkin (1979; p.9)

Boal (1980), in the tradition of Neuwirth (1969) and Phillips (Ch. 5), demonstrates the significance of a theoretical interpretation of spatial patterns of segregation in terms of the process of social closure. Exclusionary closure, mounted against Asian groups through white control over access to housing, precludes free locational choice by the ethnic minorities. In response, these groups strengthen their claim to ethnic territory as an expanding resource which facilitates the maintenance of social and cultural separation. There is also evidence of 'dual closure', the manipulation of power within the subordinate group as well as against it, as evidenced by the exclusion of Pakistani Muslims from the Hindu dominated Belgrave area. Parkin provides some explanation for the phenomenon of 'dual closure' in his suggestion that less energy is expended effecting exclusionary closure against a visible and vulnerable minority group than in mounting collective usurpationary action against a powerful dominant class. This immediately suggests a rationale for the magnitude and directedness of social reaction to crime in the ethnically mixed area examined by Smith (Ch. 2).

According to Parkin's social closure thesis, classes are defined by reference to their mode of collective action, rather than by their place in the productive process or the division of labour. They are a product of interaction and negotiation. While Park, in his interactionist sociology was less concerned with the formal properties of social structure than with the dynamic processes comprising it, we find his and Parkin's conclusion (the latter a product of a neo-Weberian stance) complementary:

> The relation between classes is neither one of harmony and mutual benefit, nor of irresolvable and fatal contradiction. Rather, the relationship is understood as one of mutual antagonism and permanent *tension*; that is, a condition of unrelieved distributive struggle that is not necessarily impossible to 'contain'. Class conflict may be without cease, but it is not inevitably fought to a conclusion. The competing notions of harmony, contradiction and tension could thus be thought of as three broad possible ways of conceptualizing the relation between classes, and on which all class models are grounded.
>
> Parkin (1979; p.112)

Here we see something of the 'dynamic disequilibrium' drawn out from Park's work by Turner. Thus our theoretical interpretation of ethnic residential segregation has necessarily drawn inspiration from those schools of thought generalizing towards social structure, while our understanding of the dynamic qualities and changing character of those patterns is dependent on Park's process-orientated interactionist sociology.

In conclusion we would stress an interpretation of Park's work which involves a more complex notion of interaction than that implied in simplistic notions of 'segregation' and 'assimilation' as the opposite ends of social and spatial continua. Such an interpretation can accommodate an equally complex notion of ethnicity as a subtly negotiable or manipulable identity whose exact formulation is contingent on the social context of particular interactions. This formulation of the concept of interaction can be used at the level of social structure in conjunction with Marxist theories of institutional racism; it can accommodate a range of managerialist perspectives together with neo-Weberian voluntaristic notions of class; and it may even be applied at the level of the individual and his choice of particular forms of ethnic behaviour. Theoretically, it has more generality and applicability than the barren tautology of the 'choice/constraint' concept.

We have attempted to demonstrate how this view of society as one of "episodes of interaction and of more durable interdependencies" (Hannerz, 1980) reflects the influence of Simmel and the pragmatists on Park, culminating in the conception of a dynamic disequilibrium between accommodation and conflict. Moreover, through Park's justly influential social distance/physical distance equation, it is a conception of the social order which gives special prominence to the spatial order and hence is of particular appeal to social geography.

References

Barth, F. (ed.) (1969). "Ethnic Groups and Boundaries: The Social Organization of Cultural Difference". Little, Brown, Boston.

Bassett, K. and Short, J. R. (1980). "Housing and Residential Structure: Alternative Approaches". Routledge and Kegan Paul, London.

Binns, D. (1977). "Beyond the Sociology of Conflict". Macmillan, London.

Boal, F. W. (1969). Territoriality on the Shankill-Falls divide, Belfast. *Irish Geography* **6**, 30-50.

Boal, F. W. (1970). Social space in the Belfast urban area. *In* "Irish Geographical Studies", (N. Stephens and R. Glassock, eds.) Queens University, Belfast.

Boal, F. W. (1980). Ethnic residential mixing in an ethnic segregation context. Paper presented at a symposium on Ethnic Segregation in Cities, St Antony's College, Oxford.

Buttimer, A. (1974). "Values in Geography". Commission on College Geography Resource Paper No. 24. Association of American Geographers, Washington DC.

Carchedi, G. (1975). On the economic identification of the new middle class. *Economy and Society* **4**, 1-86.

Castells, M. (1977). "The Urban Question: a Marxist Approach". Arnold, London.

Cullingworth, J. B. (Chairman) (1969). "Council Housing: Purposes, Procedures and Priorities". Ninth report of the Housing and Management sub-committee. HMSO, Ministry of Housing and Local Government.

Dewey, J. (1948). "Reconstruction in Philosophy". Beacon Press, Boston.

Entrikin, J. N. (1976). Contemporary humanism in geography. *Annals, Association of American Geographers* **66**, 615-632.

Entrikin, J. N. (1980). Robert Park's human ecology and human geography. *Annals, Association of American Geographers* **70**, 43-58.

Hall, S. (1981). In defence of theory. *In* "The People's History and Socialist Theory" (R. Samuel, ed.) Routledge and Kegan Paul, London.

Hall, S., Lumley, B. and McLennan, G. (1977). Politics and ideology: Gramsci. *In* "On Ideology". Hutchinson, Centre for Contemporary Cultural Studies, London.

Hannerz, U. (1980). "Exploring the City: Towards an Urban Anthropology". Columbia University Press, New York.

Herbert, D. T. (1980). Social geography and the city. Report on an SSRC Seminar Series.

Jackson, P. (1980). "Ethnic Groups and Boundaries: 'Ordered Segmentation' in Urban Neighbourhoods". Research Paper No. 26. School of Geography, Oxford.

Johnson, R. (1980). Against absolutism. *In* "The People's History and Socialist Theory", (R. Samuel, ed.) Routledge and Kegan Paul, London.

Johnston, R. J. (1981). On the nature of explanation in human geography. *Transactions, Institute of British Geographers N.S.* **5**, 402-412.

Kantrowitz, N. (1980). Ethnic segregation and public policy. Paper presented at a symposium on Ethnic Segregation in Cities, St Antony's College, Oxford.

Levine, D. (1971). Introduction to Georg Simmel *On individuality and social forms: selected writings.* University of Chicago Press, Chicago and London.

Ley, D. (1974). "The Black Inner City as Frontier Outpost: Images and Behavior of a Philadelphia Neighborhood", Monograph Series No. 7. Association of American Geographers, Washington DC.

Ley, D. (1980). "Geography without Man: a Humanistic Critique", Research Paper No. 24. School of Geography, Oxford.

Lieberson, S. (1980). An asymmetrical approach to segregation. Paper presented at a symposium on Ethnic Segregation in Cities, St Antony's College, Oxford.

Matthews, F. A. (1977). "Quest for an American Sociology: Robert E. Park and the Chicago School". McGill—Queen's University Press, Montreal.

Mercer, D. C. and Powell, J. M. (1972). "Phenomenology and Related Non-positivistic Viewpoints in the Social Sciences", Monash University Publications in Geography No. 1. Monash University, Monash, Australia.

Morrill, R. L. (1965). The Negro ghetto: problems and alternatives. *Geographical Review* **55**, 339-361.

Neuwirth, G. (1969). A Weberian outline of a theory of community: its application to the 'Dark Ghetto'. *British Journal of Sociology* **20**, 148-163.

Pahl, R. E. (1967). Sociological models in geography. *In* "Models in Geography". (R. J. Chorley and P. Haggett, eds.) Methuen, London.

Pahl, R. E. (1972). British sociological seminar, Leeds. Cited in Rex and Tomlinson (1979).

Park, R. E. (1926). The urban community as a spatial pattern and a moral order. *In* "The Urban Community", (E. W. Burgess, ed.) University of Chicago Press.

Park, R. E. (1950). "Race and Culture", (E. C. Hughes, ed.) The collected writings of Robert E. Park, Vol. 1. Free Press, Glencoe, Ill.

Park, R. E. (1952). "Human Communities: the City and Human Ecology", (E. C. Hughes, ed.) The collected writings of Robert E. Park, Vol. 2. Free Press, Glencoe, Ill.

Park, R. E. (1955). "Society: Collective Behaviour, News and Opinion, Sociology and Modern Society", (E. C. Hughes, ed.). The collected writings of Robert E. Park, Vol. 3. Free Press, Glencoe, Ill.

Park, R. E. and Burgess, E. W. (1921). "Introduction to the Science of Sociology". University of Chicago Press.

Parkin, F. (1971). "Class Inequality and Political Order". MacGibbon and Kee, London.

Parkin, F. (1979). "Marxism and Class Theory: a Bourgeois Critique". Tavistock, London.

Peach, C. (ed.) (1975). "Urban Social Segregation". Longman, London.

Poulantzas, N. (1975) "Classes in Contemporary Capitalism". New Left Books, London.

Rex, J. (1980a). John Madge lecture. London School of Economics.

Rex, J. (1980b). Urban segregation and the inner city policy in Great Britain. Paper presented at a symposium on Ethnic Segregation in Cities, St Antony's College, Oxford.

Rex, J. and Moore, R. (1967). "Race, Community and Conflict: a Study of Sparkbrook". Oxford University Press for the Institute of Race Relations, London.

Rex, J. and Tomlinson, S. (1979). "Colonial Immigrants in a British City". Routledge and Kegan Paul, London.

Robinson, V. (1979). "The Segregation of Asians within a British City: Theory and Practice". Research Paper No. 22. School of Geography, Oxford.

Robinson, V. (1980). Lieberson's isolation index: a case-study evaluation. *Area* **12**, 307–312.

Rock, P. (1979). "The Making of Symbolic Interactionism". Macmillan, London.

Shah, S. (1979). Aspects of the geographic analysis of Asian immigrants in London. Unpublished D. Phil. thesis, University of Oxford.

Simmel, G. (1955). "Conflict and the Web of Group-affiliations". Free Press, New York.

Smith, N. (1979). Geography, science and post-positivist modes of explanation. *Progress in Human Geography* **3**, 356–383.

Taeuber, K. (1980). A demographic perspective on school desegregation in the United States. Paper presented at a symposium on Ethnic Segregation in Cities, St Antony's College, Oxford.

Thompson, E. P. (1978). "The Poverty of Theory and Other Essays". Merlin, London.

Tuan, Y. F. (1976). Humanistic geography. *Annals, Association of American Geographers* **66**, 266–276.

Turner, R. H. (1967). Introduction to Robert E. Park. "On Social Control and Collective Behaviour: Selected Papers." University of Chicago Press, Chicago and London.

Weber, M. (1968). "Economy and Society" (G. Roth and C. Wittich, eds.) Vol. 1. Bedminster Press, New York.

Wilson, B. M. (1980). Social space and symbolic interaction. *In* "The Human Experience of Space and Place". (A. Buttimer and D. Seamon, eds.) Croom Helm, London.

ONE

Conflicting interpretations of segregation

CERI PEACH

St Catherine's College, Oxford, UK

Firstly, in this paper, I want to examine one of the theories which has focused the work of empirical investigators on a particular type of spatial segregation. Secondly, I want to show that while the key methodological works on segregation highlighted the mathematical inter-relationships of various indices, they hid conceptual differences which underlay those proposed indices. Thirdly, I want to show that the resulting positivist methodology produced much more accurate predictions about social interaction than did alternative theories. Finally, I want to show that Marxist considerations of segregation, which are currently being proposed as more theoretically powerful than the positivist empiricist tradition are empirically crude.

I have argued elsewhere (Peach, 1975) that an essay by Robert Park first published in 1926 gives the key theoretical idea for the spatial social analysis from which the most productive empirical work has subsequently flowed. The revolutionary idea which Park propounded in that paper was that social analysis could be treated like physical sciences: the key to that transformation was through the use of geographical space.

> Reduce all social relations to relations of space and it would be possible to apply to human relations the fundamental logic of the physical sciences. Social phenomena would be reduced to the elementary movements of individuals, just as physical phenomena, chemical actions, and the qualities of matter, heat, sound, and electricity are reduced to the elementary movements of molecules and atoms . . . Park (1926; p.13)

> It is because social relations are so frequently and so inevitably correlated with spatial relations; because psychical distances so frequently are, or seem to be the indexes of social distances, that statistics have any significance whatever for sociology. And this is true finally, because it is only as social and physical facts can be reduced to, or correlated with, spatial facts that they can be measured at all.
>
> Park (1926; p.18)

Park overstated his case, it is true. Physical sciences had already entered the era of uncertainty so that the clockwork view of the universe was already under attack. However, the method by which uncertainty itself was analysed was the positivistic, scientific method. Even when uncertainty has been absorbed into the social sciences

—as through the use of Monte Carlo simulation models—the element of determination far outweighs the element of chance (see, for example, Morrill, 1965 or Robinson, Ch. 7, this volume).

Park's view of the physical analysis of social relations in spatial terms has major intellectual attractions in that it is capable of generating hypotheses which conflict with hypotheses generated by other approaches. These conflicts are susceptible to empirical testing and solution.

Spatial intermixture and social interaction

Using Park's social physics approach leads to the prediction that specifiable amounts of social interaction should be found in Western urban societies, given specified spatial arrangements of social groups. The social interaction chosen for examination in this paper is marriage. Marriage is important as a topic since it not only measures interactions but measures those which are socially significant and which affect processes such as assimilation (Gordon, 1964; p.80); it serves as a surrogate measure for more elusive friendship patterns (Shannon and Nystuen, 1976) and it helps define mean information fields (Morrill and Pitts, 1967). Finally, data are reasonably accessible so that hypotheses may be developed from marriage patterns that relate to other social processes.

The principal means of investigating Park's hypothesis has been by operationalizing the two concepts of social and physical distance. Physical distance has been operationalized through measurement of segregation. Interaction has been operationalized through the measurement of the ability to speak English in English-speaking host societies, through the measurement of differences in socio-economic structures or indeed, through the measurement of intermarriage and so on.

Measurement of segregation

In a seminal review paper in 1955, Duncan and Duncan described segregation as a somewhat fuzzy concept. However, by demonstrating the common root of many different indices of segregation in the Lorenz curve the Duncans may have obscured the even more important fact of the very dissimilar conceptualizations of segregation involved. For example, if we were to take the situation in Fig. 1 as representing a totally black inner city and a totally white periphery, with no overlap between black and white, we could agree that the distribution was totally segregated.

If the distribution were modified so that the white population were to be uniformly distributed across the whole city, but the black population were to remain concentrated in the central area, then it would be possible to argue radically different cases as to whom or what was being segregated.

(1) It could be argued that the black population was segregated because it was confined to one area and absent from the rest (while the white population, being found uniformly everywhere was unsegregated).

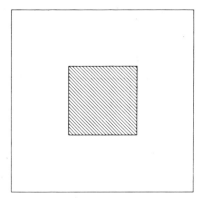

Figure 1.

(2) It could be argued that the black population was unsegregated because Whites were living in all areas where Blacks were found, while the white population was highly segregated because the majority lived in exclusively white areas.

(3) It could be argued that the centre of the city was segregated because all Blacks lived there.

(4) It could be argued that the centre of the city was unsegregated because its population was mixed.

In other words, from the *same* distribution one could argue that totally *different* places or groups were segregated. Sims (Ch. 6), for example, uses argument (4) to criticize Robinson's (1979) categorization of part of Blackburn as a 'Sikh' area, while Robinson is using a variation of argument (3) to point to the distinctiveness of the area for Sikhs.

Conceptual views of segregation differ according to whether one takes the measure to refer to one community in isolation or two together. It differs according to whether one takes it to refer to one part of the city in isolation or whether one takes it to refer to the entity. There is a profound difference between the concept of segregation advanced in my early book *West Indian Migration to Britain* (Peach, 1968; pp.87-89) which follows basically argument (2) and the concept of segregation followed in the later book *Urban Social Segregation* (Peach, 1975; pp.2-4) which uses the index of dissimilarity. Measures such as the index of dissimilarity (ID) measure the overall spatial intermixture of two groups over the totality of the city.

The literature, after two major reviews by the Duncans (1955) and by the Taeubers (1965) settled down in the 1950s, 1960s and 1970s to the use of ID and produced what Kantrowitz (1980) has identified as one of the few examples of cumulative social science. The index had a major attraction in that it dealt simultaneously with two groups over all subunits of a city. Thus, it produced a measure of spatial 'mix' which was particularly important if social interaction were related to physical intermixture of groups. The index had a direct verbal meaning: the proportion of a group which would have to move if it were to reproduce the distribution of the group with which it was being compared (i.e. what percentage would have to move to produce a zero index). The measure used and the philosophy of interpretation is essentially that used independently by the later 'social justice' or 'welfare' school. David Smith's measure of wealth inequality is essentially the ID (Smith, 1977; pp.131-140).

Duncan and Duncan also argued that ID was independent of the relative sizes of the groups examined (Duncan and Duncan, 1955). This view is, however, suspect. It had long been known that reducing the size of areal subunit used for measuring ID (from tract to block or from ward to enumeration district) increased the score of the index.* Logically, between two extremes, the size of areal unit used will affect the degree of segregation recorded. When all of the population lives in one area there can be no segregation recorded; when each member of the population lives in his or her own subarea, there will be total segregation. Thus, as the scale moves from one large unit containing all the population to a large number of small units each containing a single individual, the degree of segregation will increase. Thus, as the number of members of a subpopulation and the number of areal subunits used approach each other, the degree of segregation recorded will increase. However, this result may be obtained either by very fine areal subdivisions or by using very small subpopulations.† The two problems of areal scale and subgroup size derive from a common relationship.

Work by Reiner (1972), Winship (1977, 1978) and Falk *et al.* (1978) has shown that small groups, particularly when measured over very fine areal subdivisions, may produce high scores even if their distribution is random. However, since the problems of fineness of area and size of group are highly related, using both fine meshes and small subgroups will compound the difficulties of producing meaningful results. It is more realistic to trade off these characteristics against each other. When there are fewer group members than areal units, (see for instance, Peach, 1979) nonsense measurements will result. Thus, judgement has to be exercised and ID should not be used near the extremes of tolerance of the index. Shah (1979) has sought to avoid this problem by calculating an 'effective index' which is the observed ID minus the random level of ID. It is clear that our understanding of ID has changed and the renewed use of asymmetric measures (Lieberson, 1980; Robinson, 1980a) represents a conceptual as well as technical re-evaluation.

However, away from extreme conditions, ID has enormous importance from the behavioural viewpoint. It is clear from the literature that ID is a particularly sensitive diagnostic measure of social interaction. Where it has been used it tends to give substantial support to the basic Park hypothesis. The key empirical paper in this context is by Duncan and Lieberson (1959) in which they were able to

---

*Woods (1976) re-demonstrates this fact but weakens the case by using compounded groups such as the Cypriot/Maltese population which contain two groups which are highly segregated from each other. Thus, as the scale of unit is diminished the two groups become more spatially separate and factors other than the scale of unit area influence the results that are produced.

†This may explain the particular case of the relatively high level of segregation reported by Kantrowitz (1973) for the ostensibly rather similar Norwegians and Swedes in New York.

demonstrate the inverse relationship between segregation and assimilation of immigrants. Groups which were highly segregated were least assimilated and *vice versa*. Measures of assimilation that were used included ability to speak English, difference in employment structure between immigrants and native population, and finally a measure of intermarriage. Duncan and Lieberson's study was replicated and expanded in many different places (Lieberson, 1963; Lancaster Jones, 1967; Taeuber and Taeuber, 1964; Kantrowitz, 1973).

Attacks on the concept of segregation as a conditioner of interaction

Nevertheless the basic idea came under direct attack by Ramsøy (1966) and indirectly conflicted with a significant contribution to American assimilation theory by Kennedy.

Ramsøy's case was this: we can recognize three tendencies in urban social relations.

(1) The tendency of distance-decay to operate: people marry disproportionately those who live near them (see Table I).
(2) People marry disproportionately those of the same social class (see Table II).
(3) A tendency for social groups to be residentially segregated.

If these propositions are true—to what extent does one proposition explain the other? If segregation means that like people live near each other does this explain why like marries like over short distances? Or, are the two tendencies separate, i.e. people marry others who live close irrespective of class and marry people of similar class irrespective of distance?

Ramsøy's technique was to use contingency analysis to show that each of the tendencies (i.e. like marrying like; short distance marriage) was true and then using the same technique to show that they were independent of each other.

Contingency analysis assumes a direct proportionality of the marginal row and column totals. Table III shows the statistically 'expected' pairings between social classes if numbers alone were the determinants of interaction.

This statistical 'expectation' is, of course, unreal. But the method is to use the difference between the statistically 'expected' interaction and the actual observed interaction in order to highlight the extent to which the characteristic which is under observation (in this case social class) 'distorts' observed behaviour. In reality people marry into their own class much more than class numbers alone might lead us to suspect. Thus, in reality, the table, given the initial assumptions about numbers in each class might look differently (Table IV).

Using real figures for Oslo in 1962, Ramsøy's figures showed that observed marriages within social classes and into those immediately adjacent were much higher than the statistical 'expectation' (see Table II). Thus, she demonstrated her first point (1), like marries like.

She next demonstrated the second point (2), that the tendency to marry over short distances is much greater than statistically 'expected'. She demonstrated this point by a similar contingency analysis. If, instead of considering our theoretical Table III

Ceri Peach

TABLE I

Observed and expected numbers of couples
according to distance between residences before marriage, Oslo, 1962

Distance (miles)	1 Observed number of couples	2 Expected number of couples	Ratio of 1 to 2
Less than 0·50	267	114·2	2·34
0·50–0·99	427	203·0	2·10
1·00–1·49	339	291·1	1·16
1·50–1·99	319	305·9	1·04
2·00–2·49	239	285·2	0·84
2·50–2·99	220	279·1	0·79
3·00–3·49	219	285·7	0·77
3·50–3·99	153	229·4	0·67
4·00–4·49	119	137·4	0·87
4·50–4·99	83	141·9	0·59
5·00–5·49	54	93·0	0·58
5·50–5·99	46	60·2	0·76
6·00–6·49	33	51·0	0·65
6·50–6·99	23	38·3	0·60
7·00–7·49	17	24·7	0·69
7·50–7·99	6	15·7	0·38
8·00	9	17·2	0·52
Total	2573	2573·0	

Source: Ramsøy, 1966.

as being divided into social classes, we considered the classes to represent subareas of a city, the cells would now represent the number of marriages that take place within and between subareas of a city. These would be the number of marriages that would be expected to take place solely on the basis of the number of potential spouses in each subarea. The distance that these subareas are apart would not be taken into consideration. The resulting expected marriages may then be classified according to the real distance between areas. For the sake of demonstration, the distances between the mid-points of each of these subareas may be taken as those given in Table V.

Marriages in Table III are now classified according to the distance between subareas given in Table V. Thus the expected number of marriages over zero distance is 4 + 6 + 6 + 4 = 20. The remaining marriages are classified according to the distance between the interacting cells in the same way for the rest of Table III to give expected marriages by distance. The same classification is applied to Table V to give the corresponding observed values (Table VI).

TABLE II

Occupation of bride according to occupation of groom, Oslo, 1962*

Groom's occupation	Professional, univ. student (%)	Semi-prof. tech., admin. skilled clerical	Routine clerical	Sales	Manual, service	No occupation	Total	No. of grooms
							Bride's occupation	
Professional, univ. student	20·1	48·4	19·3	2·2	4·9	5·1	100·0	816
Semi-prof., admin., sales	2·5	42·1	29·3	7·2	10·2	8·7	100·0	1047
Routine white-collar	1·3	25·6	35·7	9·4	19·9	8·1	100·0	694
Skilled manual and service	0·3	20·5	32·2	9·5	25·0	12·5	100·0	727
Semi- and unskilled manual and service	0·6	11·9	26·6	11·3	32·3	17·3	100·0	1770
No occupation	0·9	21·5	19·6	2·8	16·8	38·4	100·0	107
All occupations	4·1	27·0	27·8	8·4	20·5	12·2	100·0	5161
No. of brides	212	1394	1438	431	1058	628		

Source: Ramsøy, 1966.

*Frequencies in the underlined cells exceed the expected numbers.

TABLE III

Hypothetical example of 'expected' intermarriage in a contingency table, between social classes

			Brides			
	Class		1	2	3	4
		No.	10	20	30	40
Grooms	1	40	4	8	12	16
	2	30	3	6	9	12
	3	20	2	4	6	8
	4	10	1	2	3	4

Thus by comparing the observed with expected figures it is possible to show that there is an overselection of those living close and an underselection of those living further away.

Ramsøy therefore tried to resolve the problem of whether nearness and likeness were related by cross-tabulating marriages by likeness (in social class) by distance

TABLE IV

Hypothetical example of 'observed' intermarriage between social classes

			Brides			
	Class		1	2	3	4
		No.	10	20	30	40
Grooms	1	40	8	12	10	10
	2	30	1	7	12	10
	3	20	1	1	8	10
	4	10	0	-	-	10

TABLE V

Distances between the four subareas of a hypothetical city

Subarea	(1)	(2)	(3)	(4)
(1)	-	1	2	3
(2)	1	-	3	2
(3)	2	3	-	1
(4)	3	2	1	-

TABLE VI

'Observed' and 'expected' marriages over distance (derived from Tables III, IV and V)

Miles	Expected	Observed
0	20	32
1	22	24
2	28	20
3	30	24

(Table VII). The surprising conclusion apparently produced by this analysis was that the same proportion of marriages of like to like took place irrespective of distance. Furthermore, the mean distance of marriage partners remained the same no matter how like or how unlike the marriage partners' social class. Ramsøy concluded therefore that likeness and nearness were totally independent factors and segregation had no impact whatever on the tendency of like to marry like or near to marry near.

Ramsøy painted herself into a corner. She showed (she believed): (1) that society was segregated by class (Table VIII); (2) that distance apart made no difference to

TABLE VII

Distribution of observed couples according to
distance between residential districts and similarity in occupational statuses, Oslo, 1962

	Similarity of bride's and groom's occupational status						
Distance between residential districts (miles)	Identical or most similar status	One occup. category distant	Two occup. categories distant	Three occup. cat. distant	Four or five occup. cat. distant	All couples	% in first two columns
0·00–0·99	201	272	156	48	17	694	68·2
1·00–1·99	198	253	131	48	28	658	68·5
2·00–2·99	140	176	98	30	15	459	68·8
3·00–3·99	103	132	95	28	14	372	63·2
4·00–4·99	64	75	46	10	7	202	68·8
5·00–5·99	38	31	24	6	1	100	69·0
6·00–6·99	10	25	15	4	2	56	(62·5)
7·00–7·99	9	7	4	1	2	23	(69·6)
8·00	1	5	2	1	—	9	(66·7)
All distances	764	976	571	176	86	2573	67·6
Distance quartiles							
Q₁	0·96	0·92	0·98	0·93	1·13	0·94	
Q₂	1·92	1·85	1·98	1·78	1·91	1·90	
Q₃	3·25	3·20	3·42	3·22	3·25	3·27	

Source: Ramsøy, 1966.

TABLE VIII

Indexes of dissimilarity in residential distribution
among occupational statuses, bridegrooms, Oslo, 1962

	Occupational status					
Occupational status	1	2	3	4	5	6
(1) Professional, university student	—	22·6	35·8	42·0	43·6	(60·5)
(2) Semi-prof., admin., sales	—	—	21·7	28·2	28·1	(48·9)
(3) Routine white-collar			—	27·0	21·6	(45·9)
(4) Skilled manual and service				—	18·7	(38·2)
(5) Semi- and unskilled manual and service					—	(41·0)
(6) No occupation						
No. of men	(417)	(538)	(336)	(412)	(820)	(50)

Source: Ramsøy, 1966.

the proportion of like marrying like; (3) that no matter how like or unlike marriage partners were, the average distance apart remained constant. She thus apparently reached a situation where average distance of doctors marrying doctors or doctors marrying factory workers were all the same, but where such groups were segregated from each other (Ramsøy, 1966).

If Ramsøy's conclusion were correct and segregation had no impact whatever on social interaction, it would mean that the whole line of argument which developed from Park, through the Duncans, Lieberson, the Taeubers and Kantrowitz, would be based on spurious assumptions. The opposite was true.

In fact there is a moral in the reason why Ramsøy's work proved wrong and that is that there can come a time in the sophisticated statistical manipulation of data when words lose contact with the categories that they are describing. What happened in this case is that words no longer meant what they seemed to mean.

The root cause of the problem lay in the classification of 'like' marriages. Ramsøy grouped together under 'like marriages', for example, all doctor to doctor marriages in the same category as factory worker to factory worker marriages. She interpreted her results of constant marriage distance, irrespective of social similarity or distance, as meaning that the mean distances were the same if a doctor married a doctor or whether a doctor married a factory worker. This conclusion was false. Her analysis was a variation of the ecological fallacy. It is impossible to tell from a classification of doctors marrying doctors and factory workers marrying factory workers what the distance is for either group, just as it is impossible to tell for a group of children with average age five what any of their ages are. The effect of her classification was to hide radically different trends in marriage distance in different classes of society. In the study in which social classes were disaggregated, average marriage distances within the upper classes were long (see Koller, 1948). Average marriage distances within lower classes were low. By amalgamating all together, the upper and lower values would disappear and the distances come out as the mean. Similarly, the effect of outmarriage for upper classes would be to lower average distance—but the effect of outmarriage at the bottom end of society to increase average distance. By putting both sets of outmarriage into the same category, the shortening and lengthening effects at opposite ends of society would cancel each other out and produce average distances. Thus, Ramsøy's finding that segregation had no impact on class marriage turned out to be a semantic confusion rather than a sociological finding. The only reason for attempting a re-analysis of these findings which seemed so secure in technique and methodology was because they conflicted with the predictions derived from the social physics approach derived from Park.

The second major research finding which conflicted with the expectation derived from Park's view of social and physical space was Kennedy's proposal of a triple 'melting pot' in American society. Kennedy (1944, 1952) had made longitudinal studies of ethnic intermarriage in New Haven, Connecticut, between 1900 and 1950. She concluded that ethnicity was breaking down, not indiscriminately into a single 'melting pot', but instead within religious divides. Thus she argued that Protestant groups such as the British, Germans and Scandinavians were coalescing within a Protestant boundary; Catholic ethnicities such as the Irish, Italians and Poles formed a separate coalescing Catholic group; while the Jews formed a third, separate group.

The conflict of this argument with the positivist dissimilarist viewpoint was that there was little spatial mixing between some of the ethnicities that were presumed to fuse socially while in other cases, the groups that were supposed to remain distinct, were merged spatially. For example, the Irish, Poles and Italians showed rather high degrees of segregation from each other in cities for which such analyses were available. For example, in Cleveland in 1930 Lieberson (1963; pp.88–89) shows the Irish population separated from Polish born by an ID of 69·3; from the Italians by 68·3; while Italians and Poles were separated from each other by 74·5. These are all high figures. At the same time, the Irish, who were supposed, under Kennedy's hypothesis, not to interact with the British and Germans, had much lower rates of segregation from those groups: 30·8 with the British and 41·3 with the Germans.

Thus, if there were truth in Park's assertion that physical and social space are related, and if there was anything to be derived from his dream that social relations could be mathematicized, then this seemed an ideal testing ground. If social interactions were related to spatial mixing then it would be predicted that the groups that were most residentially mixed would interact most with each other and least with those from whom they were most segregated. In practical terms, it would mean that the Irish would be predicted to interact most with the British, Germans and Scandinavians and least with the Italians and Poles. It would also indicate that Italians and Poles would not be expected to interact and, therefore intermarry, much with each other.

Re-examining the Kennedy New Haven data, the hypotheses formed from the spatial expectation of interaction were proved correct (Peach, 1980a). The Irish showed low rates of intermarriage with the Poles and the Italians; there was no Catholic 'pot'. On the other hand, the Irish, Germans, British and Scandinavians intermarried substantially. The supposed Protestant 'pot' contained the Catholic Irish. Furthermore, once the segregation patterns of the ethnic groups in New Haven were analysed it was shown that there was a high and significant degree of correlation between the extent ethnic groups were segregated from each other and the extent to which they intermarried (Peach, 1980b).

Alternatives to positivism

Thus, the positivist approach to social geography presents an intellectual challenge. Behavioural geography and humanist approaches which claim to have replaced positivism are not so much a breakaway from positivist modes as a development of those modes. The dramatic parting of the shopping patterns on either side of the Shankill–Falls divide demonstrated by Boal (1969) are dramatic only in relation to normative expectation derived from positivist models. The extraordinary can only be appreciated in relation to normative expectations.

All sorts of other behaviour continues to demonstrate expected social-physics effects, varying from the distance decay of marriage patterns cited in the present paper to Ley's gang wars in Philadelphia (Ley, 1974; p.132) and to Murray and Boal's analysis of doorstep murders in Belfast (Murray and Boal, 1979). Smith's (Ch. 2, this volume) examination of interethnic crime is a further development of this idea: positivism applied to negative interaction.

It is possible that the progress of the behavioural side of social geography will take it into progressively 'softer' areas of behaviour. 'Softer' does not mean easier—in fact, the opposite is more likely. 'Softer' is meant in the sense that landscape is composed of hard elements such as physical morphology and buildings and soft elements such as colour and type of foliage and texture. In social geography the hard elements are made of census and questionnaire data; the 'softer' elements will be epiphenomena—who talks to whom in the playground (Robinson, 1980b), which way the religious procession is routed (Jackson, 1980).

Both behavioural and positivist approaches continue to emphasize the importance of space as a conditioner of action: Marxist approaches are tending to argue in the opposite direction. Marxists argue that space is a record of social relations rather than a regulator. For Marxists, segregation is the end-point of economic relations rather than the starting point for social analysis.

It is not possible, of course, to write of a single Marxist approach to social geography. However, the most directly influential recent author is Castells (1977). The paradox of Castells' *The Urban Question* is that he believes that there is no independent urban question. For him the urban question is a particular conjunction of the general Marxist class relations in an urban setting. Urban features such as segregation or ecological areas are for Castells the spatial outcomes of class relationships. The role of segregation on intermarriage, for example, is one of social class convenience rather than ecological conditioning:

> ... the classic inquiries that try to demonstrate the link between residential proximity and choice of marriage partner ended by isolating a certain effect of spatial proximity (insofar as it increases the probability of interaction), but within a cultural definition of couples, itself determined by membership of different social milieux (Katz and Hill, 1958).

Castells (1977; p.108).

This view is at variance with the literature outlined in the present paper.

For Castells, studies which attempt to measure the behavioural consequences and implications of segregation are pursuing false goals. The correct path is to pursue the analysis of class relationships that produce such outcomes as segregation. For Marxists, segregation is an outcome of the problem, not the problem itself. The problem is the class struggle. Hence there is enormous resistance on the Marxist side to approaches to ethnicity that challenge the primacy of the class explanation (see, for example, Doherty, 1973). Those approaches that see ethnicity as stronger than class or as an alternative to a class approach rather than as a temporary phenomenon, operating within the class system, are seen as attempts to mystify rather than clarify the structure of society.

Castells, therefore, argues (1977; p.108) against any independent effect of segregation or ecology. He argues that although the ghetto or the slum may produce a re-inforcement of certain systems of behaviour, the ghetto or slum itself is not the product of independent supraclass effects. Instead, it is the product of the class struggle working in two different levels to produce a joint coincidental effect:

> . . . in the case of American slums, for example, racial discrimination is two fold, it is manifested, on the one hand, by the distribution of the 'subjects' in the social structure and, on the other, by the distribution of housing and amenities in space. Their high cultural specificity results, therefore, from this correspondence and from the meaning it assumes in the sphere of social relations, through the conditions of the particular organisation of the class struggle in the United states.
>
> Castells (1977; p.108).

This argument is not without force, but subjected to positivist empirical probing, structural weaknesses show. The bundles of factors that Castells cites do not coincide but overlap each other. Thus, not all of worst class of housing is occupied by the Blacks; not all Blacks are in the lowest position in society. Indirect standardization techniques applied by Lieberson (1963) and by Taeuber and Taeuber (1964) shows that Blacks have degrees of segregation massively higher than that which their economic situation alone would predict. To a much lesser extent, European ethnicities are also more segregated than their economic class structure would suggest. Inferior economic position, important though it is, plays only a small part in the explanation of the high degrees of black segregation.

Class explanations may owe much to Marx; ethnic attitudes may owe more to Freud. The view which sees ethnic segregation solely in terms of class oppression seems, to me, to be historically and psychologically impoverished. Ethnic groups do not exist in any society independently of the class system or of modes of production. However, this is not to say that their position in the class system or relative to the modes of production is the dominant factor in their ethnicity. English, Welsh or Russian ethnicity were established long before current class structures or modes of production. Ethnicity contains class rather than vice versa. The language, values, religion, culture and dress of ethnic minorities are not simply badges of degradation imposed by more powerful groups to imprison, confine and divide those whom they dominate. They are elements of group and personal identity, fostered from within the group. Ethnicity is however, contextual. To state a truism, it is unimportant where it is taken for granted. It becomes important only in the presence of other ethnicity.

Positivist analysis argues that economic structures explain only a small part of segregation. Social forces over and above those of the economic structure are more influential. There are both positive and negative forces in segregation. Positive and negative, however, are not symmetrical and equally counterbalancing forces. Positive desires of groups to stick together may dominate without being the result of some current, equally strong, negative forces preventing dispersal. Thus, as well as positive and negative forces, there are also dominant and recessive forces (Peach, 1968; pp.83-91). Most Marxist analysts interpret segregation in terms of constraint; positivist analysis argues that the situation is more complex.

However, if we follow Feyerabend (1975), progress requires conflicting theory. The common way to produce change in hypotheses is to produce conflicting facts. Facts and observations, however, depend on hypotheses and theories. If there are no conflicting theories, there will be no conflicting observations. If a theory is successful, it can prevent challenging theories which will have no competitive or challenging 'facts' from which to start. Success of the theory therefore guarantees its continuation (Feyerabend, 1975; pp.44-45).

There can be no philosophical reconciliation of the positivist and Marxist interpretations of segregation. There is, however, room for both approaches and progress is most likely to be made by highlighting those areas in which contradictory predictions of outcomes are made. Thus far, it seems to me, Marxist analysts of segregation have shown enthusiasm only for postdiction. Marxist analysts can explain everything but predict little.

References

Boal, F. W. (1969). Territoriality on the Shankill-Falls divide, Belfast. *Irish Geography* **6**, 30-50.

Castells, M. (1977). "The Urban Question." Arnold, London.

Doherty, J. (1973). Race, class and residential segregation in Britain. *Antipode* **5**, 45-51.

Duncan, O. D. and Duncan, B. (1955). A methodological analysis of segregation indexes. *American Sociological Review* **20**, 210-217.

Duncan, O. D. and Lieberson, S. (1959). Ethnic segregation and assimilation. *American Journal of Sociology* **64**, 364-374.

Falk, R. F., Cortese, F. and Cohen, J. (1978). Utilizing standardized indices of residential segregation: comment on Winship. *Social Forces* **57**, 713-716.

Feyerabend, P. K. (1975). "Against Method." New Left Books, London.

Gordon, M. M. (1964). "Assimilation in American Life." Oxford University Press, New York.

Jackson, P. (1980). "Ethnic Groups and Boundaries: 'Ordered Segmentation' in Urban Neighbourhoods", Research Paper No. 26. School of Geography, Oxford.

Kantrowitz, N. (1973). "Ethnic and Racial Segregation in the New York Metropolis." Praeger, New York.

Kantrowitz, N. (1980). Ethnic segregation and public policy. Paper presented at the symposium on Ethnic Segregation in Cities, St Antony's College, Oxford.

Kennedy, R. J. R. (1944). Single or triple melting pot? Intermarriage trends in New Haven, 1870-1940. *American Journal of Sociology* **49**, 331-339.

Kennedy, R. J. R. (1952). Single or triple melting pot? Intermarriage in New Haven, 1870-1950. *American Journal of Sociology* **58**, 56-59.

Koller, M. R. (1948). Residential propinquity of white mates at marriage in relation to age and occupation of males, Columbus, Ohio, 1938 and 1946. *American Sociological Review* **13**, 613-616.

Lancaster Jones, F. (1967). Ethnic concentration and assimilation: an Australian case study. *Social Forces* **45**, 412-423.

Ley, D. (1974). "The Black Inner City as Frontier Outpost", Monograph Series No. 7. Association of American Geographers, Washington, DC.

Lieberson, S. (1963). "Ethnic Patterns in American Cities." Free Press of Glencoe, New York.

Lieberson, S. (1980). An asymmetrical approach to segregation. Paper presented at the symposium on Ethnic Segregation in Cities, St Antony's College, Oxford.

Morrill, R. L. (1965). The Negro ghetto: problems and alternatives. *Geographical Review* **55**, 339-361.

Morrill, R. L. and Pitts, F. R. (1967). Marriage, migration, and the mean information field: a study in uniqueness and generality. *Annals, Association of American Geographers* **57**, 401-422.

Murray, R. and Boal, F. W. (1979). The social ecology of urban violence. *In* "Social Problems and the City", (D. T. Herbert and D. M. Smith, eds.) Oxford University Press.

Park, R. E. (1926). The urban community as a spatial pattern and a moral order. *In* "The Urban Community", (E. W. Burgess, ed.) University of Chicago Press.

Peach, C. (1968). "West Indian Migration to Britain: a Social Geography." Oxford University Press for the Institute of Race Relations, London.

Peach, C. (ed.) (1975). "Urban Social Segregation." Longman, London.

Peach, C. (1979). More on race and space. *Area* **11**, 221-222.

Peach, C. (1980a). Which triple melting pot? A re-examination of ethnic intermarriage in New Haven, 1900-1950. *Ethnic and Racial Studies* **31**, 1-16.

Peach, C. (1980b). Ethnic segregation and intermarriage. *Annals, Association of American Geographers* **70**, 371-381.

Ramsøy, N. R. (1966). Assortative mating and the structure of cities. *American Sociological Review* **31**, 773-786.

Reiner, A. (1972). Racial segregation: a comment. *Journal of Regional Science* **12**, 137-148.

Robinson, V. (1979). "The Segregation of Asians within a British City: Theory and Practice", Research Paper No. 22. School of Geography, Oxford.

Robinson, V. (1980a). Lieberson's P* index: a case-study evaluation. *Area* **12**, 307-312.

Robinson, V. (1980b). The social and spatial encapsulation of Asians in British cities. Paper presented at the IBG Population Geography Study Group Conference, St Catherine's College, Oxford.

Shah, S. (1979). Aspects of the geographic analysis of Asian immigrants in London. Unpublished D.Phil. thesis, University of Oxford.

Shannon, G. W. and Nystuen, J. D. (1976). Surrogate measures of urban social interaction. *Professional Geographer* **28**, 23-28.

Smith, D. M. (1977). "Human Geography: a Welfare Approach." Arnold, London.

Taeuber, K. E. and Taeuber, A. F. (1964). The Negro as an immigrant group: recent trends in racial and ethnic segregation in Chicago. *American Journal of Sociology* **69**, 374-382.

Taeuber, K. E. and Taeuber, A. F. (1965). "Negroes in Cities". Aldine, New York.

Winship, C. (1977). A revaluation of indexes of residential segregation. *Social Forces* **55**, 1058-1066.

Winship, C. (1978). The desirability of using the index of dissimilarity or any adjustment of it for measuring segregation: a reply to Falk *et al. Social Forces* **57**, 717-720.

Woods, R. I. (1976). Aspects of the scale problem in the calculation of segregation indices: London and Birmingham 1961 and 1971. *Tijdschrift voor Economische en Sociale Geografie* **67**, 169-174.

TWO

Negative interaction: crime in the inner city

SUSAN J. SMITH

Nuffield College, Oxford, UK

Introduction

Even before the extensive research on urban crime patterns completed by Shaw (1929) and Shaw and McKay (1931, 1942), the transitional and decaying 'working class' inner areas of large industrial cities were associated with high crime rates and high rates of offender residence (Engels, 1848; Mayhew, 1862). Despite some striking contrasts with earlier offence patterns revealed by the construction of 'opportunity specific' rather than 'population specific' crime rates (Lottier, 1938; Boggs, 1965; Phillips, 1973; Baldwin *et al.* 1976), the contention that parts of the inner city display many of the socio-economic and environmental characteristics persistently associated with high offence and offender rates remains undisputed. A large number of factorial ecologies completed during the 1960s point to several such crime correlates which characterize the study area cited in this essay.* It is a community of 17000 people nestling between the first generation of suburban council estates, outer zones of owner occupied housing, and central city redevelopment areas in Birmingham. It supports a relatively high proportion of low income households, high rates of unemployment (especially amongst school leavers), and the high densities and overcrowding often associated with subdivided, multi-occupied Victorian terraces. Traditionally one of the city's main immigrant reception areas, it now exhibits a high degree of spatial mixing amongst ethnically and socially distinct populations at ward and Enumeration District level. These include elderly white residents, a substantial but dispersing Irish community, and a

---

*These areal and 'ecological' analyses, mapping and comparing the distributions of 'observable' social phenomena, progressed from the simple analysis of gradients and zones, through the correlation and regression of single census variables (reviewed by Phillips, 1972) to more complex social area analyses (discussed by Baldwin, 1974), factor analyses (Gordon, 1967, provides a critical assessment of this method), principal components analyses (Ahamad, 1967) and a range of related multivariate techniques (Corsi and Harvey, 1975; Turner, 1969a). Herbert (1976) discusses the geographical significance of a number of these approaches. Later studies tend to re-affirm the social and environmental correlates of crime established by the Chicago ecologists and forecast by nineteenth century European criminologists (whose work is also succinctly reviewed by Phillips, 1972).

well-established West Indian population who were the dominant group of New Commonwealth origin in the early 1960s, but who are increasingly interspersed residentially with British, Indian and East African Asians who have arrived more recently to the area.

High densities, social heterogeneity, low socio-economic class and high rates of residential mobility, particularly accompanying ethnic transition or 'succession' have frequently been shown to correlate strongly with the locations of high crime and offender residence rates.* At a smaller scale, however, it is possible to probe beneath statistical associations among spatially aggregated environmental indicators and urban pathologies, to examine crime as one of several forms of social inter-action, differing in quantity and quality. This move is prompted by prior research among both geographers and criminologists: by Baldwin (1975), whose disillusion-ment with broad areal analyses led him to call for more detailed studies of particular 'natural areas'; by Herbert's (1977) assertion that opportunities for crime are often best understood through the micro-environment; and by Harries' (1974) emphasis, following his own large scale analyses, on the centrality of relationships at a small scale for insight into the *meaning* behind criminal events. It is also an approach closely related to a well-developed geographical literature exploring the links between spatial structure, social structure and social interaction.†

The spatial structure of social interaction

The central tenets of this latter tradition derive from a positivist interpretation of work by the Chicago ecologists. Particularly salient is Park's argument that

> It is because social relations are so frequently and so inevitably correlated with spatial relations; because physical distances, so frequently are, or seem to be, the indexes of social distances, that statistics have any significance whatever for sociology. And this is true finally, because it is only as social and physical facts can be reduced to, or correlated with, spatial facts that they can be measured at all.
>
> (Park, 1926; pp.30-31)

By implication, if marriage (a measure of low social distance), demonstrably a good surrogate for positive social interaction generally (Shannon and Nystuen, 1976) and a widely used indicator of 'assimilation', could be related primarily to spatial intermixing rather than to the tendency for like to marry like, then measures of residential segregation and intermarriage should provide useful tools with

---

*Crime has been related both to crowding (people per room) (Rengert, 1973) and to density (people per unit area) (Beasely and Antunes, 1974), particularly for 'direct contact' personal crimes (Schichor, *et al.* 1979). Links between social heterogeneity and crime, most marked among lower class neighbour-hoods, have been established by Szabo (1966) and by Willie and Gershenowitz (1964), while Kapsis (1976) links higher rates of delinquency with ethnically transitional rather than ethnically stable areas. Braithwaite's (1979) comprehensive review confirms the longstanding association between deviance and low economic class, and Osborn (1980) identifies the significance of high rates of residential mobility within rather than between cities.

†Peach (1975) provides a salient introduction to this literature.

which to assess aspects of the social structure. Measuring the *spatial* structure of social interaction should allow inferences to be drawn about the structure and organization of social relations themselves.

Empirical support for the hypothesized relationships between social and physical distance is provided by research on ethnic intermarriage and sectarian violence. These 'positive' and 'negative' forms of interaction, representing extreme measures of small and large social distances, can both be related to residential (spatial) structure. It has been shown that residentially segregated groups have high rates of inmarriage (Timms, 1969), while outmarriage is more characteristic of the occupants of ethnically mixed areas (Peach, 1974a). More recently Peach (1974b, 1980) has convincingly refuted the most influential challenges to the applicability of his spatial argument. Measures of marital dissimilarity often correlate positively and well with measures of residential dissimilarity. Moreover, propinquity of social opposites can over-ride the tendency for like to marry like in ethnically mixed areas, and where this occurs intermarriage relaxes group boundaries socially and spatially. It may even have a causal role in the process of spatial mixing (Beshers, 1962). Conversely, Boal *et al.* (1976) and Boal *et al.* (1977) suggest that periodic outbreaks of sectarian violence in Belfast, together with enduring memories of them, are powerful forces maintaining high levels of ethnic segregation and territoriality. During periods of conflict, social and spatial boundaries are intensified (Jones, 1956). During more peaceful years, they are attenuated (Mitchell, 1979). Sectarian doorstep murders (see Murray and Boal, 1979) are a form of interaction, able, if necessary, to surmount the constraint of distance in order to ensure contact with social opposites. Even when groups are spatially segregated, sectarian violence persists as a tangible force maintaining social and spatial boundaries.

Intermarriage and sectarian violence represent two extremes on a continuum of forms of social interaction between groups. Conceptually, this may be said to range from positive high quality interaction comprising intermarriage, shared leisure, primary group mixing and accommodative tolerance; to the negative low quality forms of passive intolerance, outgroup labelling, common indictable crime and various forms of sectarian and political violence. A pertinent question is whether working class (as distinct from highly organized professional or white-collar) crime in an ethnically mixed inner city, is amenable to interpretation within this framework; whether the form of crime, its geographical pattern, volume and direction, allows meaningful inferences to be drawn from it about the structure of social relations.

Together, patterns of intermarriage and sectarian violence illustrate that the form of social interaction responds to the constraints of distance and the desire (or opportunities) for contacting social similars and opposites. The relative strength of these two major constraints apparently varies with the quality of interaction. Thus, below, an initial focus on the role of distance reveals how the opportunities for crime are spatially constrained, and access to them socially structured. This prefaces a discussion of the direction of offending, which requires explicit consideration of the role of potential victims, as well as actual victims and offenders. It probes beyond a narrow definition of crime as discrete pathology to a wider view of its meaning and interpretation as one of several forms of low quality social interaction, and considers its implications for the spatial structure of group relations.

Spatial aspects of criminal and social behaviour

Empirical evidence demonstrates that distances between offender residence and crime location vary according to the type of offence and its target area characteristics (White, 1932; Baldwin *et al.*, 1976). Longer distances characterize those crimes with higher rewards (Capone and Nichols, 1976) and those committed in areas of higher socio-economic status (Pyle *et al.*, 1974). Nevertheless, as demonstrated in the text, and widely observed elsewhere, inner city offenders travel comparatively short distances to commit their offences (Baldwin *et al.*, 1976; Rengert, 1977). Spatial constraints preclude any tendency to offend against more distant social and economic opposites. Two possible explanations for this geographical containment are discussed below in terms of the distribution of opportunities for crime; and the constraints imposed by limited spatial mobility among the inner city population as a whole.

The distribution of environmental opportunities for crime has been investigated in Britain (cf. Mawby, 1977; Clarke, 1978) and in the USA (Brantingham and Brantingham, 1975; Dingemans, 1978), and its links with social organization tentatively explored (Reppetto, 1976; Rengert, 1977; Mayhew, 1979). It is clear that the location and availability of environmental opportunities exerts a major influence on patterns of crime, and that in terms both of opportunities and social organization the inner city environment provides many chances for opportunistic offending.

Despite a predominantly working class character, the inner city often contains areas of apparently high socio-economic variability over short distances. This feature may be influential on the propensity to offend (Winchester, 1978) and its explanatory power is supported both by 'structural strain' and 'frustration-aggression' theories (Merton, 1938; Wolfgang and Ferracuti, 1967; pp.143–146). Despite the predominance of ageing and often structurally unsound Victorian terraces, a mixture of housing types and tenures cuts across the sharp environmental differences between characteristic 'housing action' and 'general improvement' areas. Insecure window and door fittings, entrances exposed by the piecemeal demolition, infill and refurbishing associated with urban renewal, and easy access through vacant lots interspersed with occupied dwellings all serve to increase residents' proneness to victimization by local opportunistic offenders. Few houses have private garages, although in the study area over 40% of families own at least one car. Here, 'on street' parking is widespread and facilitates the 'game' of 'taking and driving away' which is rapidly gaining popularity among bored local youths.

High densities and crowding, together with marked social and cultural hetero-geneity themselves influence the possibilities for crime. Density *per se* yields a wide range of nearby victims (as well as greater opportunities for like-minded offenders to meet in mutual support); heterogeneity increases the range of socially dissimilar contacts; and overcrowding is a factor contributing to a lively street life. One consequence of the latter, pertinent to the present discussion, is an acute awareness of 'street offences' and offenders, either through direct observation and participation, or through verbally exchanged information about others' experiences.

Space precludes a detailed discussion of the concept of socially structured access to objectively apparent opportunities for crime. However, in order to examine its containment within the inner city more closely, data pertaining to offenders, victims and places of offence for all indictable crime charged to residents of the study area over an 18 month period (January 1978–June 1979) were obtained.* Survey material gathered in the same area during February 1979 provides additional information on population mobility and other behaviour patterns. To facilitate comparison, the offence data were aggregated to the level of 71 destination zones utilized in the survey.†

Table I presents the statistical relationship between the mean distance of each destination zone (from and including the subareas comprising the main study area, and weighted to control for variations in the total populations of these 13 origin zones), and rates of movement or linkages to them. All crime-related variables decline consistently over increasing distance; more markedly with respect to offence locations than victim origins. This is not surprising as the mobility characteristics of the victims themselves would also be expected to influence the maximum distance between offender and victim residential origins. Consequently, although there is no evidence that the most distant victims travel farthest to crime locations, victims' own 'journey to crime' characteristics are also responsive to distance such that 63·9% of offences occur within one kilometre of the victim's home, and 83% occur within five kilometres.

Despite this, and although victim origins are amongst the crime characteristics least related to distance from offender residence, the *locations of offences* against private victims decline more consistently with distance than does any other crime-related measure. It is suggested that the spatial constraints on offender and victim mobility operate independently with respect to offence locations (which represent their zone of overlap), but that because of the limited mobility of both parties this is realized in the tendency for predominantly local offending often against local victims. Thus, the second explanation for the spatial containment of crime in the inner city, a more general set of constraints on the geographical extent of population mobility, appears particularly salient.

Few attempts have been made to assess the form of crime in relation to other types of social interaction. Although Turner (1969b) found distance decay functions

---

*Altogether 615 offences were included (of which 224 were perpetrated by two or more offenders), involving a total of 702 offenders (of whom 152 were responsible for two or more crimes).

†These zones were designed by the city's public transport authority who administered the survey cited here.

‡Nevertheless, the characteristics of victims resident at relatively large distances from zones of offender origin are an important focus in their own right, and the assessment of crime locations in terms of their attraction for victims as well as offenders is a pertinent area for research.

Susan J. Smith

describing pairs of marriage licence applicants, intra-urban migration and slogan hearer–teller links could also be applied to data for offender residence and crime locations, most research has assumed rather than asserted the relationship between offender mobility and population mobility in any one area (see Baldwin *et al.*, 1976; p.96). However, if the 'journey to crime' *is* a reflection of general population mobility, as usually assumed, then the distribution and distance characteristics of offences will not only be related to the type of crime, its target area characteristics and the distribution of available opportunities, but also to the behavioural

TABLE I

*The spatial structure of population mobility and patterns of offending**

	1	2	3	4	5	6	7	8	9
(1) Distance	—	0·764	0·722	0·526	0·696	0·706	0·601	0·638	0·686
(2) All regular journeys		—	0·930	0·810	0·649	0·614	0·430	0·427	0·471
(3) Journey to work			—	0·820	0·591	0·533	0·536	0·373	0·393
(4) All journeys (non-walk)				—	0·566	0·473	0·460	0·208	0·531
(5) Offence locations (all)					—	0·930	0·879	0·619	0·534
(6) Offence locations (private victims)						—	0·893	0·737	0·620
(7) Victim origins							—	0·720	0·517
(8) Private victim residence								—	0·622
(9) Co-offender residence									—

*Each entry denotes the value of Spearman's rank correlation coefficient; for all coefficients including distance as a variable, short distances are allocated the highest ranks.

characteristics of populations from which offenders (and victims) are drawn. It is, therefore, pertinent to consider the suggestion of Horton and Reynolds (1971) that the areas of a city accessible to its population vary among residentially based subgroups, due to differences in travel and shopping preferences, workplace locations and length of residence; factors themselves related to socio-economic class and ethnicity. Knowledge of the city is acquired through regular journeys, but the extent of this knowledge may limit the subjective availability of other travel destinations. In this sense areas available to the population generally could also be seen as those available to potential offenders, with population mobility patterns outlining the distribution of potential crime locations.

Exploring this contention, the correlation co-efficients (Table I) among various mobility and crime measures show the relationships between their respective distributions.* They reveal similarities in the spatial structure of links to the 71 zones. The two sets of measures comprise distinct intercorrelated clusters bridged by 'journey to offence' destinations, with which all three measures of mobility correlate more strongly than with any other crime-related variable. In fact both measures of offence location are more strongly related to their respective regular journey destinations than to *all* journey destinations (which include irregular journeys for recreation, medical purposes, visiting and other personal reasons), which lends some support to Horton and Reynold's contention that, if anything, it is regular journeys which influence the spatial structure of other travel patterns. However, while the distribution by zone of 'all journeys' exhibits no strong correlation with offence or victim locations, there *is* a relationship between the origins of all journeys and the origins of crime 'trips' (r_s = 0·65, $P<0·05$). The *pattern* of offending may to some extent be influenced by regular journeys, but the *amount* of offending is related to a more general tendency towards socializing among the population as a whole.

Table I thus suggests that the spatial structure of population mobility is more representative of offence locations than of victim origins.† Additionally it indicates for all three measures of mobility, that the relationship between journey destinations and co-offender residence is stronger than their respective relationships with private victim residence so that, by implication, the residential origins of victims are less familiar to the population of the study area than are the zones from which co-offenders are drawn. This is explained by the greater over-representation of co-offenders nearby, and their more complete containment within the zoned area. It confirms that opportunities to commit offences against non-local victims depend on the propensity of the latter to move within offenders' spatial range, but this in turn often limits the type of victim such that many are drawn from within or nearby the study area.

Figure 1 shows the incidence of all eight variables in terms of their over- or under-representation by zone (the proportional deviation from volumes expected on the basis of zone area).‡ Trends of over-representation nearby and under-representation further away are broadly congruent across all trip categories, with irregular peaks

---

*The table compares population data (offences) with a 20% sample (journey destinations). It is obviously not necessary to test coefficients among the former for significance; those among the latter *are* all significant ($P<0·01$). Correlation coefficients among the two measures would be significant ($P<0·05$) if both were samples. Assuming that utilizing population data for one of the variables decreases the error measure, all coefficients for which an inferential test is meaningful are statistically significant at the levels of confidence specified.

†That the locations of offences against private victims are themselves related most strongly to private victims' residential origins reflects again the tendency for most victimization to occur over a narrow spatial range.

‡For victims' and co-offenders' residences, the measure is of the built-up area only. The proportion of destinations and residences excluded from the diagrams (unknown, unspecified or outside the zoned area), are as follows: all regular journeys, 7·7%; all journeys, 3·6%; journey to work, 9·8%; co-offender residence, 4%; all offence locations, 3·1%; locations of offences against private victims, 2·3%; private victims' residences, 18·5%; all victims' origins, 20·2%.

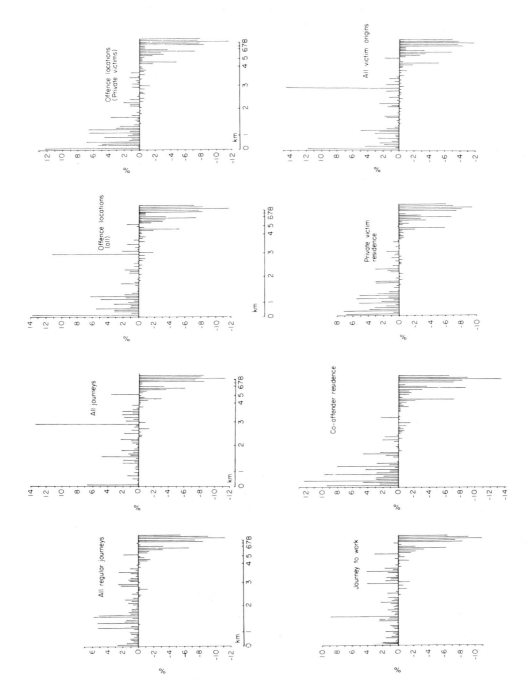

Figure 1. Percentage of over-representation and under-representation of journey destinations, victim and co-offender origins by zone.

(partly a function of zone configuration) reflecting the clusters of fixed opportunities presented by corporate victims. Particularly prominent among these is the city centre (zones 40, 42, 46). Although regular journeys (to work, school or college) were shown to be those most strongly correlated with distance (they decline most *consistently* with increasing distances from origin zones), it is the crime-related variables which are most marked in their *over-representation* nearby (particularly with respect to co-offenders' residences and the location of offences against private victims). Moreover, a much smoother decline over distance is exhibited by private victims' residential origins and the location of offences committed against them, than by the measures including all types of victim, so that despite the daytime clustering of people in the city centre, offences against private victims are not markedly over-represented in these zones. Instead, they concentrate near to offender origins, again confirming the localized nature of crimes against private individuals.

The spatial extent of offending is clearly well contained by that of the other journeys.* In effect, the incidence of all crime related variables (but particularly those involving private victims) is constrained by distance to a greater extent than more habitual activity patterns, which may in turn influence the distribution of crime insofar as they render greater subjective availability to some parts of the city than others.† While resident offenders account for almost 50% of crimes cleared in the neighbourhood, there is no evidence of long distance moves by non-resident criminals into the locality. These characteristics support Rengert's (1977) contention that inner city areas tend to be both less 'emissive' than their higher offender rates would suggest, and less 'attractive' to outside offenders than their relatively high accessibility would seem to merit.

The spatial constraints on offending discussed so far limit considerably the range of available potential victims. Under these circumstances, temporal variations in activity patterns become acutely significant as a permissive influence on the directedness of offending, and as a passive constraint on the distribution of opportunities.

Weekly and diurnal patterns of population mobility create spatial variations in the probability of contact between potential offenders and victims, and Cohen and Felson (1979) suggest that long term crime trends can be partly explained by changes in these routine activities. They argue that the postwar experience in the USA of a major shift away from activities in the home towards more widespread

---

*Not only are a larger proportion of offence locations than other journey destinations concentrated into zones where they are over-represented (80% all offence locations and 79% locations of offences against private victims, compared with 68% regular journey destinations, 61% journeys to work and 53% all journey destinations are found in zones where they are over-represented by 1% or more) but also, a much larger proportion of offence locations occur in zones less than 1·5 km from their respective perpetrators' zone of origin (52% all offence locations and 63% locations of offences against private victims, compared with 25% regular journey destinations, 16% journeys to work and 13·2% all journey destinations are found within this relatively short distance).

†The potential influence of the offender's image of the city on patterns of offending has been explored by Carter (1974).

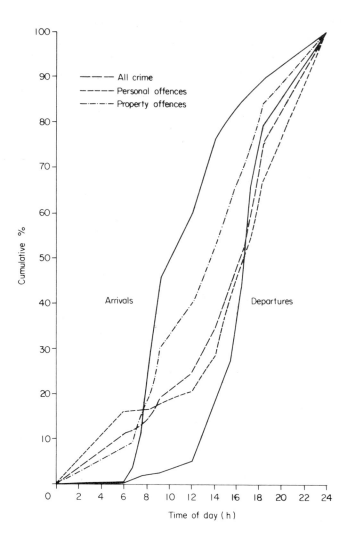

Figure 2. Arrivals at and departures from all regular journey destinations, and offence times (all known offences).

socializing, has underlain much of the increase in those direct contact personal crimes which occur less frequently at home than elsewhere. In Britain too, Sparks *et al.* (1977) have confirmed their implication that the most active and mobile sections of the population experience greater personal victimization. These short-cycle movements also affect the distribution in time of unguarded property. For instance, Reppetto (1974) identified rhythms in the pattern of residential burglary which reflected diurnal variations in aggregate journey to work characteristics.

Further inferences in the same vein may be drawn by considering all indictable crime occurring in the study area during the 12 months, July 1978–June 1979, and so including the large proportion of offences which remain uncleared (viz. 1859,

73·9% of the total).* Figure 2 shows the relationships between the known times of these offences and those of the resident population's arrivals at and departures from their regular journey destinations. The tendency for most offences to have occurred either before the majority of the population reached their regular destination, or after they left, is clear. However, there were marked differences between personal and property crimes in this respect. Within the obvious limitations of these data, it is possible to infer that during peak periods of property offending there was a higher probability for local residents to be absent. During peak times for personal offending, they were more likely to be present, in the sense that they would not be engaged in regular commitments.

To date, the 'dark figure' of unreported and undetected crime has not been extensively researched in Britain (see Sparks *et al.*, 1977), and the relationships between actual and perceived crime remain ambiguous (Balkin, 1979; Garofalo, 1979). However, it is not difficult to appreciate how the highly visible personal offences, disproportionately localized, and committed at times when they are most likely to be witnessed by residents, can become responsible for inciting fear, apprehension and patterns of avoidance such that their social significance reaches beyond the parties immediately involved. It is by considering these direct contact personal crimes, though not excluding the many burglaries against private victims (which are frequently small scale and take the form of a personal affront), that the influence of crime on the spatial structure of group relations will be considered in more detail.

Such personal offences are the type of crime most appropriately examined as social interaction, and distance has been revealed as a powerful constraint on their spatial form. It is argued that either as a result of this constraint, or as one factor contributing to it, the directedness of crime is conceptually, and often analytically, inseparable from that of the other forms of social interaction with which it is associated.

Crime and the structure of social relations

Within the study area, crime as a form of social interaction proved closely linked with several other strands in the complex web of social relations.† Over a period of ten years, the area acquired a reputation for high crime and tension among ethnic groups, and in this it is not unusual among the inner areas of many large British and American cities.

> The prevalence of rumours about street robberies at night and actual criminal acts committed against the residents (of the area), the generalised anxiety and gossip about crime are factors which account for a certain amount of racial tension.
>
> John (1972; p.14).

*Uncleared crimes are those which have not been charged to an offender, 'taken into account' with other offences or 'written off' according to Home Office instructions.
†The author was resident in the study area for two consecutive years between 1977 and 1979. Evidence presented in this chapter is drawn from ethnographic and survey material collected during this time, in addition to the 'official' statistics discussed earlier.

Newspapers reported the 'facts behind the wave of terror', noting offers to shop-keepers of 'Mafia-style protection against gangs of marauding West Indian youths' and the refusal to pay rates due to excessive vandalism.* Despite ethnic residential mixing, activity patterns became increasingly polarized and a tendency towards separate primary groups, clubs and community organizations was re-inforced by gossip, rumour and the mass media.

It is suggested below that observed spatial and temporal constraints on the extent of offending and, as a consequence, the actual or perceived responsibility of local offenders for much crime, ultimately helps explain how it became interleaved with ethnic relations.† Moreover, it is suggested that the key to this explanation *does* lie in the association between propinquity and social distance. However, the link is not straightforward, for it is only (and even here arguably) with reference to the two extremes of intermarriage and sectarian violence that the content of relationships can be approximately derived from their form. Common indictable crime sits uneasily between these two extremes, for it is a more enigmatic type of social exchange, and its objective form prompts at least two contrasting interpretations.

Crime as positive social interaction

The short geographical distances between offenders and private victims *could* be interpreted as reflecting small social distances. Crime itself could be regarded as an essentially non-directed, independent variable, integral to all social relations and contingent upon the permissive opportunities present in the density, composition and spatial arrangement of the population. Inter-group crime may then be explained with reference to patterns of primary group socializing. For although intermarriage provides a good measure of 'assimilation', the key to its inception lies in the character of primary group relations (Gordon, 1964). Primary group mixing *per se* increases the probability of randomly directed offences occurring across group boundaries, and in this sense, as an indicator of Gordon's critical stage of assimila-tion, an increase in intergroup crime *could* mark the beginning of social and spatial de-segregation and the dissolution of group boundaries.

Criminologists have observed that much crime arises out of essentially positive forms of interaction within the primary group (Driver, 1961; Luckenbill, 1977), while sociologists' research on changes in the nature of primary groups with increased densities and social heterogeneity offer further support for this

---

*For example, *Birmingham Evening Mail* 5.1.1970-8.1.1970, 9.8.1977, 14.10.1977, 6.12.1977; *Birmingham Post* 8.6.1976, 30.11.1977. Hall *et al.* (1978) and Cashmore (1979) document reports made by the mass media in greater detail. Some consequences are apparent in Rex and Tomlinson's (1979) study.

†Links between crime and race explored during the world population movements earlier this century are epitomized in the work of Sellin (1938) on 'culture conflict'. Renewed interest since the late 1960s suggests that significant differences in crime rates are experienced between ethnic groups (see Batta *et al.*, 1975; Mawby *et al.*, 1979; Mawby and Batta, 1980). There is no firm evidence, however, that a large proportion of crime is inter-racial (Stevens and Willis, 1979).

interpretation. The associated increase in transitory contacts (see Simmel, 1957; Wirth, 1938) may not replace intimate bonds, but co-exist with them (Baldassare, 1977), and as a consequence the quality of primary relations varies spatially (see Litwak and Szelenyi, 1969; Bell and Boat, 1957). This tendency is formalized by Fischer (1977) who posits distance as an important 'cost' of maintaining interpersonal relationships, a cost which necessarily influences their quality. Long distance friendships *must* be intimate because they are 'expensive' to maintain; short distance ties *may* be intimate, but they are often casual. Thus the changed character of the primary group not only offers opportunities nearby for strong ties with potential co-offenders, but also presents an increasing number and variety of less committed associations with potential victims, within a framework of ostensibly positive social interaction.*

This interpretation is consistent with the assumptions of assimilability underlying some intermarriage studies. Work in this vein by the 'spatial sociologists' threads tenuously through two interdependent themes characterizing current research on residential segregation: the specification of locational constraints imposed by structural economic or political factors (see Sims, Ch. 6, this volume) and the elucidation of residential choice guided by the positive desire of like individuals to cluster spatially (Robinson, 1979), and to exclude social opposites (Boal, 1980). Assuming locational freedom to translate social distance into spatial separation, the tradition apparently favours a residential choice model, but allowing that propinquity may promote social similarity (intermarriage) their tenets can also be applied when access to housing is constrained.

In an ethnically mixed area of limited housing resources (such as the study area in Birmingham), the latter condition might be expected to obtain. Here, the interpretation of intergroup crime as an undesirable, but nevertheless inevitable, consequence of social integration gives it at least a contributary role in the process of social 'accommodation', if not 'assimilation'. In this, with intermarriage, its form paradoxically supports Dewey's (1920) observation that social life rests in communication, Park's (1926) exposition of the importance of communication to the spatial pattern and moral order of city life, and Shibutani's (1961) argument that interpersonal contact is the basis for the formation of united social groups with distinctive cultures. It also seems in agreement with Simmel's (1957) view of the positive role of conflict, integrated with its negative aspects but empirically inseparable from them. However, for Simmel, the 'positive' role of conflict carries some very different connotations, for it is instrumental in the formation and consolidation of group boundaries.

Crime as negative social interaction

This alternative framework is offered both by Simmel (1957) and Wirth (1938) who

---

*Herbert (1977) discusses territoriality among offenders, illustrating the geographical significance of subculture theories which were originally formulated in social rather than physical space.

explore most explicitly the contention that physical proximity and social interaction need not necessarily promote 'consensus'. Density and heterogeneity (for Wirth the very epitome of urbanism), while providing a framework for contact and communication between groups, can also lead to heightened awareness of group differences. Physical contact and social interaction are necessary but not sufficient conditions for moral order. In fact contact is as likely to cause conflict and confusion as it is to provide a basis for stability and consensus.

Clarke's (1971) research in Trinidad illustrates how propinquity may be conducive to low quality forms of social interaction across group boundaries. Despite ethnic residential mixing in San Fernando, ethnic inmarriage predominates. Institutional factors prevent the translation of large social distances into spatial separation, and 'intersegmental friction' excited by national politics serves to maintain group boundaries socially where geographical segregation is precluded. Ley's (1974; p.131) description of the decline in gang confrontations over increasing distances from the home turf suggests moreover that proximity itself is of critical significance in the choice of social opposites as victims. Together, these examples suggest a second interpretation of intergroup crime: it may signify a purposive attempt to assert social distance in terms of authority, status, class, political or ethnic allegiance; or to usurp material benefits and social standing as a response to domination in these same terms. As an active response to structural positions, crime provides a means of defining and reinforcing group boundaries, of maintaining social distance where spatial separation is impossible, or even of initiating a move towards residential segregation.

It is clear from the contrasting 'positive' and 'negative' interpretations of crime that any assessment of its significance for the structure of social relations requires insight into the subjective meaning attached by participants and observers to events, as well as specification of their 'objective' form.* Thus it is suggested that the geographer's measurement of the quantity and direction of interaction be complemented by the social psychologist's assessment of its content and quality; that the 'spatial sociologist's' link between social and physical distance is combined with the symbolic interactionist's association between social structure and interpersonal relations.

Social interaction and social reaction

An interactionist approach to crime, intellectually grounded in the work of Simmel, and first gaining its distinctiveness earlier this century from psychologists, sociologists and philosophers in Chicago (who include Dewey, Mead, Park and Wirth), provides an analytical framework appropriately combined with the major tenets of criminology's 'social reaction' theorists (see Becker, 1963; Lemert, 1972). Particularly salient is their contention that offences are largely inseparable from

---

*Hannerz (1980; pp.280-296) discusses the problem of 'meaning', its negotiation during social interaction and its significance for the emergence of collective identities.

reactions to them: crime and its aftermath are both products of social interaction. Becker's assertion that "deviance is not a simple quality, present in some kinds of behaviour and absent in others. Rather, it is the product of a process which involves the responses of other people to the behaviour" (Becker, 1963; p.14), suggests that as a *low* quality form of social interaction, crime is often analytically inseparable from processes of outgroup labelling or passive intolerance. This framework offers the opportunity to understand how crime (including those offences emerging from essentially positive relationships) can ultimately prompt the replacement of tendencies towards primary mixing with a propensity for social separation. It illuminates the role of crime in the crystallization of group and individual identities, and clarifies the rationale for its association (in this particular example) with ethnicity, rather than with (for instance) economic class *per se*.

Recorded crime does remain an important indicator of social reaction, for the public plays a far more crucial role in the policing process than has usually been appreciated.[*] But over a period of 12 months in the study area, while the majority (57%) of recorded offences occurred in highly visible places (in the street or on public land, in local shops, or in places of entertainment, pubs and cafes), 'official' knowledge of their perpetrators remained limited (80%, 63% and 51% for each scene respectively remain unsolved), such that the 'objective' occurrence of crime was easily and rapidly subsumed by perceptions of it, and of its perpetrators. The resulting patterns of social avoidance and spatial exclusion may be elucidated at two distinct levels of analysis, the cognitive and the structural.[†]

Initially, it is appropriate to consider the level of 'folk' perceptions and behaviour, the role of shared meanings abstracted primarily from ethnographic material. In this vein, Hannerz (1969) identifies the public as 'consumers of danger'. They comprise actual and potential victims, minimizing trouble, fear and uncertainty by developing their 'street wisdom' and avoiding dangerous places and people. Ley's (1974) attempt to elicit behavioural responses to stress among the residents of Monroe, an inner city neighbourhood of Philadelphia, provides a graphic illustration of this strategy. Crime (usually associated with local gangs) presented residents with their greatest insecurity and, as a result, spatial avoidance of gang turfs was widely practised, even at the cost of substantially lengthened journeys in some cases.

It was apparent within the study area that residents additionally displayed an ability to adjust their definitions of danger in accordance with their need for 'safe' activity space within their own neighbourhood. There was a strong tendency to define trouble spots and offenders according to perceived neighbourhood boundaries: dangerous locales beyond the immediate neighbourhood were designated

---

[*]Chatterton (1976), noting the control exerted by members of the public over the availability of information to the police, supports the view that figures traditionally interpreted as the products of police discretion may often be attributed to citizen discretion.

[†]Mitchell (1974) provides a cogent account of the epistemological distinctions between different levels of analytical and common sense abstractions of group behaviour, which provides the basis for the conceptual separation of these levels in the text.

(and could be avoided) in terms of their physical or locational characteristics; danger within the familiar (and necessarily well-used) locality could often only be conferred upon places at specific times and, therefore, by virtue of the suspected identities and activities of their occupants, rather than because of any inherent properties of the place itself. This distinction, between danger as a property of place and danger as a property conferred upon places by the characteristics of the people associated with them, is one forecast by Hannerz (1969). Perhaps because of the blurred distinctions among contemporary socio-economic groups, and the apparently high possibilities for upward social mobility in modern British society, 'dangerous' occupants, most often envisaged by respondents to be their social opposites, were more frequently defined in terms of their ethnicity than in terms of any other social characteristic.*

It is when individual strategies can be generalized in this way to the level of group interaction patterns that the significance of the varying space requirements observed in interpersonal relations becomes clear. Thus Irving justifiably stresses social avoidance as one of the main forces underlying residential segregation.

> Social relations, especially with relative strangers, are potentially perilous. There is a serious risk of shame or even harm through behaving wrongly and one of the most obvious safety mechanisms is avoidance through the medium of space.
>
> Irving (1978; p.270)

The practise of 'distancing' (Suttles, 1972) provides one such mechanism. It is a process initiated by actual and potential victims as a means of managing perceived danger, and it is related to territoriality in terms of

> a series of sieves in which territorial differentiation is the first in a telescoped series which sorts people so the possibility of affiliation minimizes the potential of physical harm and negative judgments.
>
> Suttles (1972; p.183)

In effecting such differentiation, easily recognized extrinsic signs (Suttles' 'para-linguistic' modes of communication) are required to prompt various levels of avoidance or interaction. These signs may be communicated primarily through the symbolic use of 'style' (Cohen, 1965; Brake, 1980); the interpretation of image (appearance, dress), demeanour (expression, gait, posture) and argot (special vocabularies and their delivery). Ethnicity, embracing all of these, is therefore a logical criterion by which to exclude social opposites as part of a strategy for managing danger. In this sense the low levels of residential segregation which facilitate shared leisure and intermarriage, also permit negative forms of interaction. As a result, actual and perceived antagonisms, tending to reinforce group boundaries socially are ultimately reflected to varying degrees by spatial separation.

One extreme consequence is the 'defended neighbourhood' (Suttles, 1972; pp.189–232), a confirmation of the ability of actual and potential victims (as well as offenders) to practise territoriality as a means of regulating spatial movement to

---

*Modern trends in social mobility often make 'objective' class distinctions deriving from the occupational order fluid and intangible (see Goldthorpe, 1980), and their behavioural significance arguable; a problem for academics as well as aspiring offenders (see Parkin, 1979; pp.4–11).

avoid conflict and confusion. The most striking tendencies towards spatial differentiation for defensive purposes are found in the inner city. However, a specific example makes it clear that the phenomenological perspective offered so far can explain only in part why these tendencies arise.

The example is taken from Shah's (1979) Althusserian critique of Asian residential segregation in East London, which also sheds some light on the spurious nature of the voluntary/involuntary segregation dichotomy. Focusing on the Bangladeshi community in East London, he stresses their need to develop 'safe' areas in order to reduce the incidence of racist attacks, frequently occurring outside Spitalfields. The strategies of spatial separation required to minimize fear and victimization, which included demands from the Bengali Housing Action Group for segregated council housing are, for Shah, a reflection of political and ideological factors (the police as an embodiment of the legal superstructure) which supplement the fundamental economic bases of segregation. Thus he asserts

> There is certainly evidence, then, that one of the determinants of residential concentration of the Bangladeshi is the lack of confidence the community has in the police's ability to protect them from racial attacks which have been a dominant feature in London's East End. Certainly this is 'voluntary segregation' but inasmuch as the distinction between voluntary and involuntary segregation is related to freely determined choice, segregation as a defensive act lies more in the realm of imposed rather than self-imposed segregation.
>
> Shah (1979; p.450)

This example draws attention to the second (structural) level introduced earlier, by focusing on the differential distribution of power. Criminologists have traditionally approached this question by examining how qualities of deviance are symbolically attached to socially, economically or politically marginal groups, affecting their arrest rates, legal processing and subsequent patterns of offending.* Thus one explanation for the marked differences in crime rates associated with variations in class and race can be couched in terms of power relations played out in the authority structure. However, *within* any one area, for the pragmatic purposes of conducting everyday life, the direction of outgroup labelling is negotiated with respect to other structural axes by which power is distributed and manipulated. Social reaction figures prominently *within* the community as well as *against* it. Damer (1974) noticed this in a small Glasgow neighbourhood. "As the people of Wine Alley have no one left to scapegoat but themselves, their displaced label buzzes around the estate with no exit" (Damer, 1974; p.205). At this level, the application of Weberian principles seems appropriate, considering the finer divisions of power as it is utilized within the economic class structure, the political structure and the status order.†

---

*Whole areas may also be labelled with similar consequences for their occupants (see Damer, 1974; Gill, 1977).

†The importance of a 'received' structure, particularly the economic order, setting the wider framework in which crime arises is not disputed. Peet's (1975) geography of crime is set at this level. However, Baldwin *et al.* (1976), and Herbert (1979) also stress the significance of class positions in the distributive system. That tenure differences explain (statistically) more variation in offender rates than most other commonly used census variables offers tentative support for the role of Weber's property (housing) class schema.

One of the principal contributions of Weber's stratification scheme is the importance attached to symbolic as well as material elements. In tying the subjective notion of status with the objective concept of class, social strata can be explained in terms of the organization of attitudes and behaviour and the adoption of distinctive lifestyles, as well as by variations in income and patterns of consumption. While social reaction theories have tended to concentrate on explaining the correlation of crime with indices of low material wealth, it is suggested here that the distribution and acquisition of symbolic rewards is equally significant. In the inner city, an area whose residents' positions with respect to the political and economic structures are common and low, the concept of status, resting on the acquirement of symbolic as well as material rewards, proves particularly valuable.

The status hierarchy is determined by a measure of social esteem or 'honour', and perhaps the most explicit 'theory' of its distribution is outlined by Parkin (1971; pp.40-44) in which he links status with the economic order: nationally, the distribution of social honour provides a means of justifying inegalitarianism. Within the inner city, however, status differences may be realized first on the basis of ethnicity. Ethnic groups comprise status groups whose collective sentiments arise from a 'subjective belief in their common descent' rather than from their position in the occupational order. Consequently, what little social power *is* available is most efficiently used by excluding *ethnic* opposites from rewards and life chances.* Outgroup labelling and social avoidance are practised in order to *preserve status* as well as to minimize danger. Reporting, accusing and evading social opposites provide means of regulating group boundaries as well as aiding the management of fear or uncertainty in a complex environment.

At both the cognitive and the structural levels discussed above, ethnicity provides the most logical or economic basis upon which to construct or avoid relationships. Together, the two levels of analysis explain how crime, together with other forms of low quality social interaction, can become linked with the selection of ethnicity as a principle upon which to organize the meaning of social action, and the structure of activity or residential space.

Conclusion

The relationship between social and physical distance may be profitably explored as an outcome of negative (low quality) as well as positive (higher quality) forms of interaction. Crime is constrained by distance, and often committed locally such that intergroup crime may be indicative of social integration (and an increased probability of random offences affecting social opposites); it may occur as an

---

*Neuwirth (1969) outlines in more general terms the application of Weber's concept of status to ethnic communities. Parkin (1979; pp.89-116) discusses the significance of the exclusion and usurpation of rewards and life chances within as well as between major social groups (i.e. according to criteria which are not solely economic), and Boal (1980) has explored the geographical application of his concept of closure (an extension of Weber's own (1948) formulation) in Belfast.

essentially non-directed response to the poverty or deprivation associated with low socio-economic class;* or it may be a means of defining and delimiting group boundaries. (Certainly reactions to crime often fulfil this last function.)

For the extremes of intermarriage and sectarian murder, where the content of the relationship is relatively unambiguous, a direct link between residential segregation and the spatial form of social interaction can be posited, from which inferences about social structure and organization can be drawn. An analysis in the same vein of working class crime is obfuscated by the consideration of a set of events whose meanings are less clear-cut; but it therefore necessarily probes the crucial area of the emergence and crystallization of social structure itself. Thus interaction can be examined as it creates and sustains the social structure, which in turn mediates between an 'internal subjective order of attitudes, traditions and aspirations' and an 'external spatial order' (Buttimer, 1969).

Low quality forms of social interaction appear instrumental in the choice of criteria upon which to organize behaviour and focus group allegiance. Their spatial realization is a symptom rather than a cause of the social processes discussed in the text. In the example cited, ethnicity provided both the extrinsic traits required to categorize and avoid social opposites, and a basis for the collective sentiments required to maximize symbolic (as well as material) rewards. Social definitions and experiences of ethnicity provided the mechanism whereby fear and apprehension, the very antithesis of Firey's (1945) 'sentiment and symbolism', could also operate independently of the economic order influencing groups' attachment to urban space.

Acknowledgements

The author is indebted to the West Midlands Passenger Transport Executive for making the results of their 'inner area community bus study' available; to the SSRC for financial support; and to Dr Peter Jackson who made helpful comments on an earlier draft of this paper.

References

Ahamad, B. (1967). An analysis of crimes by the method of principal components. *Journal of Applied Statistics* **16**, 17-35.

Baldassare, M. (1977). Residential density, household crowding and social networks. *In* "Networks and Place", (C. S. Fischer, ed.) Free Press, New York.

Baldwin, J. (1974). Social area analysis and studies of delinquency. *Social Science Research* **3**, 151-168.

Baldwin, J. (1975). British areal studies of crime: an assessment. *British Journal of Criminology* **15**, 211-227.

*Rose and Deskins (1980) explain the increase in inter-racial homicide in Detroit in these terms. Youth bent on acquiring wealth or material goods seem insensitive to the racial identity of the victim.

Baldwin, J., Bottoms, A. E. and Walker, M. A. (1976). "The Urban Criminal". Tavistock, London.

Balkin, S. (1979). Victimisation rates, safety and fear of crime. *Social Problems* **26**, 343-358.

Batta, I. D., McCulloch, J. W. and Smith, N. J. (1975). A study of juvenile delinquency among Asians and half-Asians. *British Journal of Criminology* **15**, 32-42.

Beasley, R. W. and Antunes, G. (1974). The etiology of urban crime: an ecological analysis. *Criminology* **4**, 439-461.

Becker, H. S. (1963). "Outsiders". Free Press of Glencoe, New York.

Bell, W. and Boat, M. D. (1957). Urban neighborboods and informal social relations. *American Journal of Sociology* **62**, 391-398.

Beshers, J. M. (1962). "Urban Social Structure". Free Press, New York.

Boal, F. W. (1980). Ethnic residential mixing in an ethnic segregation context. Paper presented at the symposium on Ethnic Segregation in Cities, St Antony's College, Oxford.

Boal, F. W., Murray, R. and Poole, M. A. (1976). Belfast: the urban encapsulation of a national conflict. *In* "Urban Ethnic Conflict: a Comparative Perspective", (S. E. Clarke and J. L. Obler, eds.) Comparative Urban Studies Monograph Series No. 3. Institute for Research in Social Science, University of North Carolina.

Boal, F. W., Poole, M. A., Murray, R. and Kennedy, S. J. (1977). Religious residential segregation and residential decision making in the Belfast urban area. SSRC Project Report No. HR 1165.

Boggs, S. L. (1965). Urban crime patterns. *American Sociological Review* **30**, 899-908.

Braithwaite, J (1979). "Inequality, Crime and Public Policy". Routledge and Kegan Paul, London.

Brake, M. (1980). "The Sociology of Youth Culture and Subcultures." Routledge and Kegan Paul, London.

Brantingham, P. J. and Brantingham, P. L. (1975). Residential burglary and urban form. *Urban Studies* **12**, 273-284.

Buttimer, A. (1969). Social space in interdisciplinary perspective. *Geographical Review* **59**, 417-426.

Capone, D. and Nichols, W., Jr. (1976). Urban structure and criminal mobility. *American Behavioral Scientist* **20**, 119-213.

Carter, R. L. (1974). The criminal's image of the city. University of Oklahoma (microfilm).

Cashmore, E. (1979). "Rastaman." George Allen and Unwin, London.

Chatterton, M. (1976) Police and social control. *In* "Criminal Justice: Selected Readings", 1978, (J. Baldwin and A. K. Bottomly, eds.) Martin Robertson, London.

Clarke, C. G. (1971). Residential segregation and intermarriage in San Fernando, Trinidad. *Geographical Review* **61**, 198-218.

Clarke, R. V. G. (ed.) (1978). "Tackling Vandalism." Home Office Research Study No. 47. HMSO, London.

Cohen, A. K. (1965). The sociology of the deviant act: anomie theory and beyond. *American Sociological Review* **30**, 1-4.

Cohen, L. E. and Felson, M. (1979). Social change and crime rate trends. *American Sociological Review* **44**, 588-607.

Corsi, T. M. and Harvey, M. E. (1975). The socio-economic determinants of crime in the city of Cleveland. *Tijdschrift voor Economische en Sociale Geografie* **66**, 323-336.

Damer, S. (1974). Wine Alley: the sociology of a dreadful enclosure. *Sociological Review N.S.* **22**, 221-248.

Dewey, J. (1920). "Reconstruction in Philosophy." Henry Holt, New York.

Dingemans, D. J. (1978). Defensible space design in the California townhouse. *California Geographer* **16**, 95-110.

Driver, E. D. (1961). Interaction and criminal homicide in India. *In* "Criminal Behavior Systems", (M. B. Clinard and R. Quinney, eds.), Rinehart and Winston, New York.

Engels, F. (1848). "The Condition of the Working Class in England." Reprinted 1969. Penguin, Harmondsworth.

Firey, W. (1945). Sentiment and symbolism as ecological variables. *American Sociological Review* **10**, 140-148.

Fischer, C. S. (ed.) (1977). "Networks and Place." Free Press, New York.

Garofalo, J. (1979). Victimisation and the fear of crime. *Journal of Research in Crime and Delinquency* **16**, 80-97.

Gill, O. (1977). "Luke Street." Macmillan, London.

Goldthorpe, J. H. (1980). "Social Mobility and Class Structure in Modern Britain." Clarendon Press, Oxford.

Gordon, M. M. (1964). "Assimilation in American Life." Oxford University Press, New York.

Gordon, R. H. (1967). Issues in the ecological study of delinquency. *American Sociological Review* **32**, 927-944.

Hall, S., Critcher, C., Jefferson, T., Clarke, J. and Roberts, B. (1978). "Policing the Crisis: Mugging, the State and Law and Order." Macmillan, London and Basingstoke.

Hannerz, U. (1969). The management of danger. Unpublished paper. University of Stockholm, Department of Anthropology.

Hannerz, U. (1980). "Exploring the City." Columbia University Press, New York.

Harries, K. D. (1974). "The Geography of Crime and Justice." McGraw-Hill, New York.

Herbert, D. T. (1976). Social deviance in the city: a spatial perspective. *In* "Social Areas in Cities", (D. T. Herbert and R. J. Johnston, eds.) Vol. 1. Wiley, Chichester.

Herbert, D. T. (1977). Crime, delinquency and the urban environment. *Progress in Human Geography* **1**, 208-239.

Herbert, D. T. (1979). Urban crime: a geographical perspective. *In* "Social Problems and the City", (D. T. Herbert and D. M. Smith, eds.) Oxford University Press, New York.

Horton, F. and Reynolds, D. (1971). Effects of urban spatial structure on individual behavior. *Economic Geography* **47**, 36-48.

Irving, H. W. (1978). Space and environment in interpersonal relations. *In* "Geography and the Urban Environment", (D. T. Herbert and R. J. Johnston, eds.) Vol. 1. Wiley, Chichester.

John, A. (1972). "Race and the Inner City." Runnymede Trust, London.

Jones, E. (1956). The distribution and segregation of Roman Catholics in Belfast. *Sociological Review N.S.* **4**, 167-189.

Kapsis, R. E. (1976). Continuities in delinquency and riot patterns in black residential areas. *Social Problems* **23**, 567-580.

Lemert, E. (1972). "Human Deviance, Social Problems and Social Control." 2nd edition. Prentice Hall, Englewood Cliffs.

Ley, D. (1974). "The Black Inner City as Frontier Outpost", Association of American Geographers, Monograph No. 7, Washington D.C.

Litwak, E. and Szelenyi, I. (1969). Primary group structures and their functions: kin, neighbors and friends. *American Sociological Review* **34**, 465-481.

Lottier, S. (1938). Distributions of criminal offences in metropolitan regions. *Journal of Criminal Law, Criminology and Police Science* **29**, 37-50.

Luckenbill, D. F. (1977). Criminal homicide as a situated transaction. *Social Problems* **25**, 176-186.

Mayhew, H. (1862). "London Labour and the London Poor", Vols 1-4. Griffin, Bohn, London.

Mayhew, P. (1979). Defensible space: the current status of a crime prevention theory. *Howard Journal of Penology and Crime Prevention* **18**, 150-159.

Mawby, R. I. (1977). Defensible space: a theoretical and empirical appraisal. *Urban Studies* **14**, 169-179.

Mawby, R. I. and Batta, I. D. (1980). "Asians and Crime: the Bradford Experience." Scope Communication for National Association of Asian Youth, Southall.

Mawby, R. I., McCulloch, J. W. and Batta, I. D. (1979). Crime amongst Asian juveniles in Bradford. *International Journal of the Sociology of Law* **7**, 297-306.

Merton, R. K. (1938). Social structure and anomie. *American Sociological Review* **3**, 672-682.

Mitchell, J. C. (1974). Perceptions of ethnicity and ethnic behaviour: an empirical exploration. *In* "Urban Ethnicity", (A. Cohen, ed.) Tavistock, London.

Mitchell, J. K. (1979). Social violence in Northern Ireland. *Geographical Review* **69**, 179-201.

Murray, R. and Boal, F. W. (1979). The social ecology of urban violence. *In* "Social Problems and the City", (D. T. Herbert and D. M. Smith, eds.) Oxford University Press.

Neuwirth, G. (1969). A Weberian outline of a theory of community: its application to the 'Dark Ghetto'. *British Journal of Sociology* **20**, 148-163.

Osborn, S. G. (1980). Moving home leaving London and the delinquent trends. *British Journal of Criminology* **20**, 54-61.

Park, R. E. (1926). The urban community as a spatial pattern and a moral order. *In* "The Urban Community", (E. W. Burgess, ed.) University of Chicago Press.

Parkin, F. (1971). "Class Inequality and Political Order." MacGibbon and Kee, London.

Parkin, F. (1979). "Marxism and Class Theory: a Bourgeois Critique." Tavistock, London.

Peach, C. (1974a). Ethnic segregation and intermarriage patterns in Sydney. *Australian Geographical Studies* **12**, 219-229.

Peach, C. (1974b) Homogamy, propinquity and segregation: a re-evaluation. *American Sociological Review* **39**, 636-641.

Peach, C. (ed.) (1975). "Urban Social Segregation." Longman, London.

Peach, C. (1980). Ethnic segregation and intermarriage. *Annals, Association of American Geographers* **70**, 371-381.

Peet, R. (1975). The geography of crime: a political critique. *Professional Geographer* **27**, 277-280.

Phillips, P. D. (1972). The geography of crime. Unpublished Ph.D. thesis. University of Minnesota, Minneapolis.

Phillips, P. D. (1973). Risk related crime rates and crime patterns. *Proceedings, Association of American Geographers* **5**, 221-224.

Pyle, G. F., Hunten, E. W., Williams, E. G., Pearson, A. L., Doyle, G. and Kwofie, K. (1974). "The Spatial Dynamics of Crime." University of Chicago Press.

Rengert, G. F. (1973). Density, crowding and criminal activity: relationships between urban environments and human behavior in Philadelphia. Unpublished paper. Temple University, Philadelphia.

Rengert, G. F. (1977). Burglary in Philadelphia: a critique of an opportunity model. Paper presented at the Annual Meeting of the Association of American Geographers, Utah.

Reppetto, T. A. (1974). "Residential Crime." Ballinger, Cambridge, Mass.

Reppetto, T. A. (1976). Crime prevention and the displacement phenomenon. *Crime and Delinquency* **22**, 166–177.

Rex, J. and Tomlinson, S. (1979). "Colonial Immigrants in a British City." Routledge and Kegan Paul, London.

Robinson, V. (1979). "The Segregation of Asians within a British City: Theory and Practice", Research Paper No. 22. School of Geography, Oxford.

Rose, H. M. and Deskins, D. R., Jr. (1980). Felony murder: the case of Detroit. *Urban Geography* **1**, 1–21.

Schichor, D., Decker, D. L. and O'Brien, R. M. (1979). Population density and criminal victimisation: some unexpected findings in central cities. *Criminology* **17**, 184–193.

Sellin, J. T. (1938). "Culture Conflict and Crime." SSRC Bulletin No. 41. Report of the sub-committee on personality and culture. SSRC, New York.

Shah, S. (1979). Aspects of the geographical analysis of Asian immigrants in London. Unpublished D. Phil. thesis, University of Oxford.

Shannon, G. W. and Nystuen, J. D. (1976). Surrogate measures of urban social interaction. *Professional Geographer* **28**, 23–28.

Shaw, C. R. (1929). "Delinquency Areas." University of Chicago Press.

Shaw, C. R. and McKay, H. D. (1931). "Social Factors in Juvenile Delinquency." Government Printing Office, Washington, DC.

Shaw, C. R. and McKay, H. D. (1942). "Juvenile Delinquency and Urban Areas." Revised edn 1969. University of Chicago Press.

Shibutani, T. (1961). "Society and Personality: an Interactionist Approach to Social Psychology." Prentice Hall, Englewood Cliffs.

Simmel, G. (1957). The metropolis and mental life. *In* "Cities and Society: the Revised Reader in Urban Sociology", (P. K. Hatt and A. J. Reiss, Jr, eds) Free Press of Glencoe, New York.

Sparks, R. F., Genn, H. G and Dodd, D. J. (1977). "Surveying victims." Wiley, Chichester.

Stevens, P. and Willis, C. F. (1979). "Race, Crime and Arrests." Home Office Research Study No. 58. HMSO, London.

Suttles, G. D. (1972). "The Social Construction of Communities." University of Chicago Press.

Szabo, D. (1966). The sociocultural approach to the aetiology of delinquent behaviour. *International Social Science Journal* **18**, 176–193.

Timms, D. W. G. (1969). The dissimilarity between overseas born and Australian born in Queensland: dimensions of assimilation. *Sociology and Social Research* **53**, 363–374.

Turner, S. (1969a). The ecology of delinquency. *In* "Delinquency: Selected Studies", (T. Sellin and M. E. Wolfgang, eds) Wiley, New York.

Turner, S. (1969b). Delinquency and distance. *In* "Delinquence: Selected Studies", (T. Sellin and M. E. Wolfgang, eds) Wiley, New York.

Weber, M. (1948). "From Max Weber", English transn (H. H. Gerth and C. W. Mills, eds). Kegan Paul, Trench, Trubner, London.

White, R. C. (1932). The relation of felonies to environmental factors in Indianopolis, Indiana. *Social Forces* **10**, 498–509.

Willie, C. V. and Gershenowitz, A. (1964). Juvenile delinquency in racially mixed areas. *American Sociological Review* **29**, 740–744.

Winchester, S. W. C. (1978). Two suggestions for developing the geographical study of crime. *Area* **10**, 116-120.

Wirth, L. (1938). Urbanism as a way of life. *American Journal of Sociology* **44**, 1-24.

Wolfgang, M. E. and Ferracuti, F. (1967). "The subculture of violence." Tavistock, London.

THREE

Black residential distribution in south London (1971)

ERROL BABOOLAL

Department of Geography, King's College, London, UK

In 1971 the 1·69 million people of 'New Commonwealth and Pakistani ethnic origin' resident in Great Britain (including children born in Great Britain to New Commonwealth-born parents) constituted 3·1% of the total population.* This group of immigrants and their British-born descendants are characterized by a brown or black skin colour, commonly termed 'black'—a feature which above all others distinguishes this group of migrants from earlier and larger migration streams to Britain (e.g. from Ireland and East Europe). In the context of urban social geography, immigrant status and skin colour status form only part of the structural characteristics of the urban population which have been shown to be important in residential segregation. These characteristics have been grouped into economic status, family status and ethnic status (Shevky and Bell, 1955).

Studies of immigrant (black and white) distributions in Western cities have revealed a tendency for these minority groups to congregate in spatially discrete areas of the city (see, for example, Johnston, 1971; Aldrich, 1975; Jones, 1976). Considerable importance has been attached to the intensity and spatial pattern of immigrant settlement, particularly in relation to the ecology of the city and to social interaction between the immigrant and host populations (Pahl, 1968).

A major tenet of this study is that black residential distributions in Britain have been examined on too large an areal scale to enable a thorough analysis of the more fundamental aspects of such distributions, more particularly, the levels of concentration, spatial patterns and processes involved. For example, Doherty (1973), Lee (1973) and Deakin and Cohen (1970) utilized rather large borough or ward units—owing largely to the superior availability of census data for these areal units.† This study utilizes small area census data (1971 census Enumeration

---

*New Commonwealth refers to all countries of the Commonwealth except Australia, New Zealand and Canada. It is a common euphemism used to describe people of black/brown skin colour.

†A significant exception is Jones (1970, 1976) who has utilized smaller Enumeration Districts in his spatial analysis.

Districts) for the southern half of Greater London. These data make possible a more detailed examination of those features of black residential distribution which have been neglected owing to inappropriate scales of analysis.

Particular attention is given to *three* features. First, the level/intensity and spatial characteristics (morphology) of black residential distributions, since these are important manifestations of the less visible social processes which operate in urban society to bring about residential segregation (Lieberson, 1963; Scargill, 1979). Second, the relationship between black residential distributions in British and US cities, since almost all the geographical concepts concerning black residential distributions in Western cities—such as models of immigrant dispersal and concentration (see, for example, Burgess, 1928; Cressey, 1938; Duncan and Duncan, 1957)—have been developed by workers in the US. The existence of this considerable body of literature invites comparison between the well established black residential patterns in US cities and the emergent patterns observed in British cities. In particular, valuable insights into the processes involved and likely future developments may be gained from US research if developments in Britain are seen to parallel earlier developments in the USA. Third, the relationship between black population distribution and the urban structure of south London, since theories of urban structure have formed a dominant theme in the development of urban geography. Despite the importance of Greater London as the chief centre of immigrant settlement and of social and political power, little attempt has been made to investigate the influence of the city's urban structure—such as the distribution of housing and employment opportunities—on various population groups.

The data and terminology

The population groups of prime interest here are those of "black" skin colour. This study relies on birthplace data derived from the 1971 census of England and Wales (Enumeration District basis) and on data obtained from the Greater London Council (GLC) relating to the physical and social condition of housing in each Enumeration District (ED). Birthplace data are used as a surrogate for the skin colour of a number of population groups, since skin colour is not directly recorded by the national census.* The following population groups are taken to constitute the black population of Britain:

(1) West Indian-born (all islands of the ex-British West Indies and Guyana);
(2) Asian-born (India, Pakistan, Sri Lanka, Bangladesh);
(3) African-born (Commonwealth Africa including Nigeria, Ghana, Kenya, Uganda);
(4) New Commonwealth-born (all countries of the Commonwealth except Australia, New Zealand and Canada, i.e. includes Cyprus, Malta, Gozo);

---

*The General Household Survey now incorporates an interviewer's assessment of skin colour. These data relate to a relatively small sample of the national population and are of little direct use in detailed intra-urban studies.

(5) UK born with both parents born in the New Commonwealth (i.e. children born in Britain to New Commonwealth-born parents);

(6) Overseas-born black (West Indian-born, Asian-born, African-born);

(7) Composite Black Population (New Commonwealth-born, plus UK-born with both parents born in New Commonwealth).

The following birthplace group is taken to constitute *one* of the white population groups of Britain:

> British-born (England, Scotland, Wales; excludes Northern Ireland and includes the relatively small proportion of black children born in Britain).

The above population groups are not all mutually exclusive. The choice of birthplace combinations has been influenced by the nature of the data published by the Office of Population Censuses and Surveys and by the need to examine the distribution of black population groups both individually and in aggregate. The use of census data is subject to a number of limitations and 'noise' which stem principally from the mode of census data gathering and presentation (e.g. under- and overenumeration) and from the use to which these data are put. In the context of this study, the chief limitation is the use of birthplace data as a surrogate for the skin colour of various population groups. It is readily admitted here that to label the above population groups as black and white, is not strictly accurate since it involves a number of definitional and conceptual problems. These problems have been widely discussed elsewhere (see Eversley and Sukdeo, 1969; Rose *et al.*, 1969; Moser, 1972; Anwar, 1974; Peach and Winchester, 1974). Despite the skin colour 'anomalies' which arise and in the absence of more specific data, it is believed that the general association between birthplace and skin colour remains sufficiently strong to allow the labelling of groups as black and white.*

ED data of 1971 for south London were amalgamated into 'comparable areas' (CAs) which enable comparison of 1961 and 1971 small area census statistics (ED boundaries were redrawn between the two census years)—part of the larger study from which this paper is drawn.† The analysis of black residential distribution relates to the whole of the Greater London Council area south of the Thames, sub-divided into 1613 CAs. This compares favourably with the 259 wards more commonly used, for example by Doherty (1973) and Lee (1973). The average total population per CA in 1971 was 1765 compared with 10 998 for wards in south London. This data base allows a more detailed spatial analysis than hitherto in south London.

---

*It seems somewhat hypocritical to sift the wealth of population data for 'New Commonwealth-born' immigrants as opposed to, say, 'all immigrants' and yet not to admit that the *raison d'être* for such sorting is the black skin colour of the first group, albeit for scientific and social interest, not necessarily because of skin colour prejudice.

†ED boundaries for 1961 and 1971 were superimposed and contiguous boundaries extracted on the premise that they should form the smallest possible closed areal unit (comparable areas). Data for EDs falling within these CAs were then amalgamated.

The black population of south London

In 1971 the Composite Black Population group constituted 6% of the total south London population (Table I). This group consisted mainly of West Indian-born immigrants (35·6% of total Composite Black Population), Asian-born immigrants

TABLE I
Number and proportion of selected population groups in south London (1971)

Population group*	Total number in south London	Per cent of total south London population	Highest per cent total CA population in south London
Composite Black Population	170 134	6·0	55·6
Overseas-born black population	122 214	4·3	43·7
West Indian-born	60 680	2·1	31·0
Asian-born	38 414	1·3	19·2
African-born	23 120	0·8	10·4
British-born black population	51 177	1·8	22·2
Total population	2 847 474	100·0	—

*See text for definition of birthplace groups

(22·5%), African-born immigrants (13·6%) and British-born Blacks i.e. Great Britain-born, but with both parents New Commonwealth-born (30·1%).* The maximum percentage concentration of the Composite Black Population was 55·6% of total CA population. Of the individual black population groups, West Indian-born reached the highest concentration (31·0% of the total CA population), then Asian-born (19·2%) and African-born (10·4%). These percentage maxima fall between the maximum concentrations observed at larger and smaller scales. For example, Lee (1973) found the highest West Indian-born concentration in Greater London wards was 21·3%, whilst Peach *et al.* (1975) found 61·0% West Indian-born in Birmingham EDs. Clearly the scale of analysis strongly influences the degree of concentration observed. It is interesting to note that the inclusion of British-born blacks raised the observed highest concentration of the 'black population' from 43·7% for overseas-born Blacks only, to over 50% for the Composite Black Population. This may be a 'critical' barrier psychologically, if not also socially and economically, for both the black and white populations. Secondly, even with the

* Small totalling error due to data aggregation by OPCS. Composite Black Population was calculated from number/1000 born in New Commonwealth plus number/1000 born in the UK, but with both parents New Commonwealth-born.

largest possible skin colour grouping, the highest level of concentration observed in south London was considerably lower than that observed in US cities at the census tract scale (e.g. between 90 and 100% according to McEntire, 1960).

Two summary measures enable a consideration of the overall distribution of population groups—the index of residential dissimilarity (ID) and the index of isolation (P*). Since the use of ID is well established in geographical literature (Duncan and Duncan, 1955; Taeuber and Taeuber, 1965; Lieberson, 1980), it suffices here simply to reiterate that the value of ID is the percentage of a sub-group which would have to change its sub-area of residence in order to reproduce the distribution of the group with which it is being compared. The second summary measure (P*) was proposed as long ago as 1949 (Shevky and Williams, 1949), but has not proved as popular as ID.* Lieberson (1980) has advocated the resurrection and modification of P* which emphasizes variations in total group size and the relative proportions of each group living in sub-areas, since,

> there are times when one would want to take into account the asymmetric quality of group interaction. Namely, the probability of a given member of group X interacting with a member of group Y is not the same as the probability of a given member of group Y interacting with an X in the usual situation where the size of the two groups are different.
>
> Lieberson (1980; p.6)

The P* index may be interpreted as

> . . . describing for a specified group in the city the average probability of interacting with some specified population based on the distribution of persons by subareas and the assumption that interaction is with someone in the same subarea.
>
> Lieberson (1980; p.9)

The two measures, ID and P*, can be viewed as complementary rather than conflicting in that they help to analyse population distribution from somewhat different perspectives—the overall segregation of one group from another (ID) and the degree of isolation of individuals in one group from individuals in another group (P*). It is tempting here to equate these with the spatial separation and social isolation of population groups.

As measured by ID, in 1971 black population groups of south London exhibited a dual pattern of segregation, from British-born and from each other (Table II). There was a quite high segregation from the British-born, although this varied markedly according to the population group, e.g. ID (Composite Black Population) = 48·8. West Indian-born were the most highly segregated individual group (ID = 57·7), and Asian-born the least segregated (ID = 36·5). This relationship is supported by P* values which indicate that West Indian-born were most isolated from the British-born population in south London (P* = 0·7684) and Asian-born least isolated (P* = 0·8221), i.e. the average West Indian-born lived in a CA, in which British-

*See Fig. 3 for equation.

higher → more segregation

↓ better for 10

Errol Baboolal

TABLE II
Index of residential dissimilarity (ID)
for black population groups in south London (1971)

Population group	British-born	West Indian-born	Asian-born
Composite Black Population	48·8		
West Indian-born	57·7		
Asian-born	36·5	53·1	
African-born	48·2	35·1	37·2

TABLE III
Index of isolation (P★)
for selected population groups in south London (1971)

Population group	Total population	British-born	Composite Black Population	West Indian-born	Asian-born	African-born
Composite Black Population	1·00	0·7794	0·1444	—	—	—
Overseas-born black population	1·00	0·7871	—	—	—	—
West Indian-born	1·00	0·7684	—	0·0739	0·0175	0·0193
Asian-born	1·00	0·8221	—	0·0276	0·0289	0·0139
African-born	1·00	0·7777	—	0·0507	0·0231	0·0226

According to Lieberson (1980):

$$_xP_y^\star = \sum_{i=1}^{n} (x_i/X)(y_i/t_i).$$

where

x_i is the number of group X in a given sub-area;

X is the total number of members of group X in the city;

y_i is the number of group Y in the sub-area;

t_i is the total population of the sub-area.

born constituted 76·8% of the total population, whereas the average Asian-born lived in a CA in which there were 82·2% British-born (Table III). Clearly, the processes of residential differentiation have operated differently on these two groups to bring about a marked disparity in distribution.

The scale of analysis has again resulted in an increase in the observed level of segregation, e.g. ID = 34·3 for West Indian-born and ID = 38·0 for African-born in Greater London wards in 1971 (Lee, 1973). However, the Asian-born population were less segregated in south London CAs than in Greater London wards (ID = 38·8) largely owing to the presence of the west London (Southall) Asian-born concentration in Greater London. Black population groups remained considerably less segregated in south London than minority groups in US cities. For example even at the larger census tract scale, Guest and Weed (1976) found that in 1970 the average segregation of Negroes from other population groups in Cleveland was 85·5; for Puerto Ricans 77·9 and for Mexicans 74·6. Even higher values can be expected in US cities at the smaller CA scale. Lieberson (1980; p.33) presented P* (black/black) values for 13 US cities (for years 'later' than 1960). From these, the isolation of the black from the white population can be calculated using P* (black/white) = 1 - P* (black/black). In these cities the isolation of Blacks from Whites ranged from 0·12 to 0·71. In the four cities in which the black population constituted the smallest proportion of total population (5·3–8·3%), i.e. more comparable with proportions in British cities, P* (black/white) values tended to be higher (range: 0·39–0·71) but still indicative of greater isolation of Blacks in US cities than, for example, of the Composite Black Population—P* (Composite Black Population/British-born) = 0·78.

Further evidence of the differential operation of segregation processes is provided by an examination of the distributional relationship between black population groups. West Indian-born and Asian-born were considerably more segregated from each other than from African-born (Table II). Indeed, Asian-born were more segregated from West Indian-born and African-born than from the British-born population. P* values support these general relationships (Table III) in that they indicate a high degree of isolation of black population groups from each other, e.g. P* (West Indian-born/Asian-born) = 0·0175; P* (Asian-born/West Indian-born) = 0·0276, i.e. the probability of a West Indian-born/Asian-born or Asian-born/West Indian-born contact was very small.

In the trans-Atlantic context, although black segregation has been shown to be higher in the USA than in Britain, the converse is true of black isolation. Lieberson's (1980; p.33) P* values for black/black isolation in 13 major US cities ranged from 0·29 to 0·88. Even allowing for the larger size and proportion of the black population groups in US cities, black population groups in south London were considerably more isolated from themselves than in the US; for example, P* (Composite Black Population/Composite Black Population) = 0·14 compared with P* (black/black) = 0·30 in Des Moines (each group constituted 6·0 and 5·3% of total population, respectively).

In recent years there has been some tendency to consider segregation between black population groups to be evidence of the voluntary or self-segregation of black people (see, for example, Dahya, 1974; Peach, 1975). In particular, Peach *et al.* (1975) stressed that

> While there may be doubt as to the relative strengths of discrimination by the white population and self-imposed separation by the black population in explaining the degree of spatial segregation of black and white, the high levels of segregation of Asians from the West Indian population indicates that voluntary, self-segregation must be a major factor.
>
> Peach *et al.* (1975; p.406)

It certainly seems reasonable to postulate a desire among Asian-born, West Indian-born etc. to live in areas in which there are other Asian-born, West Indian-born etc. Indeed, in the writer's experience there is much animosity between these groups, particularly on the part of the Asian-born, who often consider Negroes to be 'inferior'. It is likely, therefore, that some Blacks will 'avoid' living close to different Blacks.* However, Peach *et al.*'s (1975) caution as to the relative strengths of constrained and unconstrained segregation is well founded. Differences in the segregation of these groups suggest a need to develop new models of immigrant segregation which cater for *two* or more competing groups (Rosenberg and Lake, 1976). Additionally, while the self-segregationists do not deny the existence and importance of skin colour discrimination, their isolation of a separate 'voluntary' segregation factor largely ignores this essential characteristic of the study groups. Skin colour is an omnipresent badge of identity, which generates complex and, paradoxically, often transparent reactions (favourable and unfavourable) between and within black and white population groups (see, for example, Smith, 1976). The very transparency of these reactions makes it difficult, if not impossible, to separate skin colour from such features as social class or 'voluntary' unconstrained segregation. The tendency of geographers to focus on the more easily measurable population characteristics of social class, religion etc., has resulted in an undervaluation of the role of skin colour as an explicit factor in explaining residential segregation in British cities. For example, to 'subtract' social class or between-black segregation from *total* segregation and then to attribute the remainder to skin colour discrimination or constrained segregation, ignores the initial strong influence of skin colour on social class, housing and employment opportunities etc.

Increasing emphasis on the examination of unconstrained segregation processes *within* black population groups is typified by several chapters in this book on current research in social geography (e.g. Simmons [Ch. 4]; Phillips [Ch. 5]; Sims [Ch. 6]; Brown [Ch. 9]). This trend highlights the need to re-examine the efficacy of applying well established geographical techniques and logic—initially developed to study monochrome population groups, such as the Irish and Jews in US cities—to the study of pleochroic societies (i.e. black, brown, white etc.) which forms the basis of much ethnic research.

In short, in terms of aspatial measures the fundamental feature of black residential distribution in south London in 1971 was one of segregation and isolation from the British-born population and from each other in terms of individual black population groups. Moreover, the degree of segregation differed markedly according to the black population group, with an especially strong contrast between the West Indian-born and Asian-born distributions. Despite the small scale of analysis, black population groups in south London were less segregated from the white population and more isolated from themselves than those in US cities.

---

*It is difficult to generalize about the attitudes of any group. However, the writer has lived in a black 'mixed' country, Trinidad, and has experienced both Asian and Negro attitudes towards each other. Among black people there still seems to be a skin colour hierarchy, in which to be a lighter shade of black is socially more acceptable than a darker shade.

The distribution of the black population

Summary indices have indicated the statistical/aspatial concentration of black population groups in south London. This was accompanied by a high degree of spatial concentration in 1971 (see Figs 1–4). The spatial distribution of population

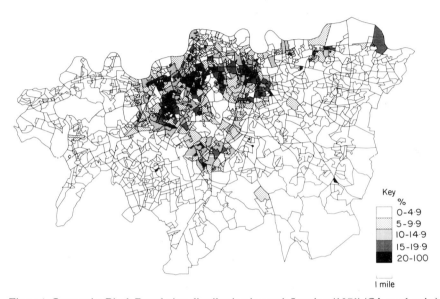

Figure 1. Composite Black Population distribution in south London (1971) (CA areal units).

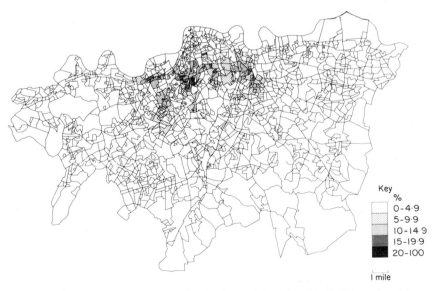

Figure 2. West Indian-born distribution in south London (1971) (CA areal units).

[handwritten margin notes: "taken for ethnic minorities", "{Eilanders not included, Wilmorrow, Ceylon}", "author boundary", "targeted training within the central S. area Acton"]

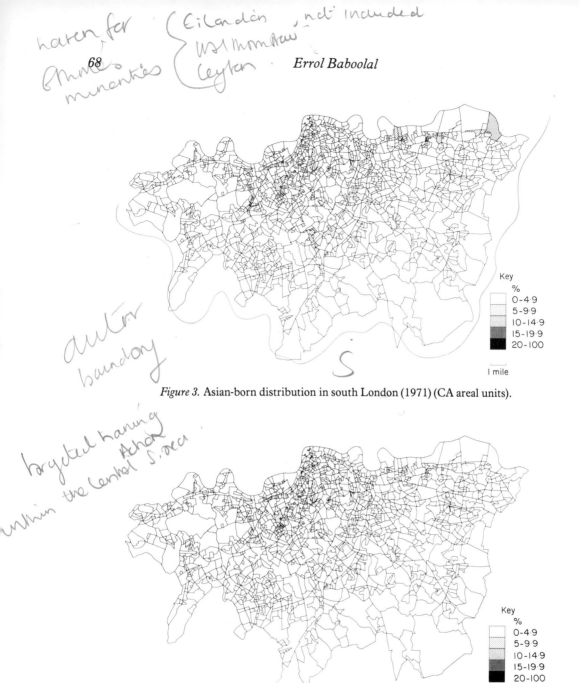

Figure 3. Asian-born distribution in south London (1971) (CA areal units).

Figure 4. African-born distribution in south London (1971) (CA areal units).

groups (black or white) cannot be divorced from the nature of the urban structure in which the residential patterns have developed. In this context, the spatial distribution of black population groups in south London is strongly suggestive of elements of three major theories of urban structure developed in the USA.

Three features dominated the spatial distribution of black population groups in south London. First, an overwhelming concentration of Composite Black Population in the inner city (relative to Greater London)—in a broad belt from West Hill/ Southfields in the west to Greenwich/Hither Green in the east (Fig. 1). If CAs in which the Composite Black Population constituted 5% or more of the total population are considered, then this inner city belt of concentration was spatially contiguous, located between the central business district of Greater London and the peripheral suburbs. This belt of concentration corresponded in both location and population composition with Burgess' (1928) 'zone of transition', a feature of which is immigrant settlement. However, within the main belt, the areas of highest concentration (20% or more of total CA population) formed four spatially discrete clusters. These clusters were centred on central Wandsworth, Upper Tooting/Balham, central Lambeth, and Lewisham. Just over one-quarter (26·1%) of the total Composite Black Population lived in the areas in which they constituted 20% or more of the total CA population, largely in the four main clusters. This multinodal pattern points to Berry and Horton's (1970) elaboration of the multiple nuclei theory of urban structure as a possible explanation of the observed spatial patterns.

Second, a secondary concentration of the Composite Black Population was located south of the main belt in the region of Thornton Heath/Selhurst. This concentration is strongly suggestive of Hoyt's (1939) sectoral development of residential areas in terms of its location in conjunction with the main belt—linked by CAs in which black people constituted 5% or more of the total population and its location in the 'suburbs' of north Croydon, rather than the inner city.

Third, individual black population groups were characterized by contrasting degrees and foci of spatial concentration. West Indian-born were more spatially concentrated than Asian-born or African-born, e.g. 1·3% of West Indian-born lived in areas in which they constituted 20% or more of the total population, compared with no Asian-born or African-born (Table IV). The principal foci of the West Indian-born distribution were central Lambeth and Lewisham with secondary foci in central Wandsworth and Upper Tooting/Balham (Fig. 2). Asian-born spatial foci were in the extreme north-east of the study area in Greenwich, Woolwich and Erith and secondary foci in Thornton Heath/south Norwood, Upper Tooting/Balham and Wimbledon Park (Fig. 3), i.e. they largely avoided West Indian-born foci. The African-born distribution was focused primarily on Upper Tooting/Balham (Fig. 4).

Despite the superior importance of Greater London in terms of size of black population and the social and political importance of developments within this city, little work has been carried out on the relationship between black residential distributions and the urban structure. The detailed spatial patterns revealed in this analysis highlight the need for further research in this direction to establish more clearly the nature of the processes which have brought about such distributions. Inadequate consideration of Greater London's urban structure has, to some extent, been due to its extremely complex nature, since it consists, in effect, of several 'cities' within the conurbation.

A major component of all models of urban structure is the nature of the housing

TABLE IV

Proportion of selected population groups living in CAs
in which they constituted stated % of total CA population in south London (1971)

CA population (%)	Stated population group's south London total (%)			
	Composite Black Population	West Indian-born	Asian-born	African-born
0·0–4·9	17·6	41·9	83·8	91·9
5·0–9·9	20·1	28·2	12·7	7·6
10·0–14·9	20·4	21·2	2·4	0·5
15·0–19·9	15·8	7·4	1·1	0·0
20·0 or more	26·1	1·3	0·0	0·0
Total	100·0	100·0	100·0	100·0

stock and the operation of the housing market, i.e. part of the physical and socio-economic fabric of the city. More specifically, models of immigrant (black and white) residential segregation emphasize the distribution of accommodation and employment opportunities and the immigrants' ability to gain access to these, as key factors influencing the distribution of immigrant groups (see McEntire, 1960). In the context of south London some indication of the nature of the housing stock is provided by a study conducted by the Greater London Council (no date). The chief objective of the GLC study was to determine which EDs contained the worst housing, with a view to their designation as Housing Action Areas (HAAs), after further investigation by local authorities. The process of identifying potential HAAs involved a consideration of the physical condition of dwellings (as indicated by the lack of basic facilities such as baths, hot water and internal WC) and the social condition of the households (as indicated by the extent of sharing basic facilities and of overcrowding). The worst 10% of EDs were considered to be potential HAAs. 432 EDs in south London were identified as potential HAAs. The CAs of south London were classified as potential HAAs if one or more of their constituent EDs were in the group of potential HAA EDs. On this basis, there were 219 CAs of potential HAA status in south London, the distribution of which is shown in Fig. 5. The 10% of areas of 'worst' housing conditions were located primarily in the inner city, although there were significant outliers in the south (Selhurst), east (Greenwich, Woolwich, Erith) and west (Mortlake, Teddington).

A visual comparison of Figs 1 and 5 reveals a remarkably close correspondence of the spatial distribution of the Composite Black Population and the potential HAAs. This correspondence extends to a detailed examination of the foci of black concentration. The four main clusters of higher concentration identified earlier coincide precisely with clusters of potential HAAs; the southward extension of black settlement into north Croydon is accompanied by an outlying potential HAA, as are

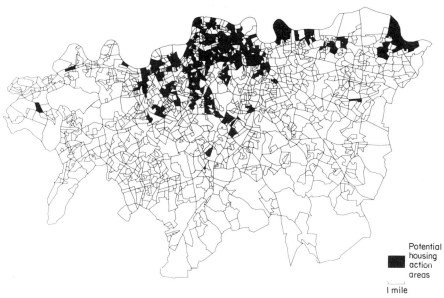

Figure 5. Distribution of potential housing action areas in south London (1971) (CA areal units).

the outliers of black concentration to the east in Greenwich, Woolwich and Erith. Of the Composite Black Population 38·5% lived in potential HAAs (Table V)—a very high proportion in relation to the British-born population (15·3%) and other immigrant groups, such as the Irish-born (23·9%).

The black people in potential HAAs were distributed mainly in CAs of higher concentration, e.g. 18·6% of the total Composite Black Population lived in potential HAAs in which they constituted 20% or more of the total population: the highest proportion in any of the percentage concentration groups used in this study and almost half (48·3%) of all the Composite Black Population in potential HAAs. However, in the case of individual black population groups a greater porportion of West Indian-born, Asian-born and African-born lived in potential HAAs of lower (less than 15% of the total CA population) concentration (Table V). This is due, in part, to the inclusion of children born in Britain to New Commonwealth-born parents in the Composite Black Population (but not in individual black population groups). These children may have contributed to higher levels of overcrowding and sharing of basic facilities, which in turn were important considerations in the GLC's selection of potential HAAs. If the number of each population group living in potential HAAs is expressed as a proportion of the group's south London total living in CAs in which they constituted 0-4·9%, 5-9·9%, etc. of total CA population, then the general association between black people in potential HAAs and CAs of higher concentration is maintained (Table VI), e.g. 22·9% of the West Indian-born who lived in South London CAs, in which they constituted 0-4·9% of the total population, also lived in potential HAAs, compared with 69·2% of West Indian-born in CAs of higher concentration (20% or more).

Individual black population groups were characterized by different relationships

TABLE V

% stated population group living in
potential HAAs, according to the proportion they constituted of the total population

Total CA population in potential HAAs (%)	Composite Black Population (%)	West Indian-born (%)	Asian-born (%)	African-born (%)
0·0–4·9	0·9	9·6	13·5	29·7
5·0–9·9	5·6	11·3	2·3	4·4
10·0–14·9	6·0	17·0	1·1	0·5
15·0–19·9	7·4	7·0	0·5	⋆
20·0 or more	18·6	0·9	⋆	⋆
Total	38·5	45·8	17·4	34·6

⋆Denotes no concentration at this level in CAs of south London in 1971.

with the areas of worst housing, with an especially strong contrast between the West Indian-born/African-born and the Asian-born distributions. A higher proportion of total West Indian-born and African-born than of Asian-born lived in potential HAAs (45·8%, 34·6% and 17·4% respectively). West Indian-born and African-born were more strongly represented in potential HAAs of higher concentration than were Asian-born (Table VI). Indeed, whilst less than half the Asian-born in each percentage concentration group in south London also lived in potential HAAs (maximum value 45·8%), in three out of the five percentage groups the majority of West Indian-born also lived in potential HAAs, especially at higher levels of concentration (maximum value 94·6%). African-born were represented in only three percentage groups in south London. All African-born in CAs in which they

TABLE VI

Stated population group living in potential HAAs as a proportion of
same population group living in all CAs of south London (1971), at various levels of concentration⋆

CA population in south London (%)	Composite Black Population (%)	West Indian-born (%)	Asian-born (%)	African-born (%)
0·0–4·9	5·1	22·9	16·1	32·3
5·0–9·9	27·9	40·1	18·8	57·9
10·0–14·9	29·4	80·2	45·8	100·0
15·0–19·9	46·8	94·6	45·5	†
20·0 or more	71·3	69·2	†	†

⋆Values in Table V as a percentage of values in Table IV for selected population groups. † Denotes no concentration at this level in CAs of south London in 1971.

constituted 10–15% of total population (their highest concentrations) also lived in potential HAAs. In aggregate, West Indian-born and African-born were considerably more strongly associated with the areas of worst housing in south London than were Asian-born.

The strong co-distribution of black population groups and potential HAAs may, in part, be due to the method of defining the potential HAAs. This included a consideration of the extent of sharing facilities and overcrowding. The predominantly young age structure and larger average family size of the black population (relative to the host population), coupled with their concentration in the lower status, lower paid occupations (see, for example, Community Relations Commission, 1976), would result in a greater incidence of overcrowding and sharing of basic facilities.

The close association of the black population distribution with a fundamental component of the urban structure of south London — the zone of worst housing — cannot be ignored and focuses attention on the need to investigate further the processes and mechanisms by which the black population gains access to housing. Bergel (1955) has suggested that the assimilation of an immigrant population into the host society is influenced by a number of factors, including the size of the immigrant group, the immigrants' social and economic status, the degree to which the immigrant culture differs from that of the host society, the degree of traditional institutionalized rejection of the immigrant group and the degree of conservatism of the host society. To these must be added more explicitly the skin colour of the immigrant/minority group, since this is an important feature of recent immigrants to Britain and has been shown to be an important consideration in housing decision-making among the white (host) population (PEP, 1967). Individual black population groups differ markedly in terms of the above factors, especially West Indian-born and Asian-born.

The nature of the disparities in the relationship between these population groups and the areas of worst housing in south London, in conjunction with contrasts in segregation discussed earlier, emphasizes the greater disadvantaged position of West Indian-born in relation to Asian-born and points to the need to investigate further not only overall urban ecological processes of residential segregation, but also the differential operation of these processes in relation to population groups of different characteristics; for example, West Indian-born and Asian-born share sufficient characteristics for their residential distribution to coincide in the zone of worst housing, but are sufficiently different for there to be some sorting of these groups within the zone, i.e. different foci of concentration. In view of the consistent 'Negro–Indian' alignment of disparities and the writer's experience, it is tempting to suggest that in a white dominated society such as in Britain a brown (Indian) skin colour allows immigrants to gain access to better housing and employment than is available to black (Negro) immigrants. It is readily admitted, however, that to prove this notion is extremely difficult, not least because factors other than skin colour distinguish the Negro and Indian populations.

Morphology of black residential clusters

If a 'cluster' is defined as a group of spatially contiguous CAs in which the black population constituted 20% or more of the total CA population, then four spatially discrete clusters dominated the distribution of the Composite Black Population in south London in 1971 (Fig. 1). These were centred on central Lambeth, Upper Tooting/Balham, Lewisham and central Wandsworth. The largest of these clusters was certainly not as dominant, at least spatially, as the primate clusters observed in US cities (see McEntire, 1960; pp.25-31 for maps of Negro concentrations in selected major US cities).*

Close examination of the clusters reveals a number of morphological similarities in terms of the disposition of areas of higher and lower concentration. The clusters were characterized by nuclei of higher concentration, surrounded by areas which decreased in concentration concentrically away from the nucleus. This is best developed in the Upper Tooting/Balham and Lewisham clusters. Concentric development was not uniform, there being some sharp boundaries between areas of highest and lowest concentration. This is best seen in the central Lambeth and central Wandsworth clusters. The higher concentration nucleus of each cluster enclosed a relatively small core of lower concentration. This is best seen in the central Lambeth cluster ('hollow' core size 1·5 miles long, 0·5 miles wide), and in the Upper Tooting/Balham cluster which has two 'hollow' cores within the nucleus (core sizes 0·6 miles long, 0·3 miles wide and 0·3 miles long, 0·25 miles wide). Each cluster was characterized by a number of close lying but spatially discrete outliers of higher concentration (20% or more). These were often connected to the main cluster by 'corridors' of CAs of lesser concentration. This feature is best developed in the central Lambeth and Lewisham clusters (Fig. 1).

The extent to which 'bands' and 'outliers' are observed is strongly dependent not only on the scale of observation—such features were not revealed in the ward analysis of Greater London by Doherty (1973) and Lee (1973)—but also on the percentage class interval used to map the distribution. Smaller and larger class intervals than the 5% grouping adopted here would tend to accentuate or mask, respectively, the detailed morphology of the clusters. What *is* important here, however, is not the number or width of bands, but their general configuration. This is represented diagrammatically in Fig. 6 which shows in essence an aureole-nebula spatial pattern. It is readily acknowledged here that this aureole-nebula spatial pattern is an abstraction and was not perfectly developed in south London. Nevertheless, the essential elements were present. Figure 7 shows the Upper Tooting/Balham cluster in more detail. If allowance is made for local deformities then the morphology of this cluster does conform to the generalized diagram shown in Fig. 6.

*A re-examination of maps of the distribution of black people in Greater London as a whole (Lee, 1973) also suggests that none of the three major clusters in North, West or South London dominated the overall spatial distribution.

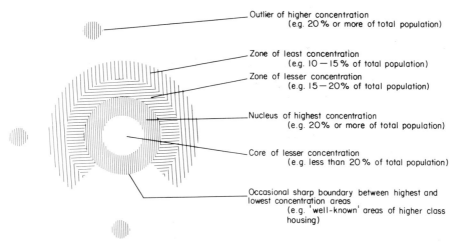

Figure 6. Diagrammatic representation of the morphology of black residential clusters in south London: an aureole-nebula spatial pattern.

The detailed morphology of clusters in south London conforms only partially to McEntire's description of Negro ghettos in 12 major US cities as a 'segregated core' surrounded by successive zones of 'concentrated', 'mixed' and 'dispersion' tracts, with some smaller separate areas of non-white residential concentration, i.e. outliers (McEntire, 1960; p.34). This correspondence of spatial form points to the need to examine further similarities in the processes and mechanisms of residential differentiation in Britain and the USA, with a view to the development of more universal geographical concepts. Equally important, however, is that differences in the spatial form of black residential clusters in British and US cities form the basis

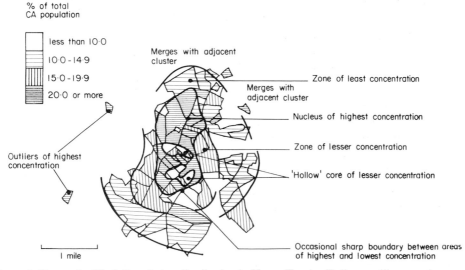

Figure. 7. Composite Black Population distribution in Upper Tooting/Balham to illustrate the aureole-nebula spatial morphology of black residential clusters.

for an examination of urban residential processes more specifically related to the British context.

South London clusters differed from those in US cities in four major respects. First, nuclei in south London were characterized by considerably lower percentage levels of concentration (20% or more) than in US cities (75% or more). Second, the 'hollow' core characteristic of south London clusters had no counterpart in the cases mapped by McEntire (at least at the census tract scale). However, recent gentrification of the inner city by private developers has resulted in the growth of white enclaves, i.e. hollow cores, in predominantly black areas in a few US cities, notably Los Angeles. Third, the spatial transition of areas from highest to lowest black concentration *appears* to be less rapid in south London than in US cities although more detailed distance decay analyses will have to be conducted in order to substantiate this view. Fourth, the CAs of south London in which black people constituted 5% or more of the total population, enclosed three relatively large areas which were characterized by less than 5% black people in 1971. These 'white' areas are of particular interest since in two of the three cases they were juxtaposed with the black residential clusters of highest concentration (20% or more), e.g. in the south-eastern sector of the central Lambeth cluster and in the southern sector of the Wandsworth cluster. The third enclosed white area was located between the central Lambeth cluster and the embryonic cluster to the south in Thornton Heath/Selhurst. These enclosed areas are represented by the 'cut-out' sector in the diagram presented in Fig. 6. It would be misleading to undervalue the three enclosed white areas as mere 'enclaves' in the broad belt of black concentration, since they are comparable in size to the black clusters and consisted of relatively 'well known' higher class residential districts, e.g. Dulwich, Upper Norwood and Southfields. Despite the existence of a few areas of white resistance, such as Beacon Hill (Boston), the persistence of white areas even when enclosed by black areas is not common in US cities. The latter are characterized by a more uniform 'retreat' of white residents in the face of ghetto expansion. It is interesting to note here that the US exceptions to the general contrasts drawn between British and US black residential patterns, occur in older US cities which are closer in urban form to British cities, i.e. characterized by a multinodal urban structure rather than by rapid, concentric urban growth. This highlights the importance of urban structure in influencing the detailed morphology of black residential clusters.

A re-examination of evidence from other studies suggests that the aureole–nebula spatial form of black population clusters is repeated in other British cities. In particular Jones's (1970; p.208) isoline maps of black population density in Birmingham and Dalton and Seaman's (1973; pp.35–36) isoline maps of black location quotients in the London Borough of Ealing strongly support the idea of nuclei of higher black concentration, surrounded by successive zones of decreasing concentration, although it is difficult to trace the 'hollow' core evident in south London. There is also evidence to suggest that this feature is not new, for example, in describing the distribution of black people in Cardiff, Little (1948) noted that 95% of the black population lived in Bute Town, mainly in the dock area of south

Cardiff. A few black families lived in the centre of the city and a few in working class districts or suburbs. Banton (1955) also suggested that in areas of black concentration ". . . there is usually a number of streets in which coloured residents may reach 50 per cent, while many more live scattered about the vicinity" (Banton, 1955; p.68). Patterson (1963) provided a clear description of the early development of the central Lambeth (Brixton) cluster. She noted that

> The Brixton coloured settlement consists of one heavily settled area in the Somerleyten-Geneva Road district, a less compact area in Angell Town and a dozen or more less concentrated nuclei within a few miles radius of Brixton market.
>
> Patterson (1963; p.213)

In view of the link between spatial form and social process (Pahl, 1968) it is somewhat surprising that little effort has been made to formalize the morphological characteristics of black residential clusters in Britain and to relate these to the processes of residential segregation. This study points to the need for a microscale examination of urban structure as a key factor in influencing the nature and location of black residential clusters. For example, it is known from field knowledge that each of the four main black residential clusters in south London was centred on a major crossroads or high road. These subcentres of the urban structure were characterized by two features which may explain the hollow core within the nucleus of highest concentration. First, non-residential land usage is more common in such areas. This is best seen in the central Lambeth cluster where retail and local government administration buildings at the crossroads of Brixton Road and Acre Lane partly account for the hollow core. The latter does, however, include some residential areas. Second, it is likely that the subcentres were characterized by the oldest housing (first to be built around the transport node) and would therefore be among the first areas to be redeveloped and replaced by local authority housing or non-residential land usage. Since up to 1971 only a relatively small proportion of black people had gained access to local authority housing these redeveloped cores contained a relatively low proportion of black people.

Conclusion

The features which distinguish black residential clusters in south London from those in US cities pose important questions *vis-à-vis* the processes and mechanisms involved in their formation (the socio-economic fabric of the city) and the importance of local variations in the housing stock (the physical fabric of the city) in influencing the location, size, shape and internal morphology of the clusters. Such questions must focus on the more specific factors which influence the ability/inability of black people to gain access to areas of better housing, and on differences in this ability according to individual black population groups; on the attitudes of the black and white population groups in influencing the intensity of black concentrations in Britain, the persistence of large enclosed white areas and the greater disadvantaged position of West Indian-born than Asian-born; and on the influence of urban subsystems on the detailed morphology of black residential clusters.

Acknowledgements

My most grateful thanks to my mother—a woman of remarkable courage, perseverance and tenacity. My thanks also to Diane and to King's College staff (Professor W. B. Morgan, Dr B. Morgan and Dr A. Warnes).

References

Aldrich, H. (1975). Ecological succession in racially changing neighborhoods: a review of the literature. *Urban Affairs Quarterly* **10**, 327-348.

Anwar, M. (1974). Pakistanis and Indians in the 1971 census: some ambiguities. *New Community* **3**, 394-396.

Banton, M. (1955). "The Coloured Quarter." Cape, London.

Bergel, E. E. (1955). "Urban Sociology." McGraw-Hill, New York.

Berry, B. J. L. and Horton, F. E. (1970). "Geographic Perspectives on Urban Systems: with Integrated Readings." Prentice Hall, Englewood Cliffs.

Burgess, E. W. (1928). Residential segregation in American cities. *Annals of the American Academy of Political and Social Science* **140**, 105-119.

Community Relations Commission (1976). "CRC Evidence to the Royal Commission on the Distribution of Income and Wealth." Community Relations Commission, London.

Cressey, P. F. (1938). Population succession in Chicago: 1898-1930. *American Journal of Sociology* **44**, 59-69.

Dahya, B. (1974). The nature of Pakistani ethnicity in industrial cities in Britain. *In* "Urban Ethnicity." (Abner Cohen, ed.). Tavistock, London.

Dalton, M. and Seaman, J. M. (1973). The distribution of New Commonwealth immigrants in the London Borough of Ealing 1961-66. *Transactions, Institute of British Geographers* **58**, 21-39.

Deakin, N. and Cohen, B. G. (1970). Dispersal and choice: towards a strategy for ethnic minorities in Britain. *Environment and Planning* **2**, 193-201.

Doherty, J. (1973). Immigrants in London: a study of the relationship between spatial structure and social structure. Unpublished Ph.D. thesis, University of London.

Duncan, O. D. and Duncan, B. (1955). A methodological analysis of segregation indexes. *American Sociological Review* **20**, 210-217.

Duncan, O. D. and Duncan, B. (1957). "The Negro Population of Chicago: a Study of Residential Succession." University of Chicago Press.

Eversley, D. and Sukdeo, F. (1969). "The Dependents of the Coloured Commonwealth Population of England and Wales." Institute of Race Relations Research Publications, London.

Greater London Council (n.d.). "Joint Working Party on Housing Action Areas." GLC Research and Intelligence Unit, London.

Guest, A. M. and Weed, J. A. (1976). Ethnic residential segregation: patterns of change. *American Journal of Sociology* **81**, 1088-1111.

Hoyt, H. (1939). "The Structure and Growth of Residential Neighborhoods in American Cities." Federal Housing Administration, Washington DC.

Johnston, R. J. (1971). "Urban Residential Patterns: an Introductory Review". Bell and Sons, London.

Jones, P. N. (1970). Some aspects of the changing distribution of coloured immigrants in Birmingham, 1961-1966. *Transactions, Institutes of British Geographers* **50**, 199-219.

Jones, P. N. (1976). Colored minorities in Birmingham, England. *Annals, Association of American Geographers* **66**, 89-103.

Lee, T. (1973). Concentration and dispersal: a study of West Indian residential patterns in London 1961-1971. Unpublished Ph.D. thesis, University of London.

Lieberson, S. (1963). "Ethnic Patterns in American Cities". Free Press of Glencoe, New York.

Lieberson, S. (1980). An asymmetrical approach to segregation. Paper presented at a symposium on Ethnic Segregation in Cities, St Antony's College, Oxford.

Little, K. L. (1948). "Negroes in Britain". Kegan Paul, Trench, Trubner, London.

McEntire, C. A. (1960). "Residence and Race". University of California Press, Berkeley and Los Angeles.

Moser, C. A. (1972). Statistics about immigrants: objectives, sources, methods and problems. *Social Trends* **3**, 20-30.

Pahl, R. E. (1968). "Spatial Structure and Social Structure". Centre for Environmental Studies, London.

Patterson, S. (1963). "Dark Strangers: a Study of West Indians in London". Tavistock, London.

Peach, C. (1975). Immigrants in the inner city. *Geographical Journal* **141**, 372-379.

Peach, C. and Winchester, S. W. C. (1974). Birthplace, ethnicity and underenumeration of West Indians, Indians and Pakistanis in the Censuses of 1966 and 1971. *New Community* **3**, 386-393.

Peach, C., Winchester, S. W. C. and Woods, R. I. (1975). The distribution of coloured immigrants in British cities. *Urban Affairs Annual Review* **9**, 395-419.

PEP (Political and Economic Planning) (1967). "Racial Discrimination". PEP, London.

Rose, E. J. B. *et al.* (1969). "Colour and Citizenship: a Report on British Race Relations." Oxford University Press for the Institute of Race Relations, London.

Rosenberg, T. J. and Lake, R. W. (1976). Toward a revised model of residential segregation and succession: Puerto Ricans in New York 1960-1970. *American Journal of Sociology* **81**, 1142-1150.

Scargill, D. I. (1979). "The Form of Cities". Bell and Hyman, London.

Shevky, E. and Bell, W. (1955). "Social Area Analysis". Stanford University Press.

Shevky, E. and Williams, M. (1949). "The Social Areas of Los Angeles: Analysis, and Typology". University of California Press, Berkeley.

Smith, D. J. (1976). "The Facts of Racial Disadvantage: a National Survey". PEP, London.

Taeuber, K. E. and Taeuber, A. F. (1965). "Negroes in Cities". Aldine, Chicago.

FOUR

Contrasts in Asian residential segregation

IAN SIMMONS

Jesus College, Oxford, UK

Current research on Asian minorities

The current data shortage in the wake of the cancellation of the 1976 sample census, added to the fact that the information from the 1971 census based on birthplace groups is outdated and inadequate, has led to something of an explosion of geographical research into Asian communities in Britain, since the Asian population can be identified by name, from the electoral register, as well by culture and appearance.

Geographers have been keen to explain the patterns of Asian residential segregation which have been consistently demonstrated to exist in many British cities on various scales.* Using a number of spatial techniques, most notably the index of dissimilarity, the extent and degree of residential segregation and concentration has been measured, interpolated and extrapolated, and inferences have been drawn based on the relationship between social and physical distance.†

The patterns so defined have been interpreted in terms of positive factors leading to group cohesion and negative factors leading to segregation. The positive factors include the desire of people to live with others from their own area and ethnic group, the desire to minimize potential contact which may have led to conflict and rejection in the past or may do so in the future, the desire to utilize the ecological base to preserve cultural identity and the possibility of using this base to gain political power (Dahya, 1974; Peach, 1975; Boal, 1976). The negative factors

---

*Geographical studies of Asian communities in a variety of British cities have consistently shown up high levels of segregation at ward and enumeration district level, as well as street levels, e.g. Jones and Davenport (1972) for Dundee; Dalton and Seaman (1973) for Ealing Borough; Kearsley and Srivastava (1974) for Glasgow; Jones and McEvoy (1974) for Huddersfield; Duncan (1977) also for Huddersfield; McEvoy (1978) for Glasgow; Cater and Jones (1979) for Bradford; Robinson (1979a, b, c) for Blackburn.

†The index of dissimilarity (ID) is the most widely used measure of segregation. It expresses that proportion of a population sub-group which would have to relocate amongst a set of sub-areas to have a distribution equal to that of another sub-group. Figures near to 100 are taken to mean social rejection and those nearer to O, social acceptance and interaction.

81

include, most notably, discrimination in housing and employment which limit the residential and market opportunities of the coloured groups (Rex and Moore, 1967; Cater and Jones, 1979). Less clearly positive or negative factors are the nature of sponsorship and the chain migration process which direct new migrants to existing ethnic areas (Peach, 1975; Community Relations Commission, 1977).

It is not, however, an easy task to disentangle the many factors leading to a particular pattern of ethnic settlement. Using spatial techniques it is possible to distil partial factors, such as the effect of social class or tenure preferences, to explain a given pattern (Shah, 1979) or to use, for instance, the segregation between sub-groups as evidence for self-segregation and polarization (Robinson, 1979a). Fuller explanations need to examine processes in a more dynamic perspective. This involves a consideration of the nature of the groups or sub-groups concerned, the local housing stock and operation of the local housing market, the way in which housing and other social rewards are allocated and the characteristics of the local population, together with the way in which these elements interact through time. Current research seems to be moving in this direction.

The nature of the Asian communities

It would seem impossible to explain a given pattern of segregation without a detailed knowledge of the segregated groups, since each will have different attitudes, aspirations and motivations. This demands an understanding of the characteristics of the sending societies, of the motives for migration, of the migrants response to and perception of their situation in the receiving society and their longer term aspirations. These latter two influences are subject to change in the light of experience which underlines the need for a dynamic component to the study.

Asian migration to Britain, as indeed to many other parts of the world, must be seen in terms of a transplantation of one social system into another and the gradual adjustment of each, not necessarily harmoniously, as they mutually interact.* Apart from the small number of Asian professionals who were highly anglicized before migrating, the majority of Asian immigrants from the sub-continent have a traditional and rural background (Desai, 1963; Rose *et al.*, 1969; Hiro, 1971). Many of them on arrival had little education and almost all remained governed by the social controls of the sending societies. The traditional status ascription of property ownership, for instance, is reflected in the Asian predilection for home ownership. Similarly, by living in close proximity, as well as being psychologically comforting, the Asian communities are able to reproduce something like a traditional social system held together by ethnic institutions. This ensures that people are governed by the social controls which regulate behaviour in the sending society and ensures that deviation is kept to a minimum (Dahya, 1974). Any such deviation may lead to a loss of status in the home village or may make re-adjustment to the home

*Asian is taken here to mean those people born in, or having a recent ancestry in, India, Pakistan, Bangladesh and Sri Lanka.

environment more difficult. Furthermore, the closeness of the Asian extended family and the dense network of mutual obligations ensure that family members overseas remain closely tied to the social system in their country of origin, as well as to the replicate social system in Britain.

The motive for migration is equally important in determining group settlement patterns and to a great extent explains group behaviour in Britain. Many commentators agree that the Asians' main motive for migration from the sub-continent was an economic one, intended to be temporary in duration, aimed at raising the family status at home through remittances and the improvement and acquisition of property often prompted by the over-fragmentation of land (Aurora, 1968; Rose *et al.*, 1969; Dahya, 1973; Ballard and Ballard, 1977). This immediately puts an emphasis on minimizing expenditure in the host society and partly explains this predilection for home ownership, often of the least desirable housing as it represents the least drain on resources (Dahya, 1974).

Migration to a strange country is a difficult process psychologically, particularly for those with only limited formal education. It is full of preconceptions which can be rapidly altered in the light of experience. Often this experience has been one of rejection and hostility in finding housing and employment. The reaction to this, and indeed the transmitted reaction to later migrants, has been to adopt a defensive attitude and a greater reliance on intra-group contacts and social life to preclude potential discriminatory and offensive contacts (Khan, 1976; Duncan, 1977).

The initial motives for migration may become less clear and the migrant's perception of his own position will, however, change with time. The decision of many Asian husbands to bring their wives and families to Britain has been interpreted as a partial reorientation of commitment away from the home region towards Britain. Most importantly, the ultimate aim of returning to the home area some time in the future, and certainly on retirement, must be seen as one of the most important factors conditioning Asian behaviour. It commits individuals to maintaining their position in the ethnic status order and to investment overseas, so as to provide for the return, thus perpetuating the sense of ethnic identity and checking any trend towards westernization. For many people this intention of return is little more than a 'myth' as they become committed economically and emotionally to life in Britain. Nevertheless it continues to condition behaviour and has a most significant bearing on settlement patterns (Jeffery, 1972; Dahya, 1974; Anwar, 1979; Robinson, 1980).

This detailed, largely anthropological, investigation of the Asian communities has led to a correct emphasis being placed on the positive factors in explaining Asian residential segregation, but these can provide only one element of the explanation although it may be the dominant one.

Local opportunities

The Asian population in Britain has similar characteristics to the West Indian in that it represents a 'replacement population', but it has a wider geographical distribution being found in the northern textile and certain southern manufacturing towns, as well as in the English industrial conurbations (Jones, 1978).* Asians have, therefore, been able to find economic niches in a variety of urban settings with a different set of housing and employment opportunities. Jones (1980) has pointed to the necessity of examining the urban morphology when considering patterns of segregation. This is because financial and access constraints, and tenure and dwelling preferences, have meant that Asians have sometimes been restricted, or have restricted themselves, to particular types of housing. Kearsley and Srivastava (1974) demonstrate how the geographical expansion of the Asian community in Glasgow was directed by the distribution of pre-1880 grey sandstone tenements. In Birmingham, Jones (1980) stresses that the 'middle-ring' containing large Victorian properties suitable for conversion and multi-occupation is one of the most important factors in explaining the pattern of ethnic settlement there. Werbner (1979) describes a process of scattering and clustering of Asian communities in Manchester since cheap, terraced housing is widely distributed. The morphology of the city, therefore, has an important impact on the patterns of settlement and it varies greatly between, say, the northern industrial terraces and the interwar semi's of the southern industrial estates. Cater and Jones (1979) would seem to sum up the Asian housing position adequately by describing them as a 'residual population' filling in the gaps where Whites no longer want to live.

The state of the local housing market further conditions the extent to which segregation may occur. If the local housing market is expanding rapidly then there are considerable opportunities for the suburbanization of the indigenous population. This is the situation Ward and Sims (1980) describe happening in Birmingham in the 1960s where members of the traditional working class were able to suburbanize leading to the creation of a 'dual housing market'. The reverse may occur where gentrification takes place. Where the housing supply is tight, choice will be restricted and there will be less opportunity for segregation.

As well as examining the local housing stock and market it is important to remember that economic opportunities vary from place to place. Levine and Nayar, (1975) in a study of immigrant adaptation in Slough, found that an integrationist path was followed where economic opportunities were highest.

> There are two ways of responding on a cognitive level to living in England. Both involve group identities and the actual socio-economic conditions. Individuals who perceived that England was open to foreigners were less likely to maintain tight group identities than were individuals who perceived that England was a closed society to foreigners. But these individuals were those who came from a more advantaged background and also had a better job in Slough. On the other hand, those respondents who came from relatively disadvantaged backgrounds and also had fewer opportunities in Slough tended to be more closed towards integration and towards English people. In both cases this was affected by a perception of widespread discrimination which

---

*Peach (1968) describes how the West Indian migrants settled in the large, older industrial cities which were losing population, where they took up jobs that Whites were becoming less willing to do. He refers to this population as a 'replacement population'.

hindered and even blocked social integration. Thus, the defensive posture on the part of most of these people was not just a set of behaviour reactions designed to reinforce "ethnic" culture in the face of culture contact (though it may have been to some extent), but it also related to the types of obstacles that these immigrants faced.

Levine and Nayar (1975; pp.362-363)

Undoubtedly, economic opportunities vary from city to city and region to region, which is bound to produce a variety of responses. Access to these opportunities is, however, as important as their actual existence.

Access to housing

A great deal of research in recent years has shown that coloured people are disadvantaged when seeking housing *vis-à-vis* equivalent Whites. While in many cases Asian families are prepared to accept and indeed enjoy lower standard housing for perfectly rational reasons this is not true for all and does not necessarily hold true for the future. It is this inequality as much as any other which determines Asian attitudes towards Whites and which conditions housing choice.

The fact that Asians are over-represented as owner-occupiers does not mean that they gain proportionally from the benefits of owner-occupation since they often own the worst housing with limited amenities and little capital appreciation (Jones, 1980). This may be owing to limited economic resources or a desire to invest less, but a number of studies have shown how the choice may be restricted by vendors, estate agents, building societies and the local authority (Daniel, 1968; Hatch, 1971; Smith, 1976). Similarly, in public housing, while the Asians may have been loath to rent, they were often unable to because of residence requirements, discrimination by housing visitors, or because owner-occupiers were ineligible for council housing (Burney, 1967; Rex and Moore, 1967; Cullingworth Committee, 1969; Smith and Whalley, 1975). Robinson (1980) has shown how the Asian population in Blackburn is becoming increasingly aware and taking advantage of the benefits of council housing. Where Asians and other coloured groups have entered council housing several studies have shown how they often receive properties considered less desirable by Whites (Parker and Dugmore, 1977; Taper, 1977; Flett, 1979; Skellington, 1980). An interpretation of this is complicated by the fact that these properties are frequently in the areas most desired by the minority groups.

It is clear, then, that access procedures to housing remain important in determining patterns of ethnic settlement and have had a significant impact in conditioning attitudes towards housing.

Synthesis

Current research on Asian minorities in Britain has considered these inter-related elements, although, by and large, individually and within different disciplinary frameworks. Geographers have been central in trying to produce a synthesis of these elements to explain patterns of segregation, as this volume testifies. It is becoming increasingly clear, however, that there is no simple explanation and that the emphasis of interacting elements may vary from place to place. What must be remembered is that the present is conditioned by the past and that the future will not be the same as the present. Current attitudes are affected by past experiences and are constantly being revised in the light of new experiences. The study of minority settlements must try to encompass this dynamic element in understanding patterns of segregation.

Choice and constraint

The debate over Asian residential segregation seems to have crystallized around two poles: those who argue that discrimination is the most important factor in explaining the high degree of segregation and those who argue that it is a result of ethnic choice. Discrimination is undoubtedly present and has affected decisions of the Asian population. As such, past discrimination and its effect on decisions is as important as the current blocking of opportunities, but choice would seem a particularly important element given the economic and social goals of the majority of the Asian population and the myth of return. It may, however, prove dangerous to over-emphasize choice, as, equally, an over-emphasis on constraint and a lack of understanding of preferences may lead to unfortunate decisions regarding dispersal and other policy matters.

There are several reasons why ethnic choice, in isolation, must be considered very carefully. Firstly, a choice is a decision taken between alternative opportunities each of which is a realistic possibility should it be chosen. The alternative opportunities available are a product of economic resources, history and experience, the knowledge and perception of alternatives, and the likelihood of their being attained. The evidence for discrimination in housing certainly suggests that there are less opportunities available to Asians than to Whites of an equivalent social class, and the experience of many of the migrants may tell them that were they to look for housing outside the ethnic enclave then they may meet with discrimination and hostility. Choice must, therefore, be seen in terms of the constraints which undoubtedly operate.

Secondly, for the new arrivals and first generation migrants the housing they occupy may suit their needs adequately (Dahya, 1974). It may also not conflict with the majority of Whites. However, there are several reasons why this may later change, leading to Asians demanding a larger choice and leading them into greater competition and conflict with Whites over housing. There is evidence of a change in orientation amongst some of the Asian community as they become more committed to living in Britain, leading them to seek better or more suitable housing (Phillips, Ch.5). The reunion of families, particularly elderly parents, bears witness to this. Furthermore, of those Asians who have decided to return to the sub-continent, only a few have found it easy to settle. In Gravesend, for instance, of the 40 Sikh families

who had decided to return to Indian only one had not returned to Britain.*
Similarly, in Hounslow the majority of those people who have returned to the sub-
continent have found it difficult to settle and have returned to England.† This
certainly represents a reorientation for these families and this trend is likely to
increase. For the second generation, return is even less of a possibility and is
considered by them to be less desirable.

For those committed to staying in Britain, and indeed for many committed to life
in the ethnic social arena in Britain, status becomes increasingly important leading
to a spatial sorting of the Asian population and a more ostentatious display of
material prosperity. Ballard and Ballard (1977) describe this process taking place
amongst the Sikhs in Leeds, and Werbner (1979) describes the behaviour of
Pakistanis in Manchester as trying to 'avoid the ghetto'. This desire for social
distancing, which may be reflected in a degree of dispersal or at least a centrifugal
expansion of the Asian enclaves, is likely to generate greater competition with
Whites for housing. Equally, some members of the Asian community, particularly
in the second generation, may wish to compete in the white status arena. For these
people with greater knowledge and different perceptions of their situation actual
choice may be less real as they come up against many of the constraints which apply.

Thirdly, choice, as the term seems to be used, is only a partial conceptualization.
Choice, as used till now, refers to the decision to take one particular form of housing
when others could equally have been easily taken. That decision in itself is not,
however, necessarily a free one, but is conditioned by the social obligations of the
person making the decision. The author was made aware of this on a visit to Mirpur
where at the Immigration Advisory Service office a father was trying to arrange for
his 18-year-old son to enter Britain. This boy could neither read nor write Punjabi,
nor could he speak English. He was obviously very frightened of the prospect of
going to Britain, but if that was what his family decreed then he had to go. Equally,
if a family decides to move out of the ethnic enclave this may lead to gossip, and any
behaviour which may lead to a lessening of commitment to the home village and to
reducing remittances is likely to meet with censure. Free choice is not in the nature
of traditional Indian and Pakistani family life.

Differences between sub-groups

A great deal of the anthropological literature on the Asian minorities in Britain
suggests that there are great differences between the various sub-groups represented.
The Asian community is multi-differentiated along religious, regional, language,
class, caste and national lines. These differences contain differences of social
control, behaviour, motivation, outlook and aspiration which greatly affect their

*Conservation with J. Austin-Walker (Senior Community Relations Officer, Bexley) and C. Revis
  (former Community Relations Officer, Gravesend), Chandigarth, April 1980.
†Conversation with Inder Singh Uppal (Senior Community Relations Officer, Hounslow), August
  1980.

life-styles and experiences in Britain and which ensure that generalizations holding true for one sub-group do not necessarily hold true for another.

The major sub-groups represented in Britain are the Pakistani and Bangladeshi Muslims, the Indian Sikhs, the Gujaratis both Hindu and Muslim, and the East African Asians. Important differences exist between these coarsely defined sub-groups and it is important to note the most significant differences.

The Muslims

The vast majority of Muslims in Britain come from Pakistan and Bangladesh and more specifically the Punjab, Frontier Province and Azad Kashmir in the former and Sylhet in the latter. They are all characterized by a background of rural poverty, although they are often from families with small land-holdings, low levels of formal education and a strict code of religious and social behaviour which governs their actions (Rose *et al.*, 1969; Hiro, 1971).

The reasons for their migration to Britain were, by and large, clear: to earn money abroad to raise the family's social and material status at home. They form very close-knit introspective communities often with people from only a handful of villages in any one British city. The restricted social activities of Muslim women means that they place a very high premium on being in close proximity to other Muslim women. The closeness of the extended family and the considerable emotional and economic investment abroad ensure that the 'myth of return' is very prominent in Muslim thoughts.

Dahya (1973) comments on the 'transient' nature of Pakistani migration and Jeffery (1972) describes the situation in Bristol of Pakistani owner-occupiers who, having paid off short-term bank loans, all chose to invest their spare savings in property in Pakistan.

The Sikhs

The Sikhs form the majority of Indian migrants to Britain. They stand in some contrast to the Muslims. Sikhism as a philosophy is much more free than Islam, and the Sikhs are by nature an enterprising people. In India the majority of Sikhs are land-owners, and they tend to do rather well for themselves in every aspect of Indian life. In Britain the Sikhs have been more ambitious than the Muslims. They are, or were on arrival at least, often better educated than the Muslims. Driven by the familial desire for success, they have moved into white-collar jobs more rapidly and have begun a process of spatial sorting along status lines at a much earlier stage, in part related to the much earlier reunion of families and an increase in familial income when children enter employment (Ballard and Ballard, 1977).

The same authors suggest that all Asian settlements can be fitted within a four stage chronological sequence: individual pioneers; all-male households; large-scale entry of wives and children and a movement to less crowded housing; movement away from most unsalubrious areas and emergence of a British educated second generation. The Ballards suggest that the Sikhs are at least 15 years ahead of the Mirpuris who are only entering the third phase.* One would, therefore, expect to find considerable differences in attitude and preference towards housing between those two abovementioned sub-groups as well as a greater material prosperity amongst the Sikhs in general.

The Gujaratis

The Gujarati communities in Britain are both Muslim and Hindu. The former sub-group have a great deal in common with the Pakistani Muslims. The latter sub-group would tend to be more similar to the Sikhs. The Hindu religion, being a very individualistic one, places less constraints upon the activities and outlook of its adherents. Tambs-Lyche (1975) describes the Gujarati premium placed on white collar occupations. Similarly, Gujaratis are loath to accept any job which involves the wearing of a uniform which many of the lower paid jobs in public service require.

The East African Asians

A large proportion of the Asian population has come to Britain from East Africa. They adhere to each of the above religions and come from all of the above regions. They often have maintained close links with the sub-continent but, by and large, they form a well educated and enterprising lower middle class, who despite considerable disadvantages in Britain, most notably a lack of capital, have been able to achieve a level of material prosperity over and above that achieved by longer settled Pakistani and Bangladeshi Muslim migrants (Commission for Racial Equality, 1978). The nature of their migration, namely political expulsion, ensures that the "myth of return" is of reduced importance in determining their behaviour which is rather more concerned with re-establishing their economic prosperity in Britain.

The other sub-groups

Excluded from the main categories above are a host of smaller sub-groups, these include: Hindus not from Gujarat, Jains, Parsees, Bengalis, Tamils and Pathans, amongst others. Sub-division is almost infinite and as such loses any generality. What is important is that generalizations made for one sub-group may not be applicable to others. One very important differentiating characteristic seems to be education. The educated classes have a more positive attitude towards integration and their negative attitude towards Britain is often a reflection of a failure to fulfil what they see as their own potential, often through no fault of their own.

*Mirpur is the district in Azad Kashmir from where the majority of Pakistani migrants to Britain have come.

Geographical considerations of sub-groups

Most geographical studies of the Asian population at the macro- and meso-scales consider the one aggregate, Asian group or else disaggregate to Indian-born and Pakistani-born. This is due to the lack of detailed data, but already with this simple disaggregation it is possible to pick out important geographical differences with large concentrations of Pakistanis in the northern textile towns and Birmingham. The Indian-born are more widely distributed with large concentrations in Greater London and the Midlands (Jones, 1978).

Certainly many of the Asian sub-groups have a history of factionalism and conflict which is unlikely to lead to group consensus (Khan, 1976). Similarly the nature of chain migration and different cultural preferences for housing are likely to lead to a spatial sorting and segregation of individual sub-groups. Robinson (1979a), in a pioneering study of Asian sub-group segregation in Blackburn, demonstrates high degrees of segregation by birthplace, religion and language. An analysis of Asian names identified by religion from the electoral register has demonstrated a similar degree of religious residential segregation in East Oxford.* Robinson concludes that

> Differences of religion, language, and birthplace ensure that community members share little, if any, consensus. Neither theory nor policy has taken this vital fact into account. Rex and Moore's housing class theory is a prime example of this. In concentrating upon explaining external conflict between whites and Asians in purely *economic* terms, it fails. The theory imposes upon the Asian community homogeneous and externally unifying economic values and aspirations where none exist.
>
> Robinson (1979a; p.38)

Robinson is, himself, in danger of committing the same error, as his Blackburn sample is 90·6% Muslim and contains only 61 Sikhs in a total sample of 4721 adults. To argue that all Asian residential segregation is largely explained by choice factors cannot be claimed from the given evidence. This does not deny that this *may* be the case but it is subject to empirical testing for a range of sub-groups in a variety of localities. As previously noted, the Muslims are amongst the least educated, most introspective and conservative sub-groups within the Asian community. Their rural peasant background, strong economic motivation, social obligations and commitment to return would seem to make them highly desirous of living in segregated communities.

Differences between areas

A consideration of the distribution of Indians and Pakistanis in Britain (see Fig. 1) again brings us back to their different geographical distributions, the problems of birthplace data and 'white Indians' notwithstanding.† The Pakistanis, whom we can

---

*Unpublished research done by the author using the 1979 Electoral Register for Oxford.

†The census, by using birthplace as a means of classification, fails to include Asians born in Britain and East Africa and includes a number of 'Whites' born in the sub-continent (see Peach and Winchester, 1974).

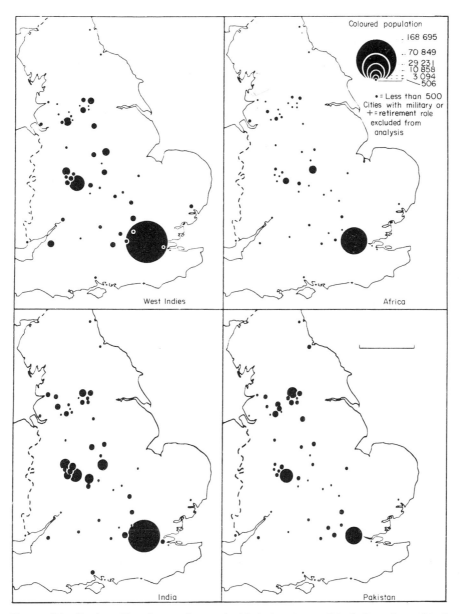

Figure 1. Distribution of immigrants from major birthplace groups (1971). From Jones (1978).

assume to be almost all Muslim, have significant concentrations in Birmingham, Blackburn, Bradford, Dundee, Glasgow and Huddersfield. The bulk of geographical research into Asian communities has been carried out in these cities. In considering segregation studies of Asian communities the danger exists of over-generalizing from non-representative samples.

Not only may the sub-groups be non-representative but housing stocks, employment opportunities and material conditions vary considerably. Whilst it is, by and large, true that the Asian population in Britain represents a 'replacement population', those living in the northern textile towns, for instance, have less opportunity for employment in anything other than semi- or unskilled manufaturing or public service jobs than someone, for example, living in Greater London. Similarly, in housing, there is often little choice other than the nineteenth century industrial terraces which are often close to the factories. Proximity to work would seem to be an important factor in the location decision of the household. This goes along with Levine and Nayar's (1975) argument that attitudes towards integration are affected by economic opportunities. The effect is cumulative as increased income is likely to afford greater housing choice and so on.

In cities such as Manchester, Birmingham and, most particularly, Greater London there are many more opportunities for employment in white-collar occupations as well as a more varied housing stock and rapidly turning over market. Tambs-Lyche (1975) comments on the prestige placed on residence in London by Gujaratis.

> The importance of London for immigrants lies almost wholly in the fact that there some white-collar jobs for the better educated immigrants are available.
>
> Tambs-Lyche (1975; p.349)

Tambs-Lyche produces a Gujarati ranking of British cities based on desirability, with Birmingham and Bradford at the bottom and Leicester and London at the top. There seems to be a trade off between those cities with cheap housing and those where the community has attained the highest standard of living. A different situation, and a different perception of that situation, might be expected in the Metropolis compared with, say, Blackburn or Bradford.

The indigenous white populations

The availability of housing opportunities and the ability of Asians to take advantage of those opportunities in part depends on the willingness of Whites to permit them. In many of the older industrial cities Asians have entered the older areas which the Whites were leaving. Where the white communities have remained stable it has been rather more difficult for the Asians to find suitable accommodation. Rex and Moore (1967) describe this situation in Sparkbrook in the early 1960s where the Pakistanis were living in multi-occupied lodging houses and had not entered the neighbouring working class terraced areas.

In certain areas of Greater London the Asians have entered twilight zones and formerly traditional middle and working class areas but the majority are now resident in the outer boroughs. This cannot be taken as synonymous with improved material conditions and material life-styles, but many of the lower class suburbs of London *would* seem to lack the traditional sense of community described by Willmott and Young (1957) in Bethnal Green 25 years ago. They have mobile and transient populations, less concerned with neighbourhood status than with living in a community without propinquity, bridged by car and telephone. Conflict between

Whites and Asians is therefore likely to be reduced, as the Whites are less concerned with status than with their location in relation to what are considered important facilities and amenities. It is for this reason that it is important to consider the characteristics of the local white population as well as the local housing stock and market when looking at patterns of Asian settlement.

Asian segregation in Greater London

At the risk of losing generality and explanatory power the trend in studying Asian communities has been to examine individual cities. This would seem necessary as the individuality of each settlement and sub-group has been emphasized and inevitably leads to a process of aggregating knowledge. In this process the major centre of Asian settlement appears to have been ignored. Just under 30% of the Asian-born population in Britain was resident in Greater London in 1971. When looking at the distribution of Asians in Greater London it is also surprising that the majority of them live in the outer boroughs (Table I) which would seem to stand in contrast with the evidence from other cities.

TABLE I

Concentration of ethnic groups
in inner and outer boroughs, Greater London, 1971

	% of total Ceylonese population	% of total Indian population	% of total Pakistani population	% of total West Indian population
Inner boroughs	47·4	33·1	50·0	68·0
Outer boroughs	52·5	66·9	50·0	32·0

Source: 1971 census, population tables.

Beyond looking at aggregate patterns using census data, geographers have been loath to investigate this apparent anomaly. Nevertheless, it is clear that there is not an even spread of Asian-born people across Greater London and that distinct concentrations occur in the suburbs of Brent, Croydon, Ealing, Gravesend, Harrow, Hounslow and Southall; as well as in the inner-city, most notably Tower Hamlets and Newham (Fig. 2). In Tower Hamlets and Newham the Asian population is mainly Bengali; in Harrow, Ugandan Asian; in Ealing, Hounslow, Southall and Gravesend, Punjabi; and in Brent and Croydon it is rather more mixed. This emphasizes the variety of sub-groups and the variety of urban environments.

A closer examination of one of these suburban concentrations, Hounslow, provides an insight into some of the contrasts emphasized above. Hounslow is a

People born in Asia
as a percentage of
the total population

8·0 or more
6·0 — 7·9
4·0 — 5·9
2·0 — 3·9
less than 2·0
0 1 2 3 miles

Figure 2. Distribution of Asians in Greater London by ward (1971). From Shepherd *et al.* (1974).

suburban borough with a large, predominantly Punjabi Sikh, Asian population.* It is not, however, comparable with the situation Nowikowski and Ward (1978) describe in south Manchester where the small Asian population represents a highly anglicized middle class. Indeed, in Hounslow Borough the Asian population forms 12% of the borough total population with 65% of the Asian population located in polling districts which are more than 15% Asian, and 44% in five polling districts which are over 30% Asian.

The borough, therefore, has much in common with the evidence presented in other studies: the minority is segregated, though not to the same degree as elsewhere,† and may reflect conscious choice, given that the Asian population is not significantly over-represented in poorer housing (67·5% of the population from the Indian sub-continent identified in the National Dwelling and Household Survey (NDHS cited Hounslow Borough Planning Department, 1977) were living in dwellings built between 1919 and 1939, and 57% of the dwellings built between 1919 and 1939 were semi-detached).

*Hounslow Community Relations Council estimate that of more than 20 000 Asians in the borough, 14 000 come from the Indian sub-continent direct and 6000 from East Africa, mainly Kenya. Of the former group 4000 are estimated to be Pakistani Muslims, 8000 Indian Sikhs and 2000 Indian Hindus; of the latter group 1000 are estimated to be Muslim, 2000 Sikh and 3000 Hindu.

†The ID for Hounslow Borough at ward level in 1979 was 43. This compares with 55·1 for Huddersfield (1974), 55·4 for Blackburn (1977), 61·1 for Bradford (1977) and 69·2 for Glasgow (1976) at the same scale.

In terms of housing characteristics Hounslow Borough Planning Department has the following comments to make from their analysis of NDHS:

Ethnic origin by use of amenities

Comment: very little difference between ethnic groups. Africans are more likely to share amenities, Whites are highest for lacking amenities.

Ethnic origin by use of bath or shower

Comment: very little difference except Africans are more likely to have to share a bathroom. Whites have the highest percentage lacking a bath, but only 2·2%.

Ethnic origin by age of property

Comment: West Indians are more likely to be in pre-1919 property, while Indians are more likely to be in 1919–1939 property.

Ethnic origin by sharing dwelling or not

Comment: not much difference. Africans and then Indians are most likely to be sharing a dwelling, but 87·1% of Africans do not share a dwelling (overall = 94·6%).

Bedroom standard by ethnic origin

Comment: the Asian group are well above average in bedroom deficiency—22% compared with 6% overall, mainly in deficiency of one bedroom rather than two or more.

Similarly, in employment, evidence from the 1971 census shows that the Asian population is only slightly over-represented in the lower paid and less desirable occupations (Table II). The Borough Planning Department further comment on NDHS:

> African heads are more likely to be professional than any other ethnic group. There is little difference across the groups as far as unskilled manual workers is concerned. West Indians and Indians have a higher proportion of semi-skilled manual workers. Indians have a low proportion of no socio-economic group (e.g. students and house-wives).

This is coupled with the fact that Hounslow has the lowest unemployment rate of any of the London boroughs.

TABLE II

Distribution of Asian and all
birthplace groups by socio-economic group, Hounslow Borough, 1971

	Socio-economic groups*				
	3/4	1/2/13	8/9/12/14	5/6	7/10/11/15/16
Asian born (%)	4·8	9·0	30·8	25·6	29·8
All birthplaces (%)	5·4	13·3	32·4	26·8	20·8

Source: 1971 census, GLC, special tabulations.

*The 17 socio-economic groups of the 1971 census are grouped into Professional (3,4), Managerial (1,2,13), Routine Non-manual (5,6), Skilled Manual (8,9,12,14) and Semi- and Unskilled Manual and Non-manual (7,10,11,15,16) categories.

In terms of housing and employment statistics, therefore, the Asian minority population is not significantly different from the resident white population in an area of good housing quality and where economic opportunities seem relatively good, with easy access to Central London, Heathrow and the industrial estates of West London.

Much of what remains to be said is still an hypothesis, forming the core of current research. Whilst the local housing stock is comprised, by and large, of interwar semi's and post-war purpose built flats, certain qualitative variations occur and the Asian population does seem to be located in the slightly less desirable areas, particularly in areas affected by aircraft noise, in what is an unfashionable suburban borough.

Local employment opportunities seem reasonable and the Asian population has not been slow to exploit them. What seems significant is that a proportion of the local white population is reasonably mobile, both socially and geographically, living within a community without propinquity. Similarly, the Asian population does, on the surface, appear to have adopted the same characteristics with a large dependence on the motor car and telephone. This is producing a more dispersed style of living but not necessarily a weakening of community coherence and commitment.

Points for attention

This chapter represents a collection of ideas about current research concerning Britain's Asian communities, particularly in social geography. Since the traditional concern of geographers has been with the spatial component, segregation studies have been a major focus of their attention. While the techniques for measuring segregation have become increasingly sophisticated and have drawn attention to the high degrees of ethnic residential segregation, these patterns have not always been adequately explained. Several studies by non-geographers have pointed to the importance of discrimination in explaining the high degree of segregation and these studies have prompted government legislation in an attempt to curb discrimination. Other studies have emphasized the conscious ethnic choice component and one hopes that these will have the same impact in making the legislators more aware of the complexity of the issue. There is a danger, however, that this may lead to an over-emphasis on choice and the turning of a blind eye towards the continuing discrimination which coloured people experience. This is particularly important as the second generation is trying to find its own place in this multi-cultural society and is likely to come into greater competition with whites for housing and jobs.

Academic research, however, in aiming at explanation has only in recent years directed itself towards public policy. In considering ethnic segregation it is first and foremost important to understand the processes which bring it about. Only when this is fully understood can policy decisions be made with any degree of certitude. The geographical approach, by assuming processes from pattern, is only of limited value. Only when the processes are adequately considered can it be of value, particularly in looking at changes in segregation over time.

It has been suggested above that there is a need to consider interrelated elements and to adopt a more dynamic approach which looks at how these elements interact with each other and how that interaction at time t_2 will be different from, yet dependent upon, the relationship at time t_1. An important example of this is the consideration of ethnic choice as being a response to closed opportunities rather than conscious defence.

It is also important to remember that several processes may be occurring simultaneously, for instance, the expansion and dispersal of Asian concentrations need not necessarily be seen as a concomitant of assimilation but a reflection of ethnic status consciousness (Werbner, 1979; Phillips, Ch.5). It would seem important, in looking to the future, to consider the attitudes and expectations of the second generation, to look at the geographical patterns of newly formed households, and to consider what is happening at the boundaries of ethnic areas rather than focusing on the cores.

It has already been noted that there are great variations within the Asian population and in the environments in which they are located. Certainly more research needs to be done into sub-group patterns considering the social and cultural differences between sub-groups and their experiences, reactions and expectations in Britain. Equally, Greater London would seem to be a particularly important social laboratory for examining Asian segregation as it has a very wide range of sub-groups and housing environments.

Acknowledgements

I am grateful to the following for permission to use copyright or unpublished material: The Editor, *New Community*; The Institute of British Geographers; Clarendon Press, Oxford; Hounslow Borough Planning Department; Mr I. S. Uppal, Senior Community Relations Officer, London Borough of Hounslow.

References

Anwar, M. (1979). "The Myth of Return: Pakistanis in Britain". Heinemann, London.

Aurora, G. S. (1968). "The New Frontiersman: a Sociological Study of Indian Immigrants to the United Kingdom." Hurst, London.

Ballard, R. and Ballard, C. (1977). The Sikhs: the development of south Asian settlement in Britain. *In* "Between Two Cultures" (J. L. Watson, ed.). Blackwell, Oxford.

Boal, F. W. (1976). Ethnic residential segregation. *In* "Social Areas in Cities" (D. T. Herbert and R. J. Johnston, eds), Vol. 1. Wiley, London.

Burney, E. (1967). "Housing on Trial". Oxford University Press.

Cater, J. and Jones, T. P. (1979). Ethnic residential space: the case of Asians in Bradford. *Tijdschrift voor Economische en Sociale Geografie* **70**, 86–97.

Commission for Racial Equality (1978). Fact sheet 3: Employment.

Community Relations Commission (1977). Housing choice and ethnic concentration.

Cullingworth Committee (1969). "Council Housing: Purposes, Procedures and Priorities". Cullingworth Report. HMSO, London.

Dahya, B. (1973). Pakistanis in Britain: transients or settlers? *Race* **14**, 241-277.

Dahya, B. (1974). The nature of Pakistani ethnicity in industrial cities in Britain. *In* "Urban Ethnicity" (A. Cohen, ed.). Tavistock, London.

Dalton, M. and Seaman, J. M. (1973). The distribution of New Commonwealth immigrants in the London Borough of Ealing, 1961-1966. *Transactions, Institute of British Geographers* **58**, 21-39.

Daniel, W. W. (1968). "Racial Discrimination in England". Penguin, Harmondsworth.

Desai, R. (1963). "Indian Immigrants in Britain". Oxford University Press for the Institute of Race Relations, London.

Duncan, S. S. (1977). Housing disadvantage and residential mobility: immigrants and institutions in a northern town. University of Sussex: Department of Urban and Regional Studies Working Paper No. 5.

Flett, H. (1979). Black council tenants in Birmingham. S.S.R.C. Research Unit on Ethnic Relations, Working Paper on Ethnic Relations No. 12.

Hatch, S. (1971). "Constraints on Immigrant Housing Choice: Estate Agents". SSRC Research Unit on Ethnic Relations, Bristol.

Hiro, D. (1971). "Black British, White British". Eyre and Spottiswoode, London.

Hounslow Borough Planning Department (1977). National dwelling and household survey: summary of additional tables.

Jeffery, P. (1972). Pakistani families in Bristol. *New Community* **1**, 364-370.

Jones, P. N. (1978). The distribution and diffusion of the coloured population in England and Wales, 1961-1971. *Transactions, Institute of British Geographers N.S.* **3**, 515-533.

Jones, P. N. (1980). Ethnic segregation, urban planning and the question of choice: the Birmingham case. Paper presented at the symposium on Ethnic Segregation in Cities, St Antony's College, Oxford.

Jones, H. R. and Davenport, M. (1972). The Pakistani community in Dundee: a study of its growth and demographic structure. *Scottish Geographical Magazine* **88**, 74-85.

Jones, T. P. and McEvoy, D. (1974). Residential segregation of Asians in Huddersfield. Paper presented at the Institute of British Geographers Conference, Norwich.

Kearsley, G. W. and Srivastava, S. R. (1974). The spatial evolution of Glasgow's Asian community. *Scottish Geographical Magazine* **90**, 110-124.

Khan, V. S. (1976). Pakistanis in Britain: perceptions of a population. *New Community* **5**, 222-229.

Levine, N. and Nayar, T. (1975). Modes of adaptation by Asian immigrants in Slough. *New Community* **4**, 356-365.

McEvoy, D. (1978). The segregation of Asian immigrants in Glasgow: a note. *Scottish Geographical Magazine* **94**, 180-183.

Nowikowski, S. and Ward, R. (1978). Middle class and British?: an analysis of South Asians in suburbia. *New Community* **7**, 1-10.

Parker, J. and Dugmore, K. (1977). Race and the allocation of public housing: a GLC survey. *New Community* **6**, 27-40.

Peach, C. (1968). "West Indian Migration to Britain: a Social Geography". Oxford University Press for the Institute of Race Relations, London.

Peach, C. (1975). Immigrants in the inner city. *Geographical Journal* **141**, 372-379.

Peach, C. and Winchester, S. W. C. (1974). Birthplace, ethnicity and the under-enumeration of West Indians, Indians and Pakistanis in the Censuses of 1966 and 1971. *New Community* **3**, 386-394.

Rex, J. and Moore, R. (1967). "Race, Community and Conflict: a Study of Sparkbrook". Oxford University Press for the Institute of Race Relations, London.

Robinson, V. (1979a). "The Segregation of Asians within a British City: Theory and Practice", Research Paper No. 22. School of Geography, Oxford.

Robinson, V. (1979b). Contrasts between Asian and white housing choice. *New Community* **7**, 195-201.

Robinson, V. (1979c). Choice and constraint in Asian housing in Blackburn. *New Community* **7**, 390-397.

Robinson, V. (1980). The development of Asian settlement in Britain and the myth of return. Paper presented at the symposium on Ethnic Segregation in Cities, St Antony's College, Oxford.

Rose, E. J. B. *et al.* (1969). "Colour and Citizenship: a Report on British Race Relations". Oxford University Press for the Institute of Race Relations, London.

Shah, S. (1979). Aspects of the geographic analysis of Asian immigrants in London. Unpublished *D.Phil.* thesis, University of Oxford.

Shepherd, J., Westaway, J. and Lee, T. (1974). "A Social Atlas of London". Clarendon Press, Oxford.

Skellington, R. (1980). "Council House Allocation in a Multi-racial Town", Faculty of Social Sciences Occasional Paper, Open University.

Smith, D. J. (1976). "The Facts of Racial Disadvantage: a National Survey". PEP, London.

Smith, D. J. and Whalley, A. (1975). "Racial Minorities and Public Housing". PEP, London.

Tambs-Lyche, H. (1975). A comparison of Gujarati communities in London and the Midlands. *New Community* **4**, 349-355.

Taper, T. (1977). The allocation of Islington housing to ethnic minorities. *New Community* **6**, 41-44.

Ward, R. and Sims, R. (1980). Social status, the market and ethnic segregation. Paper presented at the symposium on Ethnic Segregation in Cities, St Antony's College, Oxford.

Werbner, P. (1979). Avoiding the ghetto: Pakistani migrants and settlement shifts in Manchester. *New Community* **7**, 376-389.

Willmott, P. and Young, M. (1957). "Family and Kinship in East London". Routledge and Kegan Paul, London.

FIVE

The social and spatial
segregation of Asians in Leicester

DEBORAH PHILLIPS

Urban Research Group, Open University, Milton Keynes, UK

The intra-urban distribution of black minorities in Britain has been well docu-
mented, revealing a general pattern of ethnic concentration and segregation from
the host (Jones, 1976; Kearsley and Srivastava, 1974; Husain, 1975; Cater and
Jones, 1979). Positive and negative forces for the continuing separation of black and
white residential space have been reviewed by Simmons in the previous chapter
(Ch.4). Although in most urban areas coloured segregation is less dramatic than in
the USA, the continuing pattern of separation has a number of important implications for black minorities in Britain. Their concentration within the poorer inner
city areas emphasizes the social and economic disadvantage experienced by these
groups, heightens the visibility of an already distinctive minority (making them
easier targets for hostility and aggression), and reaffirms many Whites' belief in the
low status of black immigrants. It is also indicative of the level of social segregation
between the coloured minority and the host. Some early researchers attributed this
separation to the minorities' 'newcomer' or 'immigrant' status as opposed to their
racial differences (Banton, 1955; Patterson, 1965). They tentatively predicted that,
with time, the coloured immigrants would follow the pattern of the earlier white
settlers, dispersing from their initial clusters to become absorbed into white
residential areas and the socio-economic structure of the host society. However,
although there has been some decrease in West Indian segregation levels over the
1961–1971 period, Asian segregation has remained high and the group has exhibited
little desire for assimilation (Peach, 1975; Lee, 1977; Kearsley and Srivastava,
1974). More detailed analysis of the Asian pattern of residence has, nevertheless,
revealed some limited dispersal away from the traditional areas of concentration in a
number of cities. Indications from research in Leicester are that increasing numbers
of Asians are searching for and acquiring property away from the centralized
community. Other research has revealed similar trends elsewhere, for example,
Ballard and Ballard's (1977) work on the Sikhs in Leeds, Husain's (1975) analysis of
Asian dispersal in Nottingham, and the studies of Nowikowski and Ward (1978) and

TABLE I
Composition of the Asian population in Leicester, 1951–1971

	1951			1961			1971		
	Male	Female	Total	Male	Female	Total	Male	Female	Total
Asia									
India	290	279	569	1219	608	1827	6340	5170	11 510
Pakistan/Bangladesh	32	17	49	98	11	109	510	265	775
Others	4	2	6	134	42	176	400	310	710
Africa									
Kenya	8	6	14	901	729	1630	2525	2280	4805
Tanzania							540	475	1015
Uganda							565	450	1015
Others							175	185	360
Total	334	304	638	2352	1390	3742	11 055	9135	20 190

Source: census tabulations

Werbner (1979) in Manchester. Although in most cases this movement has been on a fairly small scale, it has important implications for the erosion of separate ethnic and white residential space and the social interaction of host and minority groups.

This paper attempts to examine some of the forces for Asian concentration and segregation in Leicester and the implications of the trend towards residential dispersal.* Polarization of black and white living space may be attributed to one or more of several segregating processes, including spatial sorting due to differences in socio-economic status, social avoidance through voluntary segregation by the minority, and forced segregation through rejection and exclusion of the coloured immigrants by the white majority (Boal, 1978). Significant changes in the pattern of ethnic residence imply a decline in exclusionary behaviour and a modifcation of host and minority attitudes towards the outside group. Studies of social and spatial distance between groups have largely attributed such a change to minority assimilation, through which major differences are gradually eliminated, defensive barriers lowered and cultural convergence occurs (Duncan and Lieberson, 1959; Lieberson, 1963; Taeuber and Taeuber, 1965). One might therefore hypothesize that Asians leaving the ethnic cluster would display some signs of acculturation and that the movement might represent the beginning of a trend towards structural and cultural assimilation of this group.

The evolution of the Leicester community

Leicester now has one of the largest Asian communities in Britain, with an ethnic population of over 40 000. Immigrants from India and Pakistan were initially attracted by a high demand for unskilled labour in heavy industry and the textile mills (where they acted as a replacement work-force (Peach, 1968)) and by vacancies in growth industries such as engineering. Good job opportunities for the immigrants persisted into the early 1970s, when unemployment elsewhere was rising. As a result, many Asians gravitated to Leicester from other less prosperous centres, for example, large numbers of Gujaratis left parts of Birmingham and Coventry to join friends and relatives in the city. Even though opportunities for immigrant employment in the traditional industries soon began to decline, Asian immigration remained high. Newcomers were primarily attracted by kinship links, services offered by the established Asian community and its institutions, and the rapidly developing Asian sub-economy, which could offer an increasing number of jobs to the immigrants. By 1978, it was estimated that approximately 42 000 Asians lived in the city, comprising about 15% of the total population. This was double the number in 1971 (Table I). Much of the increase in this period can be attributed to the influx of East African Asians—especially from Uganda, despite early attempts

*Data on the spatial distribution of Asian households in Leicester were collected from the Register of Electors for the period 1951-1978. A detailed questionnaire survey of 280 households throughout Leicester was also conducted (240 Asian households, drawn both from areas of high and low ethnic concentration, and 40 white indigenous households).

TABLE II

Ethnic composition of the Leicester Asian population, 1978

	Number in group★	Proportion of Asian population (%)
Ugandan Asians	10 500	25·0
Kenyan Asians	7000	16·7
Tanzanian Asians	2000	4·8
Punjabis (Sikh)	8000	19·0
Pakistanis/Bangladeshis	3000	7·1
Rest of Indian Subcontinent (mostly Gujaratis)	11 500	27·4
Total	42 000	100

★The figures are estimates based on a combination of sources including the electoral register and 1971 census, and are therefore only approximate.
Source: Leicester Council for Community Relations.

by the Ugandan Resettlement Board to divert this group away from major immigrant centres such as Leicester (Bristow and Adams, 1977). East African immigrants (Kenyans, Ugandans and Tanzanians) now constitute the dominant sub-group in the Leicester Asian community and, as far as can be assessed, form one of the largest clusters of these refugees in the country (Table II).

The rapid growth of the Leicester Asian population in the post-war years has placed severe pressures on housing in traditional immigrant areas close to the city centre. This has resulted in a gradual expansion into transitional neighbourhoods adjacent to the established Asian core. The residential space now occupied by the central ethnic community includes a range of housing types and quality, permitting internal differentiation on the basis of socio-economic status and housing needs. Further spatial organization within the community is encouraged by cultural, religious and linguistic differences (Figs 1–3). These provide a basis for social interaction, community organization and voluntary segregation, particularly at street level.

Several distinct phases in the evolution of the Asian settlement may be identified, each with different social and spatial implications. The general pattern is similar to that noted in other immigrant reception centres such as Birmingham (Rex and Moore, 1967; Jones, 1970), Coventry (Winchester, 1974) and Nottingham, (Husain 1975). The early post-war years saw the first major influx of male immigrants from the Punjab, Gujarat and Pakistan. The main motive for migration was economic and the visit to Britain was intended as a short-term solution to problems facing the family in the homeland (Desai, 1963; Aurora, 1967). Most sought private rental accommodation in the cheap lodging houses along the Narborough Road and in the transitional neighbourhood of Highfields (east of the city centre). Chain migration and the availability of suitable accommodation encouraged other newcomers to join

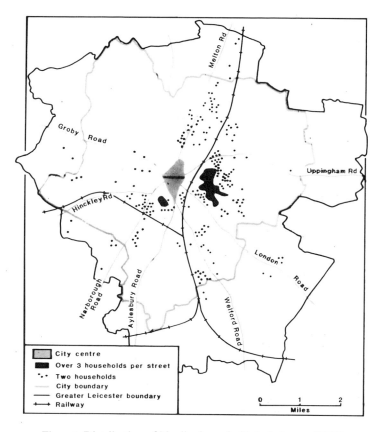

Figure 1. Distribution of Muslim households in Leicester (1978).

these clusters, which have since become the focus of two of the three main areas of immigrant settlement in the city. Early concentration and segregation within these neighbourhoods was mainly voluntary, with little inter-ethnic conflict over this cheaper, less desirable housing (Rex and Moore, 1967). Immigrant choice of accommodation and location was principally governed by frugality and a desire for social isolation from the host.

Despite the initial intention of early immigrants to return home rapidly, the 1960s saw increasing numbers of dependants joining their male relatives and a gradual transition to a more balanced demographic structure (Table I). This led to a progressive stabilization of the Asian community in Leicester as elsewhere (Lomas, 1974; Jones, 1978). The Pakistani Muslims were the only group not to participate fully in this period of reunion, largely due to fears of cultural contamination of the women and the desire to maximize remittances to Pakistan (Dahya, 1972; Jeffery, 1976; Anwar, 1979). The trend is nevertheless still evident, with the male:female ratio for this sub-group in Leicester decreasing from 9:1 to 2:1 over the 1961–1971 period (Table I).*

*This broadly supports Dahya's (1973) estimate that, in 1972, 40% of the Pakistani households in Britain had been reunited.

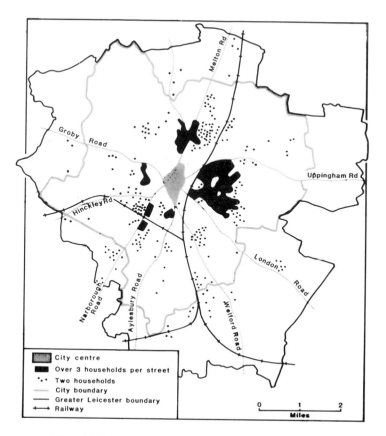

Figure 2. Distribution of Sikh households in Leicester (1978).

This phase of family reunion initiated important changes in immigrant housing demands and the pattern of ethnic residence. Firstly, many families abandoned the private rental sector and the lodging houses lining the main roads in the immigrant reception areas, opting instead for owner-occupied property in the Victorian terraces in the crowded backstreets of these areas. This modest accommodation, often lacking basic amenities, could be purchased for a few hundred pounds. The move, nevertheless, represented an important step in terms of investment of funds in the host country rather than the homeland. The arrival of the family and entry into property ownership may therefore be seen as the first stage in a more permanent commitment to Britain, although most still adhered to the myth of return (Anwar, 1979). Secondly, this period strengthened the Asians' desire for social and spatial encapsulation. The arrival of the women and children initiated a cultural revival, with a return to the traditional lifestyle. Any tenuous links between the minority and host were severed and the social exclusiveness of the group reinstated. This social isolation was paralleled by a desire for spatial separation, leading to a strong preference for property in predominantly Asian streets. Approximately 87%

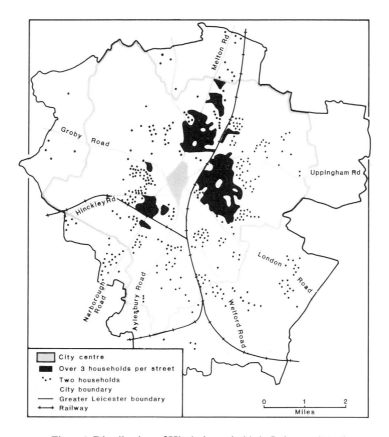

Figure 3. Distribution of Hindu households in Leicester (1978).

of the minority households interviewed maintained that proximity to other Asians had influenced their choice of a family dwelling in Leicester. This voluntary segregation was motivated by fear of cultural contamination (this being especially important for the Muslims) and the desire to recreate a traditional Indian or Pakistani lifestyle based on intense social interaction within the group and a complex network of kin and friendship links. The degree of spatial separation between Asians and Whites for this period is illustrated by a Dissimilarity Index of 67·8 for 1969 (calculated at the electoral parish scale).

As in many other cities, the movement during this period of family reunion simply represented a gradual expansion into adjacent owner occupied areas (Husain, 1975; Jones, 1970). The immigrants encountered little resistance from the indigenous population, many of whom were vacating the area in preference for newer accommodation in the private suburban housing estates or in the local authority sector. The Asians therefore constituted a replacement population in a neighbourhood no longer highly valued by the Whites. In Highfields, a traditional immigrant reception area, a steady process of residential succession ensued, with

Asians displacing a large proportion of earlier immigrants from Eastern Europe. This group has subsequently dispersed through the city.

The concentration and segregation of the Asian minority was greatly intensified by the arrival of 20 000 East African Asians in Leicester between 1968 and 1978. Their presence has had a significant effect on the structure and development of the community and the spatial pattern of settlement. The East African refugees differed greatly from the immigrants who had hitherto settled in the city. Predominantly from Gujarati trading communities, many came to Leicester equipped with entrepreneurial skills, a good education and some knowledge of English. They also tended to migrate as a complete family unit, often bringing ageing parents and relatives with them. Their initial demands for housing were therefore substantially different from their predecessors. The Kenyans also had sufficient financial resources for the immediate acquisition of property, allowing them to bypass the rental stage. The Ugandans, however, were forced into the well developed ethnic rental sector, although most managed to accumulate sufficient capital to purchase a dwelling after three to five years. While some East Africans settled in the traditional reception areas, especially Highfields, a main focus for the Gujarati community, others pioneered new ethnic space in the Belgrave neighbourhood to the north of the city centre. Although this area is again characterized by Victorian terraced housing, the properties generally provide larger, more substantial accommodation, more suited to the extended family. Kenyan Asians pioneering this new area encountered the first real white hostility and resistance to Asian movement in Leicester. Although the character of this area was already mixed, with a significant number of East European and Irish inhabitants, the residents valued it and were prepared to defend it as white residential space. However, market conditions favoured residential succession, and initial resistance declined as increasing numbers of indigenous households moved into the recently completed housing estates adjacent to this area.* This led to the rapid development of a flourishing East African community, supported by numerous Asian-run businesses and institutions. This proved an important attraction to the later Ugandan refugees, who have clustered here in great numbers.

Belgrave has subsequently evolved as one of the more prestigious central Asian residential areas, although it has remained predominantly East African territory. This internal differentiation within the community has been prompted by both religious and status considerations. The majority of the East African Asians are Hindu and the social organizations, ethnic institutions and religious facilities available within Belgrave strongly reflect this. While a number of East African Sikhs have settled here, Pakistani Muslims have generally avoided the area (the only mosques are in Highfields) and in some cases their access has been firmly denied through discrimination by Hindu vendors. The relative homogeneity of the Belgrave community may also be explained in terms of social stratification within

---

*The influence of local market conditions on ethnic concentration and segregation has been stressed by Ward and Sims (1980).

the minority and the power of the dominant East African group. Evidence suggests that these Asians have attempted to segregate themselves from the lower status immigrants from the sub-continent, irrespective of religious affiliations. Many of the former (who generally came from urban rather than rural origins, are better educated, and have greater financial resources than the earlier immigrants) perceive themselves to be superior to the 'peasant' community in Highfields. Structural and economic developments within the Asian community have permitted these East Africans to maintain some degree of separation. The Belgrave community is based on a thriving Asian sub-economy and the group has significant control over the allocation of residential space in this area. This is achieved through the operation of East African estate agents, financiers, solicitors etc. (who by their own admission 'look after their own'), and by widespread individual property ownership (60% of these homeowners admitted they would only sell to one of their own sub-group). The East Africans therefore have the power to exclude undesirable groups from their territory in a way hitherto only possible for Whites (Pahl, 1975; Palm, 1979). Voluntary segregation for this sub-group in Leicester would therefore seem to imply some measure of forced segregation for the remainder of the community. While many of the latter would themselves support the continued isolation of their own sub-group in Highfields or Narborough Road, some Gujaratis would certainly favour a move to the protected space of the Belgrave community.

Concentration and segregation in Leicester: an assessment

By the end of the 1970s, the Asian population had formed a cohesive and highly distinctive community in central Leicester. This was characterized by a high level of concentration and segregation from the indigenous population, as illustrated by the Dissimilarity Index of 71·1 for 1978. This clear separation of ethnic and white residential space may be seen as a reflection of social distance between the groups, suggesting that there are important cultural differences and minimal interaction between the minority and host in Leicester.

Two alternative interpretations of ethnic residential concentration and segregation have been presented in the literature: (1) voluntary clustering based on housing preferences and cultural differences (Deakin and Cohen, 1970; Hiro, 1973; Kearsley and Srivastava, 1974), and (2) forced isolation based on conflict over housing and other resources between the minorities and the more powerful white majority (Rex and Moore, 1967; Pahl, 1975; Cater and Jones, 1979). The relative importance of these factors is likely to vary with the size and character of the minority group, the history and context of their immigration and the extent to which immigrant accommodation needs can be met by the housing supply. Their importance may also vary over time, according to developments within the community and changing demands for residential space.

Voluntary concentration and segregation from the indigenous population seems to have played an important part in the current pattern of Asian residence in Leicester. This was particularly important in the early stages of settlement, when choice of location was governed by the availability of property, the desire for cultural exclusiveness and proximity to the ethnic group (Dahya, 1974). Initial clustering has been reinforced by chain migration, which has strengthened bonds within the community and provided a sound basis for intense interaction within the group (Desai, 1963; Hiro, 1973; Dalton and Seaman, 1973). The emergence of a well developed Asian sub-economy and community infrastructure has also helped to emphasize the positive aspects of concentration. Now nearing a position of 'institutional completeness', the community is able to offer many religious facilities, shops and services, which provide employment, reinforce ethnic values and constitute a framework for the traditional way of life (Breton, 1964; Dahya, 1974; Driedger and Church, 1974). They also allow the community relative autonomy and free many members from unwanted interaction with the host.

The segregated ethnic neighbourhood may therefore be seen as a separate territory, which serves to heighten and proclaim the distinctive identity of the minority, and provide support and protection for the immigrant (Boal, 1969; Deakin, 1970; Ley, 1974). The spatial separation enables the community to enforce social closure, thereby excluding outside groups and maintaining social and cultural isolation from the host (Parkin, 1979). It has been hypothesized that, with time, the immigrants will become acculturated and feel less need to seek refuge within the spatial confines of the ethnic cluster (Cressey, 1938). Greater inter-group mixing should therefore ensue. However, for many Leicester Asians, including the early immigrants, the concentrated and segregated community remains important. The questionnaire survey revealed that more than three-quarters of the immigrants who had lived in the city for 12 or more years still had no desire to move away from their compatriots. Complete segregation from the white indigenous population was advocated by only 37% of the respondents living within the ethnic community. They justified their feelings in terms of culture preservation (90% of the group), irreconcilable differences between the minority and host (63%) and conflict avoidance (36%). However, 77% of the centralized population strongly endorsed the less extreme principle of clustering, referring to the positive benefits it brings. The continuing role of the community was also underlined by the finding that over half the respondents would not be prepared to live in a predominantly white area (13% were not even happy with the prospect of living in an all white street). Most cited the importance of Asian services and institutions available within the established ethnic space (85%), the threat of cultural contamination (64%) and the significance of a traditional Asian orientated environment for bringing up the children (61%). While the remainder maintained that they would be prepared to live outside the main area of ethnic residence, less than 10% had any firm intention of leaving in the near future.

While minority choice has undoubtedly contributed to ethnic segregation in Leicester, this only provides a partial explanation of the pattern. Completely voluntary separation implies that the Asians would be free to disperse whenever they wished (Deakin and Cohen, 1970). However, studies suggest that coloured groups face a number of barriers to dispersal (Burney, 1967; Smith, 1976). Social closure by the Whites, who can use their dominant position to control access to the more desirable housing and living space, can effectively exclude outside groups from large areas of the city. The result is forced segregation of the minority.

Evidence of forced segregation may take several forms. Firstly, it is possible to identify 'manifest' conflict between the groups through evidence of discrimination within the housing market (Daniel, 1968; Brown, 1972; Williams, 1976). Nearly half of the segregated group of Asians felt they had experienced discrimination, including 20% who maintained they had been denied access to the area of their first choice, away from the established ethnic space. A survey of Asians using high street estate agents in Leicester suggested that the mobility and preferences of approximately half of these immigrants was constrained either by the estate agents (e.g. by funnelling prospective purchasers away from more prestigious white neighbourhoods such as Stoneygate to more mixed areas such as Evington) or through discrimination by the vendor. Twenty per cent decided to abandon their decision to move as a result, and remained within the segregated area. Secondly, forced segregation may be the product of 'latent' conflict. This highlights the constraints placed on immigrants' housing choice and aspirations by the fear of white hostility, discrimination and rejection (Deakin and Cohen, 1970; Lambert and Filkin, 1971; Fenton, 1977). In this case, social and physical isolation is a means of defence and no attempt may be made to move away from the security of the ethnic cluster (Stea, 1965; Boal, 1978). The strength of this force for segregation is more difficult to assess since immigrants may continue to stress only the positive aspects of clustering. However, a number of survey respondents revealed, either directly or indirectly, their underlying fears about leaving the protective ethnic territory. Nearly 30% perceived white hostility as a problem and referred to clustering as a means of conflict avoidance, while others felt it would be impossible to acquire housing in white areas because of discrimination. A further 11% maintained that they definitely favoured suburban living, but feared that hostility from the neighbours would make life intolerable.

Finally, the minority's ability to compete for housing in more desirable areas is also indirectly constrained by discrimination in employment. This leads to a forced separation of black and white groups through economic differences. It might be hypothesized that some of the ethnic clustering interpreted by Lee (1977) and others in terms of socio-economic characteristics might be more meaningfully attributed to forced segregation through racial prejudice. Evidence suggests that coloured workers earn significantly less than their white counterparts, that they are frequently forced to take unskilled jobs despite good educational qualifications and that economic advancement is often blocked (Castles and Kosack, 1973; Smith, 1976). Again, it is difficult to assess the full effect of job discrimination without a more detailed analysis of immigrants' employment careers, which is beyond the scope of this research. However, a comparison of Leicester Asians' occupations before and after migration indicated a significant decline in job status, suggesting constraints upon their earning power. In 1971, 55% of the clustered group were still employed in unskilled or semi-skilled jobs compared with 25% of the indigenous population. Nearly half of these Asians felt they had been subjected to discrimination with the job market, and many feared that coloured workers would suffer more prejudice and blocked socio-economic mobility in the future.

The pattern of ethnic concentration in Leicester may therefore be attributed to both voluntary and forced segregation. Until the 1970s, inter-group contact was characterized by social avoidance and mutual exclusion, and race relations appeared good. Indigenous Whites and the more established East European immigrants displayed relatively little resistance to the Asian invasion of the poorer inner residential areas, perceiving better housing alternatives in the suburbs. As Ward and Sims (1980) have stressed, since white demand for such property was falling, it was frequently in the economic interests of these residents to sell to the incoming minority. In short, Asian housing preferences and their desire for segregation from the host coincided with the pattern of residence preferred by the white majority and provided little basis for conflict. The 1970s, however, have seen increasing numbers of Asians searching for property away from the main ethnic concentration, with greater conflict occurring over this more highly prized residential space. This movement has taken two forms. Firstly, there has been a progressive expansion into areas of better quality, semi-detached housing adjacent to the main ethnic cluster, e.g. the Evington area near Highfields. These are now characterized by a fairly high level of residential intermixing between black and white groups (e.g. an ID of 19·8), although the areas are still transitional and their stability not assured. Secondly, there has been a small scale dispersal away from the main cluster to scattered locations within the higher status white residential areas. This re-location has important implications in terms of the attitudes and behaviour of both the minority and the white indigenous population in Leicester.

Residential dispersal

A small number of Asians were to be found in isolated locations throughout Leicester even during the 1960s. Evidence suggests that these households fell into Nowikowski and Ward's (1978) category of Asian professionals, a group having little in common with the main immigrant community and few links with them. This research, however, is more concerned with families who have made a conscious decision to leave the familiar ethnic territory where they have been closely involved with the local Asian community.

Successful residential dispersal by coloured immigrants depends on several factors. Firstly dispersal is often, although not inevitably, associated with movement away from poorer low rent districts into higher status neighbourhoods of more expensive housing. Acquisition of property within these areas demands access to adequate financial resources. Secondly, barriers to movement away from the assigned ethnic space must be lifted by the host population. The conflict interpretation of minority segregation stresses the importance of white control and defence of established white territory. The arrival of coloured households in these neighbourhoods suggests that either the housing occupied is no longer in great demand by the

Whites or that the host group no longer perceives the minority as a threat. In Leicester, the white residential space now being entered by the dispersing Asians is characterized as follows. (1) Local authority housing, located predominantly to the south and south-west of the city. Flett (1977), Robinson (1980) and Skellington (1980) have provided evidence of the increasing demand for council housing from the Asian minority. However, most allocations are to inner city housing in Leciester, as elsewhere, and movement to outer local authority estates accounts for less than 5% of immigrant dispersal in the city. (2) Better quality private sector housing, still in demand from the white population. The location of this is varied, ranging from inter-war housing within fairly easy reach of the city centre to newer developments outside the city boundary. By 1978, nearly 400 Asian households had dispersed outside the city itself to locations at least five miles away from the major ethnic concentration. Superficially at least, this physical displacement would appear to represent a break with the centralized community.

Finally, immigrants who wish to disperse must not only be willing to pioneer potentially hostile white areas, but must also feel able to survive outside the confines of the protective community and be willing to forsake many of the benefits which accrue from clustering. While this may not be significant for immigrants forced together by ascriptive group membership, it has important social and cultural ramifications for traditionally cohesive and exclusionary groups such as the Indians and Pakistanis. Although relocation away from the main minority settlement may entail some re-clustering, these newly formed nuclei are often too small to support many ethnic institutions or services, or to recreate the atmosphere of the larger centralized community. It is, therefore, generally hypothesized that minority group members leaving the ethnic cluster are characterized by some degree of cultural and structural assimilation, which eases their transition into the residential environment of the host.

By 1978, approximately 830 Asian families had dispersed away from the main ethnic cluster to areas of low ethnic concentration.* Interviews were conducted with 130 of these households living in scattered locations within the private housing sector. The implications of their relocation and their ability to bypass some of the barriers to dispersal are evaluated below

Constraints within the housing market

Coloured minority groups occupy a weak position within the housing market, as highlighted by Rex and Moore's (1967) theory of housing classes. Disadvantage stems from several factors but low socio-economic status and discrimination are of particular significance (Burney, 1967; Smith, 1976). Coloured minorities tend to be

---

*In the absence of any objective definition of high or low concentration, thresholds were chosen on the basis of the proportion of the total Asian population living in any ward. The lowest quartile of the range (i.e. 0·1–1·6%) was chosen to define areas of low concentration. All these areas had a Location Quotient of less than 0·2.

over-represented amongst the lower income groups, which places severe restrictions upon their housing choice. Over a quarter of the households living within the main ethnic cluster maintained that economic constraints had permitted them no choice in the type or location of their property. While the residential decision of dispersing Asians was also obviously bound by financial considerations, members of this group were clearly in possession of a larger disposable income, for example, 55% paid more than £11 000 for their property and 22% over £13 000. The ability to finance such a move was related to a number of factors.

(1) A significant proportion were employed in higher status occupations, and nearly 10% were prosperous businessmen. However, 20% were still employed in semi-skilled or unskilled jobs.

(2) About a third had some form of additional income, which had helped them to accumulate capital for the move. This included a number of landlords owning a single property within the ethnic core. This provided both financial and emotional security. Not only was it regarded as a source of income, but also as a permanent tie with the central community and a refuge to which the family could return if the need arose.

(3) A significant difference was found in the number of immigrants sending regular remittances to the homeland and in the proportion of the household income sent by families in the high and low concentration areas.* While most of the latter still emphasized their cultural and emotional links with the sending society, only 20% spoke of strong economic ties in the form of investments to which they might return. Many had chosen instead to invest their funds in businesses and property in Leicester, a symbol of their more lasting commitment to life in this country.

The availability of financial resources with which to compete in the housing market does not necessarily ensure access to white residential space. Nearly two-thirds of the Asian households maintained that they had encountered some form of discrimination in their attempts to disperse into the white housing sector. This had prolonged the length of their search (53% took over six months) and frequently denied households access to their first choice of housing. Whereas many Asians now living within the centralized community might have been discouraged from moving by such experiences, this group exhibited a strong determination to succeed and a faith in their ability to do so despite the racial barrier. For example, many were characterized by a positive attitude towards the host population in general (72%), which encouraged them to persist in their search until they found households willing to sell.

About 15% of the dispersed Asians managed to bypass prejudice from the private vendor by opting for newly built housing in suburban estates, while others chose to avoid institutional discrimination through the use of ethnic banks, estate agents and solicitors. However, as Cater (Ch. 8) has shown for Bradford, Asian estate agents in

*East African Asians were excluded from this analysis since their migration was motivated by political rather than economic reasons and relations with the homeland are different.

Leicester tend to deal mainly with cheaper inner city properties (80% fall within the £2000–6000 price range). Most of the dispersing Asians were therefore forced to use the white-run high street agents (82%) or other information sources. Two-thirds opted to secure a mortgage through a white building society, and those with skilled or high status occupations apparently encountered few problems. Only 16% chose to acquire funding through an Asian financier, mainly due to high interest rates. Finally, none of the sample had purchased from an Asian vendor, but as more immigrants disperse this may become an important means of access to suburban property in the future.

Reaction of the white indigenous population

Throughout much of the history of Asian immigration into Leicester, race relations have appeared good. However, in recent years, with the rapid expansion of the Asian community, growing number of more vocal second generation immigrants and the problems of unemployment facing both Blacks and Whites, new tensions have arisen, heightening the potential for conflict. Asian entry into previously separate white territory has only exacerbated the problem as perceived by the Whites. A small-scale survey of the indigenous population suggested that nearly 60% favoured continuing separation of black and white residential space, 53% of the total agreeing that coloured immigrants lower the status of a neighbourhood. Over a third were convinced that race relations in Leicester would only become worse if the Asians were to move out from their traditional segregated clusters.

The prevailing white attitude is therefore one of continuing opposition to black entry into their territory. Asians who have successfully dispersed have, nevertheless, managed to overcome this barrier. Two explanations may be offered.

(1) Despite a general reticence, white vendors may well sell to coloured households if it seems in their economic interests (Ward and Sims, 1980). This may be particularly important if the vendor is experiencing difficulty in selling. Also, not all white owners are bound by the same status considerations which encouraged discrimination. However, these sales may be accompanied by some price discrimination, with the vendor exploiting the difficult situation faced by the minority (Fenton, 1977; Banton, 1979). Evidence from the Leicester survey suggests that 65% of those Asians entering white residential space paid the full asking price for their property.

(2) Prospective Asian purchasers may seem more acceptable to the vendor if they exhibit some signs of cultural assimilation. While this does not eradicate deeply rooted prejudice based on colour, it does partly reduce the uncertainty and fear surrounding strangers with different customs and behaviour from the host (Banton, 1959, 1967). Indeed, 60% of the indigenous sample felt that Asians should be encouraged to adopt English ways and customs, suggesting that the continuing preference for ethnic and cultural isolation was a basis for conflict.

Characteristics of the dispersing Asians

Representatives of all the major Asian sub-groups were to be found in areas of low ethnic concentration, although the Muslims had participated least in the dispersal due to their preference for cultural exclusiveness and their greater financial commitments to the homeland. Dispersing immigrants must be willing to forsake both the protection offered by spatial isolation within the community and the positive aspects of clustering. A number of researchers have attributed this to the process of cultural assimilation, suggesting that dispersal symbolizes both rejection of the ethnic community and its traditional way of life, and a gradual merging with the host society (Park, 1926; Duncan and Lieberson, 1959; Lieberson, 1963). Broad indicators of total assimilation such as naturalization and intermarriage have frequently been used to demonstrate the strength of social and spatial association (see, for example, Lancaster Jones, 1967; Timms, 1969). However, these are not particularly useful in the investigation of social and spatial patterns in Leicester, where ethnic assimilation has not advanced to the stage of intermarriage. The recent trend towards dispersal here may, nevertheless, be interpreted in terms of a change in the cultural orientation and attitudes of some of the Asian minority and a move towards their social and spatial integration with the host.

The survey revealed a number of significant differences between those immigrants living in areas of high and low concentration. These broad differences generally cut across areal and religious affiliations. Firstly, the protective function of the community was no longer significant for the dispersed group. Any perceived threat or earlier uncertainty of the host had subsided and limited mixing occurred in most cases. Most used host institutions in their search for housing and, despite experience of prejudice and discrimination, 79% felt that race relations were good or improving. This strongly contrasts with the negative reaction of many of the segregated Asians. Secondly, most dispersed immigrants placed a high value on the acquisition of material possessions, a good standard of living, and on displaying their wealth in this country. The purchase of a good quality spacious house in a better residential area was viewed both as an investment and a symbol of success, and it constituted the main motive for dispersal. This represents a significant departure from the traditional immigrant philosophy of deferred gratification (Desai, 1963; Dahya, 1974). In contrast to many of the segregated immigrants, most of the dispersed group had only weak links with the homeland (or none at all in the case of the East Africans) and were committed to spending most of their life in this country. They had therefore modified their goals and aspirations accordingly. Finally, all the dispersed Asians displayed some signs of acculturation. For example, a higher proportion could speak English than amongst the segregated population and many of the women at least occasionally wore Western dress. These attributes may have helped them gain access to the suburban areas by removing the stigma of strangeness surrounding the minority and encouraging a more favourable reaction from characteristically defensive Whites.

The profile of the dispersed Asian population would superficially seem to indicate a trend towards full cultural and structural assimilation. However, a closer analysis revealed significant variations in the character of dispersed households, reflecting differences in behavioural adaptation and cultural orientation. It was possible to divide these households into three main sub-groups.

(1) Non-traditional, assimilating immigrants, comprising approximately 20% of the households. This group was generally better educated than the majority of immigrants and most were in high status or professional occupations. Similar groups have been identified by Nowikowski and Ward (1978) and Ballard and Ballard (1977) in suburban Manchester and Leeds. Dispersal for these immigrants represented a clear break with the ethnic community and a move towards cultural and structural assimilation, although the latter may be inhibited by discrimination (Ballard and Ballard, 1977). Social interaction was characterized by a high level of both primary and secondary contacts with the host, and full use was made of white institutions and services. About half still participated in religious festivals with the centralized community, but otherwise ethnic links were few. Nearly all agreed that marital assimilation was desirable and nearly 80% maintained they would not oppose an inter-racial marriage by their children.

(2) Traditional, non-assimilating immigrants, comprising about 45% of the dispersed population. Dispersal for this group was motivated by a preference for good quality housing and the desire to elevate the family status within the ethnic social hierarchy. The increasing size and permanence of the Asian population has encouraged the development of a well defined minority social structure. This provides an important framework for social organization and interaction, and a basis for competition amongst immigrants not bound by the principle of deferred gratification. Prestige not only depends on the acquisition of material possessions and property, but also on strict religious and cultural observance, which provides the basis for the cohesion of the community.* Hence, physical re-location for this group was not accompanied by any change in cultural orientation. In some cases, the move stimulated even stricter adherence to cultural tradition, for example, women were more confined to the house to avoid cultural contamination. Social interaction with the host was restricted, with contacts being mainly of a 'secondary' nature. In contrast, great emphasis was placed on maintaining links with the ethnic community through regular social contact (nearly all owned a car which aided their mobility) and participation in community organizations and activities.

(3) A transitional group. Although predominantly traditional in orientation, this group exhibited some indications of a trend towards cultural and structural assimilation. Participation in social and religious activities in the Asian community was declining and an increasing number were seeking greater social interaction with the host.

*As Nowikowski and Ward (1978) have noted in Manchester, the ethnic lifestyle adhered to by these groups does not strictly conform to the traditional culture inherited from the homeland, but has been modified to suit the urban life of an Asian minority in Britain.

Conclusion

The pattern of Asian residence in Leicester suggests that the minority's propensity to disperse is not simply a function of length of residence in the community, but is governed by the immigrant's cultural orientation, aspirations and experience of the host society. It is possible to identify three principal sub-groups within the Asian community as a whole, each with different reference groups and implications for social and spatial mixing: (1) those strongly orientated towards the homeland, dispersal is unlikely for this group unless it is in their economic interests and social and cultural isolation is assured; (2) those who are fairly prominently settled in Britain and have chosen the Asian community based in this country as a frame of reference; prestige is sought within the Asian social hierarchy, which might encourage dispersal; (3) those orientated towards the white host society and aspiring to social and spatial assimilation.

Given the desire to disperse, movement will only occur if certain preconditions are fulfilled, e.g. immigrants have sufficient financial resources, and the ability to overcome enforced segregation. The research indicates that although Whites retain a dominant position in the allocation of residential space, determined Asians have managed to bypass barriers and force residential integration on the Whites. However, the potential for dispersal is limited by both voluntary and imposed forces, suggesting that spatial segregation will persist.

Finally, the research suggests that residential dispersal does signify a change in immigrant attitudes towards both the indigenous and minority communities. Dispersing Asians clearly place higher value on achieving their housing aspirations and elevating their socio-economic status than being physically close to the immigrant community, and they are prepared to tolerate some measure of interaction with the indigenous population. However, this change may not always be equated with cultural assimilation into the host society. While all exhibit superficial signs of acculturation and limited structural assimilation through secondary inter-group contact, most remain culturally isolated. Rather than a precursor to total assimilation, dispersal for many of the immigrants may at best be seen as a step towards partial integration in the host community.

Acknowledgements

This work forms part of the author's doctoral research at the University of Cambridge, and was funded by a grant from the Social Sciences Research Council and Girton College, Cambridge.

References

Anwar, M. (1979). "The Myth of Return: Pakistanis in Britain". Heinemann, London.
Aurora, G. S. (1967): "The New Frontiersmen: a Sociological Study of Indian Immigrants in the UK." Popular Prakashan, Bombay.

Ballard, R. and Ballard, C. (1977). The Sikhs: the development of South Asian settlement in Britain. *In* "Between Two Cultures", (J. L. Watson, ed.) Blackwell, Oxford.

Banton, M. (1955). "The Coloured Quarter". Jonathan Cape, London.

Banton, M. (1959). "White and Coloured". Jonathan Cape, London.

Banton, M. (1967). "Race Relations". Tavistock, London.

Banton, M. (1979). Two theories of racial discrimination in housing. *Ethnic and Racial Studies* 2, 417-427.

Boal, F. W. (1969). Territoriality on the Shankill-Falls divide, Belfast. *Irish Geography* **6**, 30-50.

Boal, F. W. (1978). Ethnic residential segregation. *In* "Social Areas in Cities: Processes, Patterns and Problems", (D. T. Herbert and R. J. Johnston, eds.). Wiley, London.

Breton, R. (1964). Institutional completeness of ethnic communities and personal relations to immigrants. *American Journal of Sociology* **70**, 193-205.

Bristow, M. and Adams, B. (1977). Ugandan Asians and the housing market in Britain. *New Community* **6**, 65-77.

Brown, W. H. (1972). Access to housing: the role of the real estate industry. *Economic Geography* **48**, 66-78.

Burney, E. (1967). "Housing on Trial: a Study of Immigrants and Local Government". Oxford University Press.

Castles, S. and Kosack, G. (1973). "Immigrant Workers and Class Structure in Western Europe". Oxford University Press.

Cater, J. and Jones, T. (1979). Ethnic residential space: the case of Asians in Bradford. *Tijdschrift voor Economische en Sociale Geografie* **70**, 86-97.

Cressey, P. (1938). Population succession in Chicago: 1898-1930. *American Journal of Sociology* **44**, 59-69.

Dahya, B. (1972). Pakistanis in England. *New Community* **2**, 25-33.

Dahya, B. (1973). Pakistanis in Britain: transients or settlers? *Race* **14**, 241-277.

Dahya, B. (1974). The nature of Pakistani ethnicity in industrial cities in Britain. *In* "Urban Ethnicity", (A. Cohen, ed.). Tavistock, London.

Dalton, M. and Seaman, J. (1973). Distribution of New Commonwealth immigrants in the London Borough of Ealing. *Transactions, Institute of British Geographers* **58**, 21-39.

Daniel, W. (1968). "Racial Discrimination in England". Penguin, London.

Deakin, W. (1970). Race and human rights in the city. *In* "Developing Patterns of Urbanization", (P. Cowen, ed.). Oliver and Boyd, Edinburgh.

Deakin, W. and Cohen, A. (1970). Dispersal and choice: towards a strategy for ethnic minorities in Britain. *Environment and Planning* **2**, 193-201.

Desai, R. (1963). "Indian Immigrants in Britain". Oxford University Press.

Driedger, L. and Church, G. (1974). Residential segregation and institutional completeness: a comparison of ethnic minorities. *Canadian Review of Sociology and Anthropology* **11**, 30-52.

Duncan, O. and Lieberson, S. (1959). Ethnic segregation and assimilation. *American Journal of Sociology* **64**, 364-374.

Fenton, M. (1977). Asian households in owner occupation: a study of pattern, costs and experience of households in Greater Manchester. SSRC Research Unit on Ethnic Relations Working Paper on Ethnic Relations No. 2.

Flett, H. (1977). Council housing and the location of ethnic minorities. SSRC Research Unit on Ethnic Relations Working Paper No. 5.

Hiro, D. (1973). "Black British, White British". Penguin, Harmondsworth.

Husain, M. S. (1975). The increase and distribution of New Commonwealth immigrants in Greater Nottingham. *East Midlands Geographer* **6**, 105-129.

Jeffery, P. (1976). "Migrants and Refugees: Muslim and Christian Pakistani Families in Bristol". Cambridge University Press.

Jones, P. N. (1970). Some aspects of the changing distribution of coloured immigrants in Birmingham, 1961-1966. *Transactions, Institute of British Geographers* **50**, 199-219.

Jones, P. N. (1976). Colored minorities in Birmingham, England. *Annals, Association of American Geographers* **66**, 89-103.

Jones, P. N. (1978). The distribution and diffusion of the coloured population in England and Wales, 1961-71. *Transactions, Institute of British Geographers N.S.* **3**, 515-532.

Kearsley, G. and Srivastava, S. (1974). The spatial evolution of Glasgow's Asian community. *Scottish Geographical Magazine* **90**, 110-124.

Lambert, J. and Filkin, C. (1971). Race relations research: some issues of approach and application. *Race* **12**, 329-335.

Lancaster Jones, F. (1967). Ethnic concentration and assimilation: an Australian case study. *Social Forces* **45**, 412-423.

Lee, T. R. (1977). "Race and Residence: the Concentration and Dispersal of Immigrants in London". Oxford University Press.

Ley, D. (1974). "The Black Inner City as Frontier Outpost". Association of American Geographers, Monograph Series No. 7, Washington DC.

Lieberson, S. (1963). "Ethnic Patterns in American Cities". Free Press of Glencoe, New York.

Lomas, G. B. G. (1974). "Census 1971: the Coloured Population of Great Britain." Runnymede Trust, London.

Nowikowski, S. and Ward, R. (1978). Middle class and British?: an analysis of South Asians in suburbia. *New Community* **7**, 1-10.

Pahl, R. E. (1975). "Whose City?" Penguin, Harmondsworth.

Palm, R. (1979). Financial and real estate institutions in the housing market. *In* "Geography and the Urban Environment". (D. T. Herbert and R. J. Johnston, eds.) Wiley, London.

Park, R. E. (1926). The urban community as a spatial pattern and a moral order. *In* "The Urban Community", (E. W. Burgess, ed.). University of Chicago Press, Chicago.

Parkin, F. (1979). "Marxism and Class Theory: a Bourgeois Critique". Tavistock, London.

Patterson, S. (1965). "Dark Strangers: a Study of West Indians in London". Tavistock, London.

Peach, C. (1968). "West Indian Migration to Britain: a Social Geography". Oxford University Press for the Institute of Race Relations, London.

Peach, C. (1975). Immigrants in the inner city. *Geographical Journal* **141**, 372-379.

Rex, J. and Moore, R. (1967). "Race, Community and Conflict: a Study of Sparkbrook". Oxford University Press for the Institute of Race Relations, London.

Robinson, V. (1980). The development of Asian settlement in Britain and the myth of return. Paper presented at the symposium on Ethnic Segregation in Cities, St Antony's College, Oxford.

Skellington, R. (1980). "Council House Allocation in a Multi-racial Town". Faculty of Social Sciences Occasional Paper No. 2, Open University.

Smith, D. J. (1976). "The Facts of Racial Disadvantage: a National Survey". Political and Economic Planning, London.

Stea, D. (1965). Space, territory and human movements. *Landscape* **15**, 13-17.

Taeuber, K. E. and Taeuber, A. (1965). "Negroes in Cities". Aldine, Chicago.

Timms, D. W. G. (1969). The dissimilarity between overseas-born and Australian-born in Queensland: dimensions of assimilation. *Sociology and Social Research* **53**, 363-374.

Ward, R. and Sims, R. (1980). Social status, the market and ethnic segregation. Paper presented at the symposium on Ethnic Segregation in Cities, St Antony's College, Oxford.

Werbner, P. (1979). Avoiding the ghetto: Pakistani migrants and settlement shifts in Manchester. *New Community* **7**, 376-390.

Williams, P. (1976). The role of financial institutions and estate agents in the private housing market. CURS Working Paper No. 39, University of Birmingham.

Winchester, S. W. C. (1974). Immigrant areas in Coventry in 1971. *New Community* **4**, 97-104.

SIX

Spatial separation between Asian religious minorities: an aid to explanation or obfuscation?

RON SIMS

SSRC Research Unit on Ethnic Relations, University of Aston, Birmingham, UK

It is perhaps a reflection on the nature of the academic disciplines that whilst sociologists have tended to "assume that the behaviour of coloured people can be understood solely in terms of external constraints, such as racial discrimination in jobs and housing" (Ballard and Ballard, 1977; p.52), geographers, for their part, have placed greater emphasis on the primacy of ethnic choice and the positive forces of ethnic association in determining the housing decisions of coloured immigrants, particularly those of South Asian origin. In particular, Dahya's (1972, 1973, 1974) stress on the voluntary non-participation by Asians in white society "has had a more widespread acceptance in the geographical literature than has the discrimination thesis" (Robinson 1979; p.8).

An anthropological perspective, which more realistically straddles these contrasting views, acknowledges that an understanding of racial and ethnic minorities and, by implication, their spatial patterns "rests on a consideration of both internal preferences and external constraints which act simultaneously" (Ballard and Ballard 1977; p.53). Theoretical recognition that an analytical separation of these forces is necessary does not answer the problem of how one might empirically test their relative importance.

To address this problem various methods have been used, ranging from questioning minority groups on their housing preferences, aspirations and their experiences of discrimination, to the examination of the practices and ideologies of the so-called urban gatekeepers. Questioning minority groups and others in relatively weak market positions has been severely criticized for its naive implication that many groups, particularly immigrants from the New Commonwealth, have a wide range of choice in the housing market (Gray, 1975). A greater weakness in this approach is the pertinent point made by Duncan (1977) that

> It is perhaps all too easy, in looking closely at the experiences of particular people to fall prey to the misleading assumption that the only socially effective forces are those of which the people involved are aware.
>
> Duncan (1977; p.16)

A common method often used by geographers has been to interpret the different levels of spatial separation exhibited by various immigrant groups, both from the rest of the population and from each other, in an attempt to illustrate the relative importance of the positive forces of ethnic association and the negative forces of discrimination. The underlying rationale for this interpretation is summed up by Winchester (1974) when he suggests that

> . . . if segregation between New Commonwealth sub populations is higher than that between the sub populations and the remaining white population . . . this may be assumed to be evidence of motives for clustering internal to the group.
>
> Winchester (1974; p.98)

Coupled with this assumption was his belief that one might use the lowest index of segregation for any of the 'coloured' groups as some kind of maximum base figure for racial discrimination. In Coventry in 1971, as in a number of other cities, (Birmingham (Woods, 1975), Nottingham (Husain, 1975)), the population born in the West Indies had a lower index of segregation than any of the Asian minorities. On the strength of this, the segregation of West Indians formed Winchester's base figure of racial discrimination, above which the higher indices of Asian segregation were interpreted as a reflection of ethnic choice. In Coventry, the very high index of segregation of Pakistanis was felt to confirm their popular image of deliberately choosing not to disperse for fear of cultural contamination.

These interpretations are questionable for a number of reasons. Firstly, they ignore the very obvious differences in housing tenure between ethnic minorities, the different timing of their main migration streams and their subsequent patterns of family reunion, all of which play a part in producing different levels of spatial separation. For example, there can be no doubt that far higher proportions of West Indians than Asians are living in council housing (Flett, 1977). Whatever the faults of the public sector it has attempted, in recent years at least, to allocate housing on grounds theoretically based on need. The private sector, on the other hand, is based on allocative procedures firmly rooted in discrimination, whether it be on grounds of income, class, status or colour. In these circumstances, ethnic minorities who have moved into the public sector might be expected to be less segregated. Indeed, in Birmingham for a time the local authority was deliberately attempting to reduce residential clustering amongst black council tenants by operating a covert dispersal policy (Flett, 1979).

A greater inadequacy of this form of interpretation is the woolly assumption of some blanket kind of discrimination based on skin colour. It assumes that the discriminating policies of urban gatekeepers and perhaps more importantly, the discriminating actions of white owner-occupiers are completely insensitive to differences between coloured minorities. In most areas outside of London it is Asian minorities who feature more prominently in the process of racial residential succession in the private sector of housing. In these circumstances it might be argued that the coloured minority whom white owner-occupiers are most keen to keep out, for fear of rapid racial residential succession and the associated threat of status decline (Ward and Sims, 1980), are Asians. It seems just as plausible to argue that higher levels of Asian segregation are a function of greater discrimination towards them than the positive forces of ethnic association.

The most obvious empirical weakness of these attempts to assess the relative importance of discrimination and ethnic choice has been that many of the accounts were based on census derived birthplace figures which may have little relevance in ethnic terms. Census birthplace categories for the Asian population may include a substantial white component, and even more damaging is the fact that there may be a poor relationship between birthplace and a recognizably ethnic component such as nationality, religion or language. Both Anwar (1979) in Rochdale and Robinson (1979) in Blackburn illustrate the large number of Indian-born ethnic Pakistanis, which is a result of a wholesale population transfers following Partition. For example, in Blackburn, although the majority of the Asian population (53%) were born in India, the overwhelming majority were Muslim (91%).

The work of Robinson is of particular theoretical and substantive interest. Its theoretical interest lies in the fact that it is the most detailed geographical exposition of Dahya's (1974) stress on the peripheral and transient nature of Asian immigrants in Britain and the importance for them of the myth of return. Robinson's emphasis is on the primacy of ethnic choice in determining the housing behaviour of Asians, and, in particular, their desire for voluntary self-encapsulation, both from the host society and from other minorities. Substantively, the work breaks new ground with its macro-scale analyses of patterns of Asian settlement based on more realistic ethnic divisions within the Asian population, such as religion and language.

There is no dispute over the importance of being able to analyse patterns of religious and linguistic differences within the Asian population, the concern is rather with the use of certain indices of residential clustering and the kinds of conclusions that are derived from them.

There appear to be three major themes underlying Robinson's interpretation. The first is the suggestion that there is a strong desire for spatial encapsulation by distinctive religious and linguistic Asian minorities, both from non-Asians and from the rest of the Asian population. The second is that the pattern of Asian intra-community spatial separation in Britain can be viewed as a manifestation of patterns of historical conflict prevalent on the Indian sub-continent, and finally, that there is evidence of increasing intra-ethnic polarization within the Asian population over a period of time.

The major accounts of the spatial patterns of the religious and linguistic differences within the Asian population of Blackburn (Robinson, 1979, 1980) are based on an enumeration of all Asian households for 1977. Many of the problems associated with using indices of dissimilarity and other related techniques appear to have been ignored. As has been noted in the literature many times, the index of dissimilarity is sensitive to both the size of the sub-group and the areal unit of study. For example, Woods (1975; p.179) notes that in Birmingham: "The Maltese and Cypriots and the Africans represent such a small group anyway that one might expect their separation from the total population to be considerable even if they were relatively evenly distributed". Peach's (1979) advice that one must be cautious when interpreting indices of dissimilarity when there are more units of analysis than minority group members is also of importance. The use in Blackburn of 14 wards for the spatial inter-ethnic indices of dissimilarity does not violate the letter of this law. However, the small numbers involved may be thought to violate the spirit of this arbitrary rule of thumb. For example, Bangladeshis form less than 1% of Blackburn's adult Asian population which means that there are 57 Bangladeshi individuals in the town. On the strength of this, the finding that Bangladeshis are the most highly segregated birthplace group, from both the non-Asian population and from the other Asian birthplace groups, must be interpreted with care. To interpret the high degree of spatial separation between Pakistanis and Bangladeshis as "to be expected in the light of events in 1971" (Robinson, 1979; p.20) is most questionable. Whether internecine ethnic conflict in the homeland leads to ethnic polarization in Britain is an interesting proposition, particularly as it might relate to the substantial Catholic and Protestant populations from Northern Ireland now settled in Britain. While much of the literature, including that cited by Robinson, indicates the high levels of segregation between Pakistanis and Bangladeshis, few conclusions can be drawn specifically from the spatial activities of 57 individuals in one town. The linguistic and religious group that Robinson singles out as demonstrating the highest degree of choice-based segregation, although never violating the above rule of thumb, is in each case by far the smallest group (Robinson, 1979).

To emphasize the importance of religion as the 'major catalyst' of the ethnic divisions of Blackburn's Asian population, use is made of Weaver's Crop Combination Index. This index can be a useful device and has a respectable academic pedigree in geographical accounts of immigrant settlement (Jones, 1976). In the case of Blackburn it is a little unfortunate that the overwhelming majority of the Asian population are Muslims (91%). In this context, the finding that "over 90% of the Asian community live in enumeration districts that effectively contain members of only one of the major Asian religions" (Robinson, 1979; p.21) is not unexpected. In fact, if Muslims were distributed in each area in proportion to their overall dominance then each area would be a 'one crop' Muslim area and the finding that all Asians live in 'one crop' Muslim areas (i.e. homogeneous areas) is not only to be expected but hardly worth demonstrating. Indeed, it is the size of the residual heterogeneous areas that points to some religious clustering not the size of the homogeneous group, which only informs us what a lot of Muslims there are.

Even more questionable than the use of these techniques to indicate the strength of ethnic divisions within the Asian population, is the procedure for mapping the spatial patterns of community clustering in the town. This procedure has its roots in the much used Location Quotient and carries all its attendant problems. Given the relative sizes of the different religious, linguistic and birthplace minorities within the Asian population, rather strange results arise. For example, in Blackburn, six Enumeration Districts are identified as the Sikh areas of the town. Yet it is evident from the analysis and the very small number of Sikhs that these areas are probably over 80% Muslim. An alternative explanation would be that in every single

Enumeration District Muslims form the majority of the Asian population and therefore share residential space with all other religious groups. This degree of residential intermixing is neither evidence for nor against there being high levels of internal conflict within the Asian population.

Perhaps the most surprising omission in this attempt to substantiate the importance of ethnic choice and the divisions within the Asian population concerns the evidence of clustering in suburban areas of Blackburn. It is noted that "St. Mark's ward (a higher class residential area) contained 22 Asian families, yet 17 of these families lived in only six streets out of a possible 73" (Robinson, 1979; p.16). This is viewed as a further indication of the operation of housing choice rather than constraint. Yet no attempt is made to analyse whether these suburban clusters have their roots in ethnic homogeneity. As will be demonstrated later, it is precisely the degree of detailed clustering in Birmingham, not based on ethnic homogeneity in outer and inner suburbia, that points to alternative forces in operation rather than those of simple ethnic choice.

Robinson's most compelling argument for the acceptance of Dahya's stress on the importance of the myth of return for Asians, and their continuing "non-participation in the housing schemes of the host society" (Robinson, 1979; p.38), rests on an attempt to substantiate the notion of Ballard and Ballard (1977) that some kind of development cycle of ethnic polarization is in operation in Britain. Robinson (1980) argues that this cycle has two spatial components. The first is a decline in the index of segregation of Asians, not because of any weakening of the desire for voluntary encapsulation from non-Asians but as a consequence of the expansion outwards from the original areas of Asian settlement. It is argued that this expansion is to permit the second component, that of the desire for increasing levels of spatial distancing between Asian minorities. Unfortunately, no evidence is presented for Blackburn to illustrate these increasing levels of internal spatial and social distancing on the grounds of either religion, language or birthplace. In an attempt to clarify some of the issues raised, the remainder of this chapter draws on material from Manchester and Birmingham.

Religious separation in Manchester and Birmingham, 1971–1976

The data on religious differences in both cities are based on material from local authority records and electoral registration data collected for five yearly intervals for the period 1951-1976. A number of surveys was also carried out, in part, to substantiate the findings from the secondary data sources. Asian names from local authority records and from the electoral register were divided into religious categories by a group of Asians from the major religious, linguistic and birthplace groups. Checks between this and survey material revealed a high level of accuracy. Use of the electoral register as a source material for Asian numbers is hardly novel (Kearsley and Srivastava, 1974; Cater *et al.*, 1977; Cater and Jones, 1979), nor is dividing the names into religious categories (Duncan, 1977). In this account, however, the electoral register was greatly enhanced by the material from the rate records which not only served as an indicator of Asian under-enumeration on the electoral register, a perennial criticism of its use, but provided information on the activities of Asian landlords, rateable values, house descriptions and details of present and previous ownership of property.

Only the simplest indices of dissimilarity based on electoral register data have been included, to examine what appear to be two cornerstones of the thesis which stresses the importance of ethnic divisions within the Asian population. The first is that the pattern of ethnic, particularly religious, separation between Asian minorities in Britain can be interpreted in terms of the religious conflicts of the homeland, largely unchanged in Britain by the process of migration and the constraints of the metropolitan housing market. Secondly, that with increasing family reunion and the desire for voluntary self-encapsulation these divisions within the Asian population will widen (Table I).

TABLE I
Ward indices of dissimilarity (Manchester)

		1976	
	Muslim	Hindu	Sikh
1971			
Muslim	—	27·1	41·8
Hindu	28·8	—	44·9
Sikh	47·8	51·7	—

Despite suggestions (Robinson, 1979) that one might expect high levels of residential separation between Hindus and Muslims, in Manchester consistently low levels of spatial separation are the case. It is also evident that separation along religious lines was declining in the city over the period. In Birmingham, as Table II indicates, the changes from 1971 to 1976 are less consistent than in Manchester, with considerably higher levels of spatial separation between religious groups and some evidence of increasing polarization between Hindus and Sikhs. This polarization cannot simple be interpreted as reflecting an increased desire by Hindus and Sikhs for less cultural contamination over the period, but rather has its roots in the great increase of Gujarati Hindus over the period (Table III).

One problem with religion as a category is that it is extremely catholic, encompassing a wide range of linguistic and regional groups. Without the benefit of detailed data on language and nationality, Table IV is an attempt to illustrate the strength of intra-religious separation. Hindu names were divided into those which emanate from the Gujarat region of India, those which originate from the Punjab and, finally, a heterogeneous 'others' category which has no meaning in ethnic terms. As one might have anticipated, there is a strong association between Punjabi Hindus and Sikhs, and high levels of spatial separation between Gujarati Hindus

TABLE II

Ward indices of dissimilarity and segregation
(Birmingham); above the diagonal 1976, below the diagonal 1971

	Index of segregation	Muslim	Hindu	Sikh	Asian
	segregation	63·1	60·5	70·9	63·7
Muslim	61·7	—	44·6	51·8	—
Hindu	61·8	48·5	—	39·0	—
Sikh	70·2	53·8	32·5	—	—
Asian	61·3	—	—	—	—

TABLE III

City and selected ward totals by religion (Birmingham)

	Muslims (%)	Hindus (%)	Sikhs (%)	Hindu Gujaratis	Asian	% of electorate
1971	12 677 (53·8)	3347 (14·2)	7536 (32·0)	1782	23 559	3·3
1976	18 457 (50·8)	6533 (18·0)	11 367 (31·3)	4170	36 357	5·2
Sparkhill 1971	995 (49·1)	604 (29·8)	429 (21·2)	495	2028	11·3
Sparkhill 1976	1997 (43·9)	1684 (37·0)	868 (19·1)	1512	4549	24·9
Saltley 1971	1319 (93·7)	28 (2·0)	61 (4·3)	10	1408	7·9
Saltley 1976	2108 (95·3)	34 (1·5)	69 (3·1)	15	2211	13·5
Washwood Heath 1971	579 (92·8)	10 (1·6)	35 (5·6)	3	624	3·2
Washwood Heath 1976	1065 (92·3)	24 (2·1)	65 (5·6)	6	1151	6·2

TABLE IV

1976 ward indices of dissimilarity (Birmingham)

	Muslim	Sikh	Hindu Gujarati	Hindu Punjabi
Muslim	—	51·8	44·2	53·8
Sikh		—	52·5	16·8
Hindu Gujarati			—	50·8
Hindu Punjabi				—

and Punjabi Hindus. Many of the Gujarati Hindus in Birmingham have arrived
from East Africa, particularly Uganda, a feature borne out by the dramatic increase
of Gujaratis from 1971 to 1976, the period covering the Ugandan expulsion.
Unfortunately, it is impossible to distinguish satisfactorily this group by name,
though there are some distinctive East African Gujarati names.

Table V attempts to examine the spatial separation between 'new' and 'old'
groups in the city, here defined as those groups who have moved into an area over
that period, and those where the householder has remained the same. As one might
have anticipated from the earlier figures on the overall changes from 1971 to 1976,

TABLE V

1976 indices of dissimilarity by length of residence (Birmingham)

	(1)	(2)	(3)	(4)	(5)	(6)	(7)	(8)
(1) Old Muslims	—	11·5	51·7	48·7	56·3	53·3	50·8	48·2
(2) New Muslims		—	45·2	42·1	52·9	49·0	46·2	41·7
(3) Old Hindus			—	16·9	35·2	29·5	—	—
(4) New Hindus				—	46·8	39·4	—	—
(5) Old Sikhs					—	16·2	51·0	58·8
(6) New Sikhs						—	47·0	51·7
(7) Old Gujaratis							—	15·7
(8) New Gujaratis								—

all the 'new' groups show increasing spatial similarity with each other except for the
'new' Gujarati Hindu group which is apparently becoming more spatially separate
from Sikhs. The increasing intra-religious polarization between Hindus and Sikhs
which ran counter to the general pattern of increasing spatial association, is, in part,
a result of this increase in Gujarati Hindus, in particular their increase in Sparkhill
(Table III). Sparkhill had been traditionally an area with a large Muslim population.
A large increase of Gujarati Hindus in a Muslim area, rather than a predominantly
Sikh area, helps to explain the small amount of increasing polarization between
Sikhs and Hindus without needing to resort to some cyclical notion of inter-ethnic
polarization.

Clearly, differentiating the Asian population in terms of their length of residence
is only one way of dividing up the population. Tenure is another obvious division
and a particularly important feature of the housing market in Britain. Indeed, one of
the most important distinctions in comparisons between black residential settlement
in Britain and America is the availability and size of the public sector. With a third
of the stock owned by the local authority it has been suggested, with particular
reference to ethnic minorities, that "Britain possesses in incipient form, the most
powerful levers for the socio-spatial engineering of society" (Peach *et al.*, 1975;
p.414). Although relatively few Asians are council tenants, their moves into council
housing have been regarded as a means of providing an arena where non-discriminatory

action by urban gatekeepers allows one to study the operation of ethnic choice apparently untramelled by racial discrimination (Robinson, 1980). In the only major study of Asians in the council sector it is suggested that the "social distancing which exists in the private sector is being recreated in the public sector" (Robinson, 1980; p.23). Table VI illustrates the high levels of spatial separation along religious lines in the council sector in Manchester, where in 1976 over 10% of the Asian families in the city were living in council property.

TABLE VI

Ward indices of dissimilarity (council property, Manchester); above the diagonal 1976, below the diagonal 1971

	Muslim	Hindu	Sikh
Muslim	—	50·4	33·7
Hindu	71·4	—	58·3
Sikh	64·9	88·5	—

Certainly religious polarization is high in the public sector. It is, however, difficult to support the view that the public sector is simply a recreation of the private sector, as the indices of dissimilarity are along very different lines from the overall pattern of religious separation. The marked changes in the indices of dissimilarity in the public sector in Manchester from 1971 to 1976 are more a function of the local authority's choice of demolition areas than changes in the desire for self-encapsulation.

The figures for the public sector in Birmingham (Table VII) are complicated by the distinction between those properties that have been acquired by the council and those which have been erected by them. Again, high indices of dissimilarity are a feature of the public sector, particularly in housing built by the local authority; but as in Manchester, the patterns are not those of the private sector.

This difference between the private and the public sector can also be seen in Blackburn (Robinson, 1979, 1980), despite assertions that the public parallels the

TABLE VII

Ward indices of dissimilarity (Birmingham); above the diagonal public sector acquired (1976), below the diagonal public sector erected (1976)

	Muslim	Hindu	Sikh
Muslim	—	52·1	29·7
Hindu	52·3	—	56·6
Sikh	58·8	63·6	—

private. In the public sector the linguistic groups who are the most spatially separate and, by implication, socially divided are Gujarati and Urdu speakers; in the private sector these two are the least socially divided.

Table II also reveals the consistently high indices of religious segregation at both a ward and sub-ward level. It is interesting to note that, as in Blackburn, it is Sikhs who are the most segregated religious group. The reasons for this high level of segregation in Birmingham, running somewhat counter to the popular images of Sikhs being more willing to integrate than, for example, Muslims, are two-fold. First, as a result of the arbitrary nature of the city boundaries, one of the major areas of Sikh residential expansion from Soho ward in Birmingham is likely to be into the district of Warley, which is outside the city. Second, in Birmingham the Sikh religious group is far more homogeneous in terms of background and timing of arrival than, for example, the category Muslim which ranges from Mirpuris with a rural peasant background to the highly urbanized Ismaili Muslims from Uganda.

As has been noted by a number of authors, a single overall figure marks very different patterns of intra-ethnic residential mixing which exists in different areas of a city (Lee, 1977). For example, Table VIII illustrates the much lower levels of sub-ward religious separation that occur in two of the most Asian wards in Birmingham, in comparison with the overall picture.

TABLE VIII

Indices of dissimilarity (polling districts 1976);
above the diagonal Sparkhill, below the diagonal Sparkbrook

	Muslim	Hindu	Sikh
Muslim	—	28·2	28·7
Hindu	44·1	—	27·8
Sikh	16·8	34·5	—

Birmingham

	Muslim	Hindu	Sikh
Muslim	—	56·6	59·6
Hindu	—	—	46·9
Sikh	—	—	—

A more graphic, if less conventional illustration of inter-religious mixing is contained in Table IX. This shows that in a city with nearly 12 000 Asian addresses, over 3000 of them have an Asian next-door neighbour to their right. One-third of these neighbours are from a different Asian religion. Admittedly, the overall figures ought to be seen in the context of the proportions Asians form on individual

TABLE IX
Next-door neighbours (Birmingham 1976)

	Next-door neighbour from same religious group (1)	Next-door neighbour from different religious group (2)	Total number of Asian properties (3)
Acocks Green	14	7	144
All Saints	58	34	335
Aston	77	53	495
Billesley	0	0	31
Brandwood	1	1	54
Deritend	75	66	592
Duddeston	9	0	56
Edgbaston	50	8	263
Erdington	2	2	43
Fox Hollies	0	0	40
Gravelly Hill	18	2	165
Hall Green	2	8	94
Handsworth	111	96	881
Harborne	18	12	152
Kings Norton	1	1	58
Kingstanding	0	0	12
Ladywood	0	0	34
Longbridge	0	0	24
Moseley	68	37	369
Northfield	10	1	26
Newtown	24	29	218
Oscott	0	0	15
Perry Barr	0	0	32
Quinton	1	0	44
Rotton Park	98	42	520
Saltley	248	7	712
Selly Oak	84	49	664
Shard End	0	0	22
Sheldon	0	0	16
Small Heath	202	80	980
Soho	337	203	1397
Sparkbrook	302	110	1230
Sparkhill	233	189	1428
Stechford	0	1	31
Stockland Green	1	0	39
Washwood Heath	87	5	428
Weoley	0	1	39
Yardley	0	0	29
Total	2131	1044	11 712

Birmingham streets; despite this, it does point to a high degree of intra-religious mixing at a detailed level. The high incidence of Asians moving into streets to locate next door to other Asians clearly echoes the pattern of black colonization in the USA (Schelling, 1972). The frequency of these moves by Asians into houses next door to another Asian family often from another religious group casts doubt on the notion that this is an understandable response to the need for close ethnic association; it points rather to a distinctive structural response of the housing market with the onset of racial residential succession.

In conclusion, there is no evidence from Manchester and Birmingham that there is some general underlying trend in the spatial pattern of religious separation which can be viewed as a response to the conflicts on the Indian sub-continent. Nor is there evidence in the two cities, and the evidence for Blackburn is questionable, that ethnic polarization is increasing. This is not to suggest that ethnic considerations play no part in structuring the housing decisions of Asians. The existence of wards like Washwood Heath and Saltley in Birmingham, which are overwhelmingly homogeneous in religious composition, belies this. These wards, despite their numerical influence on indices of dissimilarity, must be set against the pattern of wards where residential clustering occurs in tandem with high levels of religious intermixing.

In some respects the differences between Manchester and Birmingham compared with Blackburn are to be expected. Blackburn is a small town with a limited economic base, drawing on immigrant Asian labour from a rural peasant background. In these circumstances one might anticipate there to be greater stress on ethnic spatial association compared with a city like Manchester whose Asian population has a large middle class and status conscious component (Nowikowski and Ward, 1978). The danger is in extending the results for one town to suggest "that the Asian element in urban areas neither sees itself as part of, nor is concerned with, the larger white society" (Robinson, 1979; p.38).

References

Anwar, M. (1979). "The Myth of Return: Pakistanis in Britain". Heinemann, London.

Ballard, R. and Ballard, C. (1977). The Sikhs: the development of South Asian settlements in Britain. *In* "Between Two Cultures", (J. L. Watson ed.). Blackwell, Oxford.

Cater, J. and Jones, T. (1979). Ethnic residential space: the case of Asians in Bradford. *Tijdschrift voor Economische en Sociale Geografie* **70**, 86-97.

Cater, J., Jones, T. and McEvoy, D. (1977). Ethnic segregation in British cities. *Annals, Association of American Geographers* **67**, 305-306.

Dahya, B. (1972). Pakistanis in England. *New Community* **21**, 25-34.

Dahya, B. (1973). Pakistanis in Britain: transients or settlers? *Race* **14**, 241-277.

Dahya, B. (1974). The nature of Pakistani ethnicity in industrial cities in Britain. *In* "Urban Ethnicity", (A. Cohen ed.). Tavistock, London.

Duncan, S. S. (1977). "Housing Disadvantage and Residential Mobility: Immigrants and Institutions in a Northern Town". Urban and Regional Studies Working Paper No. 5, Sussex.

Flett, H. (1977). Council housing and the location of ethnic minorities. SSRC Research Unit on Ethnic Relations, Working Paper on Ethnic Relations No. 5.

Flett, H. (1979). Dispersal policies in council housing, arguments and evidence. *New Community* **7**, 184-195.

Gray, F. (1975). Non-explanation in urban geography. *Area* **4**, 228-235.

Husain, M. S. (1975). The increase and distribution of New Commonwealth immigrants in Greater Nottingham. *East Midland Geographer* **6**, 105-129.

Jones, P. N. (1976). Some aspects of the changing distribution of coloured immigrants in Birmingham. *Annals, Association of American Geographers* **66**, 89-102.

Kearsley, G. W. and Srivastava, S. R. (1974). The spatial evolution of Glasgow's Asian community. *Scottish Geographical Magazine* **90**, 110-124.

Lee, T. R. (1977). "Race and Residence: the Concentration and Dispersal of Immigrants in London". Oxford University Press.

Nowikowski, S. and Ward, R. (1978). Middle class and British?: an analysis of South Asians in Suburbia. *New Community* **7**, 1-10.

Peach, C. (1979). Race and Space: a comment *Area* **11**, 82-83.

Peach, C., Winchester, S. W. C. and Woods, R. I. (1975). The distribution of coloured immigrants in Britain. *Urban Affairs Annual Review* **9**, 395-419.

Robinson, V. (1979). "The Segregation of Asians within a British City: Theory and Practice." Research Paper No. 22. School of Geography, Oxford.

Robinson, V. (1980). The development of Asian settlement in Britain and the myth of return. Paper presented at the symposium on Ethnic Segregation in Cities, St Antony's College, Oxford.

Schelling, T. C. (1972). A process of residential segregation: neighbourhood tipping. *In* "Racial Discrimination in Economic Life", (A. H. Pascal ed.). D. C. Heath, Lexington, Mass.

Ward, R. H. and Sims, R. M. (1980). Social status, the market and ethnic segregation. Paper presented at the symposium on Ethnic Segregation in Cities, St Antony's College, Oxford.

Winchester, S. W. C. (1974). Immigrant areas in Coventry in 1971. *New Community* **4**, 97-104.

Woods, R. I. (1975). Dynamic urban social structure: a study of intra-urban migration and the development of social stress areas in Birmingham. Unpublished D.Phil. thesis, University of Oxford.

SEVEN

Segregation and simulation:
a re-evaluation and case study

VAUGHAN ROBINSON

Nuffield College, Oxford, UK

The advent of Monte Carlo modelling techniques in geography can be firmly linked with the work of one author and with the analysis of one type of phenomenon. The technique had been widely used in other fields such as biology, sociology and communications, and it may have been work in this last area that encouraged Hägerstrand (1967) to apply the concept to the study of innovation diffusion via personal contact or the 'neighbourhood effect', as he termed it.

To Hägerstrand, and many of those who followed him, the approach had a great deal to offer. As with all other models, the Monte Carlo approach conferred several practical and conceptual benefits upon the potential user. Firstly, modelling necessarily involved a degree of simplification or crystallization and was one of the few techniques available for studying the totality of a complex system. All the major elements within a system could be considered simulataneously, within the correct context, and in this way holistic and dynamic relationships between variables could be highlighted. In short, modelling produced simplified order out of complex chaos. Secondly, at a time when geography was undergoing a change in form from an idiographic art to a nomothetic science, modelling was firmly within the mainstream of the new geography. It followed Warntz (1959) in advocating the search for regularities. It epitomized Schaefer (1953) and Bunge's (1962) desire to see geography placed in the logical-positivist mould as a social science, and it was closely attached to the influential Washington school (Johnston, 1979) which thrived upon a strong mathematical base with a substantial policy orientated output.

Modelling in general, and simulation modelling in particular, consequently closely followed what Harvey (1969) has since termed the scientific method, and hence bestowed upon its users the kudos and respect that were such necessary parts of career advancement during a period of academic revolution (Taylor, 1976; Johnston, 1979). However, in addition to those benefits accruing to the user of all models, Monte Carlo simulation modelling offered additional advantages. In particular, it was an ideal tool for the study of black- or grey-box situations where understanding was partial. As Morrill (1965a; p.16) stated, even in conditions where "we haven't the information to reproduce exactly the real world, and to predict just what will happen" we often have "sufficient understanding to generate similar patterns, one of which could, by its properties, be a real one". Such insight was potentially invaluable at the early stage of theory building, and promised a much needed focus. The Monte Carlo approach also overcame one of the major disadvantages of other techniques in that it blended deterministic and probabilistic stances by disaggregating forces into macro-scale constraints and micro-scale choices. This successfully operationalized Jones' (1956) plea for dual scale laws which could parallel the classical theory and quantum mechanics of contemporary physics, and therefore effectively defuse the argument about the merits and demerits of determinism which had threatened to re-appear in the UK in the 1950s (Martin, 1951; Montefiore and Williams, 1955; Jones, 1956). Finally, the Monte Carlo simulation approach provided "feasible, risk-free, economic, and in some cases reproducible, ways in which artificial experience of a real system may be obtained" (Bracken, 1978). The opportunity to experiment or explore within a system without disturbing the operation of that system recommended simulation modelling not only to the social scientist but also to the socio-spatial engineer. To the former the model represented a substitute for the natural scientist's laboratory (Bartholomew, 1967), whilst for the latter it allowed the application of pre-tested policies and initiatives. Such policy orientated research was becoming more important for, as Hägerstrand (1971; p.1) noted, "after a short period of belief in the mechanisms of automatic progress, we have now reached a stage when the world is perceived by many as increasingly chaotic. The opinion is spreading that if mankind shall have a future at all, we need to be able not only to forecast coming events but consciously and purposely to invent this future".

With such a large number of potential advantages it is not difficult to see why Monte Carlo simulation attracted interest in fields as disparate as the spread of Dutch elm disease in the UK (Sarre, 1978) and the growth of urban systems in south Sweden (Morrill, 1965a). Since many of those studies employing the technique did so for different motives, Bracken (1978) has developed a useful three-fold typology of simulations. He groups them into those which aim to further 'Decision and Policy' through the construction of the model itself, through the specification and testing of alternative social and spatial states, and through long-term monitoring; those which aid in 'Investigation and Research' by means of the scientific method, by providing a stimulus to inter-disciplinary co-operation, or by re-constituting partial data and theories; and, finally, those which assist purely through the pedagogic nature of the process.

The use of Monte Carlo simulation modelling in urban social geography

The 1960s, particularly in America, witnessed not only a change in societal values and concerns but also the beginnings of a parallel shift in academic emphases. As Smith (1973; p.1) notes, although "there is a long history of professional and philanthropic anxiety over the existence of social problems such as poverty, the conditions in the slums, and the decline of conventional morality", the 1960s witnessed growing popular concern over these issues and rising expectations "that the government will do more about these problems than simply issuing formal expressions of concern and offering ineffectual remedial programs". A key issue among these was the problem of racial disadvantage—a topic forcibly brought to the attention of the American population by the Civil Rights movement, and also increasingly publicized in Britain. Geographers had not been slow to take an interest in the problem at a variety of scales, an early inkling of what later became known as the 'relevance revolution'. At one level, geographers concentrated upon the description of ethnic patterns in residential space but it was the inter-disciplinary work which concerned itself primarily with the social processes underlying such spatial patterns, which promised to be of the greatest value for both administrators and intellectual liberals. Work on the form and process of neighbour-hood transition such as that by Duncan and Duncan (1957) and Rapkin and Grigsby (1960) all paved the way for the more directly policy-orientated statements such as those of Downs (1968) in the USA and Deakin and Cohen (1970) in the UK. Increasingly, social geographers became conscious of the fact that their efforts had to be directed towards both the explanation of ethnic segregation and towards the improvement of conditions through policy initiatives. Morrill (1965b) answered this call in his study of the expansion of the Seattle ghetto by employing Monte Carlo simulation techniques. The latter, he considered, were

> an ideal vehicle for the characteristics of ghetto expansion—a process of growth in time, concerning behaviour of small groups in small areas in small units of time, in which a powerful element of uncertainty remains, even though the general parameters of the model tend to channel the results. This randomness is evident in the real situation, since we observe that the ghetto, like a rumour or an innovation, does not progress evenly and smoothly in all directions but exhibits an uneven edge and moves at different rates in different directions . . .
>
> Morrill (1965b; p.349)

Morrill's purpose in applying the technique was "to discover and illustrate the nature of the ghetto expansion process, in full knowledge that the detail of the ultimate step is omitted—how the actual individual decides between his specific alternatives". He considered that the central factors in the process were those of natural increase, Negro in-migration, the nature of resistance to Negro dispersion, land values and housing characteristics, and the population size limits of the recipient blocks. Morrill formalized these factors and incorporated them into a simulation which closely followed Hägerstrand's earlier lead, i.e. probabilities were assigned to each cell on the basis of their characteristics, their spatial proximity to the sending cell and their likely resistance to entry. Households were then created by internal migration, natural increase, or in-migration to Seattle, and these were then relocated using random numbers over ten two-year time periods between 1940 and 1960. Morrill (1965b; p.359) was not rigorous in his testing of the results and although he proposed criteria for verification (that "the simulated pattern of spread, had the right extent (area), intensity (number of Negro families in blocks), and solidity (allowing for white and Negro enclaves)"), he was content to apply primarily visual tests of conformance. The results of these suggested that the model had failed to take into account the quality and the value of dwelling units, and had also ignored the impact of topography. Nevertheless, Morrill (1965b; p.359) declared the exercise a success since "the simulated patterns *could have* occurred according to the operation of the model".

Morrill's reliance upon the mechanism of 'invasion–succession' involving active Negro pioneers and passive Whites was later taken up by Hansell and Clarke (1970) who considered the ghetto in Milwaukee between 1950 and 1960. Their hypothesis was

> that the direction, extent, and degree of expansion of the Negro ghetto is proportional to the differential value of dwelling units, to the number of Negro dwelling units already in an area, to the location of ethnic groups within the city, and to the increasing area of influence of the CBD.
>
> Hansell and Clarke (1970; p.270)

Like Morrill, Hansell and Clarke operationalized their ideas through an empirically derived probability field with the added component of barriers to represent the inpenetrability of high rent zones and stable ethnic communities of Eastern European origin. The model was run through five two-year generations spanning the decade up to 1960. Although their work was based upon that of Morrill, Hansell and Clarke were more rigorous in their testing procedures, although the techniques which they employed were still rudimentary. They reported a correlation coefficient of $+0.87$ between the actual and simulated 1960 distributions, but were quick to point out that the model had overdiffused the population as a result of unrealistic initial assumptions made necessary by a pre-existing computer program. Despite this inaccuracy the authors (Hansell and Clarke, 1970; p.275) felt sufficiently confident to state that "the hypothesis around which the model is built seems to be basically sound and is not rejected. The direction, degree, and extent of the 1960 ghetto core were replicated with some degree of success".

The evidence presented by Morrill, and by Hansell and Clarke, was strongly suggestive of the dominance of invasion-succession in the process of ghetto expansion. This confirmed Burgess' early ideas, graphically demonstrated for ethnic groups in Chicago by Cressey (1938). On the basis of this new understanding of the process at work, Hansell and Clark (1970; p.277) were able to encourage additional studies which might progress one stage further and outline "possible policy decisions on a more desirable speed of ghetto expansion and hence dilution".

Simultaneous with Hansell's and Clarke's work, however, was that of Rose (1970). Rose disbelieved the evidence for invasion–succession and pleaded instead for a re-consideration of the filtering-down model with an active suburbanizing white population and a passive 'supply-led' black population. Rose therefore structured his simulation so as to contain three components: the demographic component deterministically estimated housing demand using age- and colour-specific birth and death rates; the producer component deterministically estimated housing availability. This was the key to both Rose's model and his theoretical vindication, and it revolved around a white leaving rate curve which supposedly quantified white reaction to the threat of Negro proximity. Rose, however, generated the curve 'intuitively' and did not present it in the paper; the third component (the consumer component) probabilistically matched housing demand and vacancies and therefore created the simulated pattern. The model was operationalized for Milwaukee and data were presented for the whole city up to 1968 and for sub-areas up to 1965. Analysis of the former revealed excessive dispersion outside the ghetto and insufficient concentration upon its fringe. The latter produced similar conclusions. In view of this, Rose (1970; p.17) was cautious in his claims, noting only that the results had "provided evidence of deficiency in some of the basic assumptions incorporated in the model". He still felt, however, that modelling generated greater understanding and that it had potential value in the planning process. With regard to the latter he suggested (Rose, 1970; p.16) that alternative models might be constructed to "generate specific levels of ghetto escapement on the basis of changing patterns of behaviour, growing out of modified economic policies and social relations".

In 1972 Rose went on to answer some of his critics by applying a similar, but more detailed model to black residential clusters in seven US cities (Rose, 1972). In this later paper Rose still did not fully explain the workings of his model, and in particular he continued to rely upon an 'intuitively-derived' white leaving curve. Evaluation of results revealed that housing demand, in all but one case, was seriously overestimated, whilst "like the demand component . . . the spatial assign- ment was characterized by wide ranging results in its ability to predict accurately the emerging pattern of black occupance". Rose concluded that "the amount of error associated with the simulated outcome is serious, regardless of the scale employed to analyze the error" (Rose, 1972; pp.59-60). He then went on to consider the spatial arrangement of errors, and closed by suggesting an alternative but untested model. In total then, Rose proved incapable of validating the filtering- down mechanism.

Following the early lead set by North American workers, it was only a short period of time before the technique was employed in the context of ethnic areas within British cities. Woods (1973) first presented his family of simulation models in 1973, although more detailed explanations of these can be found elsewhere (Woods, 1975; Woods, 1980). Woods was clearly aiming his model not only in the direction of academic understanding of the processes at work but also in the direction of policy and planning initiatives. In his earliest paper (Woods, 1973) he noted that the rationale behind his work was "the improvement of race relations by establishing a greater understanding of how segregation and discrimination work and thus their eventual elimination". He emphasized this point in the 1980 paper by setting his models within the context of a discussion of housing policy and its implications for ethnic areas in Birmingham. Woods' models thus fell firmly into Bracken's (1978) 'Decision and Policy' category rather than the more abstract type concerned with 'Investigation and Research'.

Woods built his family of models around three general principles since "immigration, relocation and housing structure can be regarded as the major elements contributing to the spatial concentration of the coloured population" (Woods, 1980; p.5). These general propositions were converted into formal inputs via the use of surrogate data. The future increase of the coloured population was predicted by estimating anticipated levels of West Indian and Asian immigration to the UK, and then assuming that Birmingham would continue to attract the same percentage of incoming migrants as it had during the 1960s. Woods (1975) admitted that this calculation was based upon 'pure supposition', but argued that extant demographic projections of the coloured population were even less accurate. 'Relocation' was operationalized by the assumption that 5% of a cell's population would change its address per annum. No evidence was presented to support this assumption, although Woods did, at a later stage (Woods, 1980), claim that such a figure had empirical support, at least within Handsworth. In 1975, however, he concluded (Woods, 1975; p.27) that "it is by no means clear just what influence the fixing of the turnover rate at 5% had on the different simulation patterns". The potential movers were to be relocated by using a distance–decay function constructed from a random sample of 62 white marriages found in a local paper during August 1972. Woods drew encouragement from the fact that this function was also supported by a study of the residential mobility of Birmingham's elite between 1950 and 1970, although he failed to indicate why the mobility patterns of non-English speaking, non-car-owning, coloured immigrants should bear any resemblance to this. The 'housing structure' component, which was designed to inject data on the suitability of areas to coloured occupancy, revolved around the location of lodging houses within the city in 1970. Woods admits that this assumes that the distribution of multi-occupied dwellings remained static throughout the decade, an assumption which he demonstrated to be untrue; he failed, however, to point out that the component also relied upon a belief that patterns of Asian and West Indian occupance had remained constant during the same period. High levels of Asian owner-occupation and increasing levels of West Indian public renting by 1971 demonstrated this to be false. Woods' omission of more detailed information on differential resistance to coloured occupance by certain housing sectors represents a major failing of all his proposed models.

Woods used the three building blocks described above to construct a series of simulations for Birmingham relating to the period 1960–1970. Model 1 distributed immigrants on an annual basis such that new arrivals were scattered in proportion to the existing immigrant population found in each cell. After each increment had been added, a new Mean Information Field (MIF) was constructed with altered probabilities. This then went forward to act as the basis of the next iteration. Model 2 replicated Model 1 but, in addition, allowed 5% of existing coloured residents to change their place of residence; Model 2a employed a fixed MIF whilst 2b used a floating 5 × 5 cell grid. Model 3 again used the previous simulations as its basis but it introduced a weighted MIF on the basis of the percentage of houses in multi-occupation. Again 3a relied upon fixed probabilities whilst 3b used a floating grid.

Each of these models was run separately for the aggregated New Commonwealth group, for West Indians and for Asians.

Woods' major contribution was not the structure of the models themselves but the techniques which he employed to test their accuracy. He was considerably more conscientious and rigorous in this sphere than were any of his predecessors, employing visual conformance, correlation coefficients, coefficients of determination, and the more advanced shape related statistics pioneered by Moran (1950) and popularized by Cliff and Ord (1973). Woods' testing was more sophisticated even if the models were not. The product of this evaluation procedure was that Model 1 formed a 'sound basis' for simulation being most accurate for the New Commonwealth and West Indian groups and least accurate for the Asian groups. The diffusion of the West Indian group was over-estimated, whilst the concentration of Asians in the inner city was less in reality than in the simulation. Model 2a was not a significant improvement although Model 2b performed better than any of the others for the West Indian population. The results of Models 3a and 3b were disappointing, in general, although the incorporation of housing data sharpened the accuracy of the simulations relating to Asians. Woods concluded that the modelling process had lent ". . . support to the aggregate effects of chain migration, the presence on a limited and restricted scale of internal movement, and the impact of multi-occupied dwellings in the housing situation" Woods (1975; p.29). On the basis of this he went on to discuss possible policy initiatives, suggesting that this might be aided by "a more theoretical model . . . which, given a desired pattern of immigrant distribution, could work backwards to develop simulation rules to generate that pattern" (Woods, 1975; p.30). Contrary to the practice of his US co-workers Woods proceeded to simulate the diffusion of the New Commonwealth population of Birmingham up until the year 1991.

The contribution of Monte Carlo simulation modelling to urban social geography

The chronological survey of works employing Monte Carlo simulation to date reveals that neither the theoretical nor practical contribution of the approach has been great. Despite the early enthusiasm generated by the technique, an understanding of the exact causes of residential segregation is little nearer, whilst policies directed at the problem have benefited slightly, if at all, from such an approach. The reasons for this failure are many and varied, but centre on the inherent methodological weakness of the technique and its injudicious employment.

The technique has been employed overwhelmingly as a tool to improve understanding of the underlying causes of the residential concentration of ethnic minorities, i.e. to aid in the development of theory. Morrill (1965b; p.349) stated that "the purpose and hope are to discover and illustrate the nature of the ghetto expansion process"; Hansell and Clarke (1970) used the technique to prove or disprove their hypothesis concerning Negro diffusion; Rose (1970; p.16) stated that "whereas models of this type have some predictive value, the real merit derived from them is the gaining of additional understanding of the process one is attempting to simulate"; and Woods (1975; p.1) noted that "interpretation comes before change". However, to use a tool in such a way assumes that it is both sharp and precise, and that its results can be interpreted unequivocally. In the case of simulation modelling within this field such assumptions are clearly fallacious. The process of residential segregation is caused by the complex interaction of a large number of geographical, economic, sociological, psychological and historical factors. The use of simulation modelling under such conditions assumes a belief that the complex interaction of these factors can be successfully condensed into two or three simple mathematical relationships without loss of accuracy. In view of the complexity of the subject matter and the uni-disciplinary nature of many of the studies employing the technique it is, according to Guelke (1971; p.42), hardly "surprising that few geographers in this tradition have gone beyond the first step of pattern identification: the patterns they simulate and describe are frequently beyond their competence to explain". This failing is emphasized by Lindsay and Barr (1972; p.56) who state that "most applications of stochastic models in geography are essentially descriptive rather than explanatory. The imprecise nature and great number of variables in geographic problems has frequently resulted in models that are over-simplified."

Even assuming that it is possible to condense the process of residential segregation into a small number of simple relationships there remains the added problem of operationalizing the simulation. Even allowing for the over-simplification of the models published to date they have been conspicuously unsuccessful in their attempts to produce a working model from theoretical constructs. Problems of scale are ignored, most notably in Rose's (1970) contribution where the ultimate limit of potential ghetto expansion was not determined on any objective criterion but merely by the arbitrary initial definition of ghetto space; wholly inappropriate surrogates are used such as Wood's (1973) employment of a white MIF and multi-occupation; the 'ecological correlation' is ignored; arbitrary assumptions are introduced to replace verifiable fact as in Woods' (1973) estimation, rather than calculation, of residential turnover rates; since inputs must be in a quantitative form, emphasis is placed upon variables which are readily quantifiable to the exclusion of the more complex but more useful psychological variables such as housing preference or fear of status loss; estimates of future demographic trends are weak or non-existent, thereby forcing models to rely upon incremental growth dependent purely upon arbitrary assumptions such as that of Morrill (1965b) who postulated a 5% increase per iteration; and inputs are frequently introduced not because of empirical proof but because of mathematical or computational simplicity. Hansell and Clarke's (1970; p.275) incorporation of a 100% turnover rate is an excellent example since this was purely "to use the available computer routine". One is left with the impression that even were the simplified inputs capable of explaining some degree of residential segregation, the choice of inaccurate, inappropriate or arbitrary data to operationalize these would ensure that it remained difficult, if not actually impossible, to judge the veracity of the hypothesis. This last point also raises the parallel questions of technique and verification once the model is operationalized, albeit imperfectly. Few of the authors state whether their models were run more than once and if this was not the case, none provided any proof as to why a single simulation derived from a set of random numbers should be considered more representative than any other of the universe of possible outcomes. Woods' work is the exception here since he ensured 100 runs of each of his models to gain validity. Finally, once a model has been created, operationalized and run, the most crucial step remains, that of testing the outcome of the model and therefore verifying the hypothesis upon which it was based. This process forms the crux of the scientific method, yet, surprisingly in view of the supposed theoretical orientation of the authors, it has remained largely ignored. Again, Woods is the exception, but his forerunners were content to validate their hypotheses by means of visual comparison of maps or correlation of serially dependent data. In addition to this statistical problem of verification there also remains the two intractable obstacles of 'multi-causality' and 'process from form' reasoning. Similarity of outcome need not necessarily result from similarity of cause whilst it is obviously hazardous to use a distribution pattern as the input for an analysis of its own causes (Hägerstrand, 1967).

The studies employing Monte Carlo simulation have thus attempted to make precise quantitative statements about sophisticated and complex theories on the basis of simplistic assumptions, imprecise data and faulty methodology. In view of this, it is hardly surprising that geographers have been unable to gain greater insight into the causes of residential segregation through the use of the technique. It therefore follows that the construction of theory has advanced little, if at all, from the employment of simulation. All too often the difficulties of operationalizing and testing the model, and the satisfaction of gaining some measure of self-determined success, ensure that the original aim, that of theoretical understanding, is forgotten. Guelke (1971) seems right to argue that

> the application of general but relatively simple theories and models to concrete, complex situations almost inevitably leads to a situation in which the goal of investigation becomes the explanation of the discrepancies between theoretical constructs and reality, rather than the explanation of reality itself.
>
> Guelke (1971; p.49)

Lindsay and Barr (1972) seem equally justified in claiming that the inability of simulation modelling to help either in the testing of existing theories or in the development of new theories did not ensure that the technique was abandoned, simply that it was used as an end in itself. Geographers could usefully take note of Bunge's (1967; p.316) warning then, that "in general no amount of technique, whether empirical or mathematical, saves us the labour of inventing new ideas, although it can effectively conceal the lack of ideas".

It is doubly unfortunate that social geographers have not halted their attempts to use simulation modelling, at the level of a theoretical verification procedure. Whilst early workers such as Morrill (1965b) were sensitive and realistic enough to halt at attempted explanation, others have gone on to prediction. Morrill (1965b; p.359) noted that "no prediction from 1964 has been attempted, because of risk of misinterpretation by the residents of the area". No such reservations were entertained by Woods (1975, 1980) who predicted patterns of New Commonwealth residence up to 1991 and concluded pessimistically that "the evidence of continued segregation and limited dispersal of coloured immigrant groups in Birmingham does not seem to auger well for their assimilation or integration into urban society . . ." (Woods 1975; p.30). Such prediction was undertaken despite Rose's (1972) earlier objections that there is a serious weakness in estimating ghetto growth over a period as short as a decade, let alone twice that time. One can only assume that the desire to forecast is not "unrelated to a rather vague notion that the power to predict is a characteristic of scientific activity" (Guelke 1971; p.44).

A re-evaluation and application of Monte Carlo methods to urban social geography

If simulation modelling is of little value in the area within which it has most frequently been used (i.e. theory building and verification), does it have value elsewhere? Perhaps the two areas where the criticisms outlined above have least impact are those concerning education and the provision of a status quo reference point against which to compare reality. In the former, the inadequacies of data sources, the imprecision of technique and the failure with regard to theory are all subservient to the didactic simplicity and dynamism of the approach. As Bracken (1978; p.69) notes, "the task of designing a simulation game is in itself an instructive activity involving scientific principles. Hypothesis testing, data collection and analysis, study of inter-relationships and causal system are required" if in a relatively diluted form. Moreover even for the more advanced researcher "they can be considered to play useful heuristic roles in geographical inquiry in that they often help one to clarify vague concepts and aid one to find certain hidden assumptions in one's thinking" (Guelke, 1971; p.49). The simulation thus forces the student or researcher to make explicit what is currently implicit.

Of considerably greater potential utility is the employment of simulation as part of a monitoring system to alert academics and policy makers to changes in the degree and form of residential segregation. Inevitably, the recognition of change must come before its explanation. Berry's (1971) use of simulation techniques was for precisely this purpose although he chose to employ Markov chains to study changes in the racial composition of school rolls. His intervention was in response to the 'Summit Agreement' in Chicago which sought to create a unified and nondiscriminatory housing market within the city under pressure from the Chicago Freedom Movement and Martin Luther King. Berry's team sought to monitor the impact, or lack of impact, of the new initiative. To achieve this, they began by developing "a sensitive reading of the ongoing processes of ghetto expansion before 1968, so that we could simulate what would have been likely to happen in 1968, 1969 and thereafter in the absence of the Council's work" (Berry, 1971; p.203). Having constructed a 'more-of-the-same' simulation of future conditions "formal evaluation of success in changing the system could then be made in terms of movement away from the 'present trend' future towards the integration goal . . ." (Berry, 1971; p.203). Sadly, but not unexpectedly, Berry discovered that the predicted and actual extent of the ghetto were very similar and he was forced, therefore, to conclude that the Leadership Council's efforts had failed and that as a consequence "housing in Chicago essentially remained locked into a racist real estate system that continued to constrain and pattern residential choice".

Berry's use of simulation was a significant advance since it employed the technique as a less precise tool requiring fewer, and less stringent, assumptions for its success. The simulation sought only to extrapolate existing conditions; it was consequently immune to the oft quoted criticism that such techniques produce only more-of-the same and are therefore tools of the status quo. In Berry's case, this was the sole aim of the simulation. In addition the simulation neither required nor needed a sophisticated theoretical understanding of the causes of residential segregation since theoretical advancement was not its purpose. The inadequacy of testing and verification procedures was also circumvented since interest centred on *differences* between simulated and actual patterns, not their *similarities*; and finally the use of conditions apertaining to one time period to predict the outcome of another became not a weakness of the approach but an advantage. In short the use of simulation as a bench mark against which to compare reality retains the strengths of the approach and minimizes the conceptual and practical drawbacks. Despite this, the work of Berry has not been replicated at the macro-scale and British workers have continued to ignore the potential of this mode of enquiry.

The remainder of this paper consequently presents an attempt to analyse changes in the degree, extent and form of Asian residential segregation within Blackburn CB through the construction of a stable additive Monte Carlo simulation for the period 1971-1977. Once the model has highlighted significant changes, some suggested causes of these may be discussed. Simulation is consequently regarded as an indirect rather than direct means to understanding.

Since the model sought only to extrapolate extant patterns the major data source was the 1971 census although additional inputs were empirically derived where the literature suggested their relevance. The producer component, which as in Rose's models sought to create a probability matrix to allocate new families, was heavily dependent upon housing characteristics although factors were included to take account of the proximity of employment opportunities, the nearness of public transport routes, and the strong attraction of existing community settlement with its religious, economic and social functions. The exact inputs which were utilized and their sources are listed below:

    (i) housing value—derived from an 18 month search of local newspapers and estate agents' lists which resulted in 850 traceable transactions.
    (ii) housing size—1971 Census Small Area Statistics.
    (iii) housing age—derived from a representative sample of surveyed houses
    (iv) housing amenities—more correctly the presence of all three census-defined amenities as shown in the 1971 Census Small Area Statistics

(v) council ownership—1971 Census Small Area Statistics

(vi) rented accommodation—1971 Census Small Area Statistics

(vii) access to public transport—operationalized by considering the location and frequency of corporation and national bus services.

(viii) access to relevant employment opportunities—more strictly proximity to employers in those industrial categories with an overconcentration of Asians (see Anwar, 1979; p.98). Locations derived from 'Yellow Pages' and local 'phone directory in addition to field search.

(ix) the attraction of community centrality—i.e. the known propensity of Asians to reside in sub-areas of a given level of ethnic concentration: source—1971 Census Small Area Statistics.

In the case of each of these variables, average values were assigned to every one of the town's 210 Enumeration Districts (average population—$c.480$). The range of values of each variable was then sub-divided to create more general classifications. The percentage of the Asian population resident in Enumeration Districts (EDs) in each of the general classifications on each of the nine variables was then calculated. As a consequence, it was possible to say that in 1971 20·3% of the Asian population was resident in EDs where the average value of property was between £4001 and £5000 or alternatively, that only 1·4% of Asians lived in EDs where over 70% of the housing stock was publicly owned. Aggregation of these calculated propensities created an 'attractiveness index' for each ED; in simple terms this represented the known propensity of Asians to reside in an ED with those particular housing, accessibility and employment characteristics. The 210 'attractiveness indices' were then converted to probabilities, using the ED base map as an irregular lattice possibility matrix.

Since data concerning the demographic characteristics of the Asian population in Britain are neither common nor detailed the Demographic Component was inevitably less detailed. Although this is regrettable, the use of certain statistics does allow the measurement of the extent and form of residential segregation irrespective of group size. Any inaccuracies should consequently have little impact upon the monitoring value of the process. The simulation relied upon a predicted annual net increase derived from the use of age- and ethnic-specific birth, death and marriage rates. These rates are found in Allen (1971), Krausz (1974), Peach and Winchester (1974), Rose *et al.* (1969), Thomas (1970), and Waterhouse and Brabban (1964). They were applied to the detailed information on the demographic structure of the minority found in the 1971 Small Area Statistics. In combination, these provided an estimated number of births, deaths and marriages for the minority in each of the years between 1971 and 1977; these were distributed using random numbers and specially constructed probability matrices relating to the location of young married couples, old people and unmarried girls. The final input to the demographic component related to in-migration derived from *pro rata* disaggregations of national totals. In retrospect this would have been more accurately measured by the use of Electoral Registers or unemployment data (Robinson, 1980a). Finally, the population totals were not altered for under-enumeration or the problem of 'white Indians', although they were adjusted to take into account the sizeable black British population of the town: the former two factors create only a maximum possible error of 3·2%.

The consumer component, as in Rose's model, reconciled the new households created through marriage or in-migration with those areas most likely to attract Asian residents. This was accomplished by the use of random numbers and the probability matrix generated in the producer component by the attractiveness index. The model underwent six iterations at one-year intervals. This decision was taken in the light of Lindsay and Barr's (1972) study of inter-regional growth and migration in the Peace River area of Alberta between 1921-1961; the authors sought to compare the results of one simulation with reality and then contrast this with the comparison of a 50-run average solution with reality. They concluded (1972; p.64) that "the difference is small between the results of the single simulations and the average of fifty runs. When both distributions were grouped into classes, the frequencies were very close and identical in some instances." Despite these findings it must be admitted that, in general, multiple runs are preferable, where resources allow this. Lindsay and Barr's study also provided the justification for employing Monte Carlo simulation in preference to Markov chains; in this context they found that "the simulation model performs slightly better than the Markov model because the overall variation between observed and expected values is less, and the prediction of the scores of individual regions is closer to the oberved figure" (Lindsay and Barr, 1972; p.65).

The results of the simulation are presented in Fig. 1 where the darkest shading represents EDs found in the quartile with the largest Asian population. This simulated 1977 pattern can then be compared with the actual 1971 distribution found in Fig. 2. According to the simulation, the intervening six years should have seen a steady but localized expansion of ethnic core territory. In particular, the areas of maximum concentration should have become a unified inner ring as a result of expansion to the south west. In general though, the distribution of the most densely settled areas remains remarkably constant. In contrast, the distribution of those EDs in the second quartile should have undergone a more substantial change. The predicted outcome groups such EDs in close proximity to the more concentrated areas thereby creating a wave front of penetration as described by Morrill (1965b). This simulated pattern is at variance with the scattered and peripheral distribution actually found in 1971; the intervening period should, therefore, have been one of contraction and re-organization of intermediate areas. During the same period, the simulation predicts a wider diffusion of the Asian population into peripheral areas such that, by 1977 the minority would be represented in 169 of the town's 210 EDs (80·5% of the total). This would represent a net gain (despite predicted withdrawal from certain EDs) of 19 EDs from the 1971 figure, when Asians were found in 71·4% of the town's EDs. In total then, the simulation predicted that, if current trends continued, the 1970s would see a centralization of community core areas into a contiguous inner ring and a measure of suburbanization or dispersal to peripheral districts.

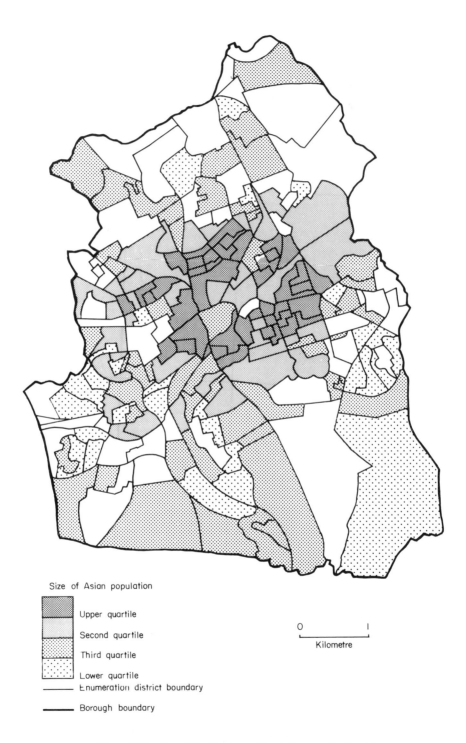

Figure 1. Predicted distribution of the Asian population (1977).

Size of Asian population

Upper quartile

Second quartile

Third quartile

Lower quartile

_____ Enumeration district boundary

━━━━━━ Borough boundary

0 ————————— 1
Kilometre

Figure 2. Distribution of the Asian population (1971).

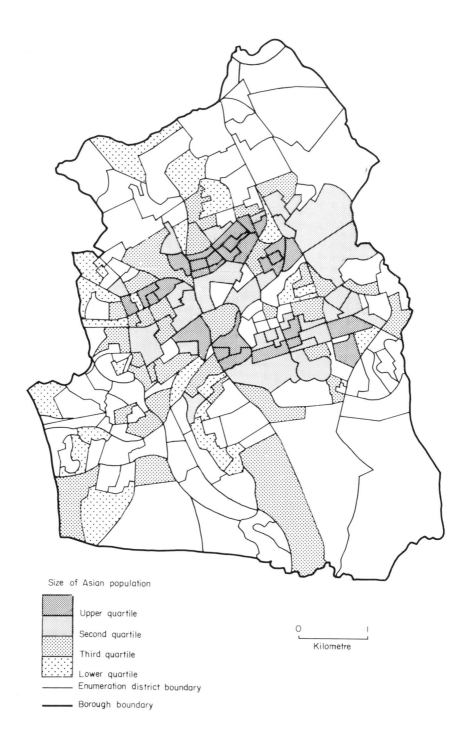

Size of Asian population

■ Upper quartile

▨ Second quartile

░ Third quartile

· Lower quartile

—— Enumeration district boundary

━━ Borough boundary

0   1
Kilometre

Figure 3. Distribution of the Asian population (1977).

Comparison of Figs 1–3 shows the contrast between predicted and actual outcomes. A simple visual comparison of Figs 2 and 3 reveals the actual changes in distribution which took place between 1971 and 1977. It is immediately apparent that there has been a localized centrifugal movement of the inner area population within a broader trend of centralization. The predicted inner ring has failed to materialize, and the most concentrated districts are now found in a more scattered distribution orientated along axial routes to the west, north-east and east. Several of the areas which were predicted to become important ethnic space have in fact lost their minority populations entirely, whilst conversely other 'unattractive' districts have gained considerably in importance. Again, in contrast to the predicted pattern, the overwhelming trend in the more peripheral areas has been one of loss, as a result of substantial re-concentration towards the middle ring. In practice then, Asians were found in only 117 of the town's EDs in 1977, barely 56% of the total. The period since the census has thus seen a real net loss of 33 EDs to ethnic space, as opposed to the predicted gain of 19 EDs. At this relatively coarse and unsophisticated level of analysis it would seem that the period 1971–1977 has not seen a continuation of pre-existing trends, and that there is, therefore, a considerable discrepancy between predicted and actual outcomes that is in need of explanation. The period should have witnessed decentralization from an increasingly ordered inner ring but in practice saw centralization into a scattered middle ring containing isolated core areas.

However before conclusions may be drawn about the causes of any observed changes it is necessary to prove that these are significant and not a casual outcome of the random element within the simulation. The simplest, but least satisfactory method of doing this is by correlation. The real and estimated 1977 distributions of the Asian population (by EDs) were thus correlated to give a coefficient of $Rs = 0.86$. However since both these populations were derived from a common 1971 base it is perhaps more accurate to correlate actual and predicted levels of change between 1971 and 1977. This produced a coefficient of $Rs = 0.36$. However, since the likely growth of the minority population in a sub-area is dependent to a certain extent upon the pre-existing minority population this was also felt to be an inaccurate measure. In consequence, attention was turned towards the more sophisticated pattern-related measures. The development in the geographical literature of an interest in spatial autocorrelation provided both the techniques and tests. The rationale behind such tests is most clearly stated by Cliff and Ord (1973; pp.69–70). who note that "if the observed map is a realization of the stochastic process underlying the theoretical map, then the non-zero residuals should be randomly located in the differences map; in other words, the observed and expected maps should differ only by chance". If this is not the case, and spatial autocorrelation of residuals is present then it is clear that the predicted and actual patterns differ significantly. To test for this, initially, a contiguity ratio test was employed based upon the binary K-colour classification shown in Fig. 4. Non-free sampling was assumed, and the test was applied to the irregular lattice of the Borough's EDs. It was decided to use the 'queen's case' (see Cliff *et al.* 1975 for explanation) which

Figure 4. Residuals between predicted and actual Asian populations (1977).

measures contiguity in all directions rather than the more common 'rook's case' which searches for contiguity only in the four cardinal directions. The results of the test revealed that the two spatial patterns were significantly dissimilar at the 0·01 level, since the number of BB joins was greater than expected and the number of BW joins less. However the simple contiguity ratio test has been criticized (see Ebdon 1977), and Cliff and Ord (1973) have shown that Moran's (1950) I statistic is significantly superior. To ensure that the predicted and actual outcomes are dissimilar, this test was also used, again assuming the queen's case and randomization. The outcome was a standard normal deviate of 9·87, a value which allows the rejection (at the 0·001 level) of a null hypothesis assuming randomly distributed non-zero residuals. It is clear then that the actual 1977 distribution of Asians differs markedly and significantly from that produced by the simulation. It remains to analyse the form and cause of such differences.

One of the most important points revealed by a comparison of simulated and actual data is that the Asian population of the town has grown much more rapidly in the period 1971-1977 than was expected. Predictions on the basis of current demographic estimates of the growth of the Asian population at a national level indicated that the minority in Blackburn should have numbered 7704 in 1977. In practice, the Asian population was 15·4% larger than expected with a total enumerated size of 8887. It is clear, therefore, that there is a need for more accurate demographic estimates of the growth of Britain's coloured population. In Blackburn, two factors can be suggested which have a bearing on the inaccuracy of demographic projections. Firstly, such estimates took no account of the arrival of substantial numbers of East African Asians in Britain in the early 1970s. In 1971 there were only 500 such people in Blackburn and these formed only 9·6% of the enumerated Asian-born population. In contrast, by 1977, East African Asians numbered 1377, thereby constituting nearly 16% of the Asian population. It is not clear why Blackburn acted as such a pole of attraction to these migrants but it may result from the rather anomalous decision to declare the town a reception area despite its substantial pre-existing Asian population. It may also have resulted from labour shortages in the local textile industry. Nevertheless the arrival of a large number of East African Asians has expanded the minority by a large and unforeseen amount. The different aspirations, values, and background of this group sets them apart from the other Asian inhabitants of Blackburn and undoubtedly adds a further dimension to community structure (Robinson 1982a). It is likely that this added dimension has been reflected in changes in residential patterns. The second factor to disturb demographic projections is the continued high birth rate of the minority. National projections have usually been based upon an assumption that the preferred family size of ethnic minorities will, in the long term, approximate that of the indigenous population. Whilst this may be true in the very long term, the rural origins and religious taboos of many Asians currently militates against a sharply declining birth rate. In Blackburn then, although Asians form only 11% of the total population, over 30% of births in the town's maternity wards are to parents of Asian origin. This factor has therefore made a significant and continuing contribution to a growth in the Asian population in Blackburn over and above that anticipated.

Scrutiny of Fig. 4 reveals the spatial patterning of discrepancies between anticipated and actual residential location. Several general points emerge from this. The Asian population had grown more rapidly than expected in 91 EDs (43·3% of the total). In these, the number of Asians was, on average, 43 more than anticipated. Such EDs were found mainly in the inner and middle rings of the town, although there were exceptions to this rule, with several peripheral EDs experiencing unanticipated growth. In contrast, 95 EDs (45·2% of the total) had experienced less growth than expected, with an average of 22·6 fewer Asian inhabitants than predicted. These EDs were found in two locations, either in contiguous blocks within the inner area or in a more widespread distribution towards the periphery of the town. The 24 EDs where predicted and actual changes in the size of the ethnic population coincided were located, in the main, in the better, owner-occupied suburbs towards the edge of the town. Further analysis of the characteristics of those areas where growth has been greater than, or less than, expected suggests several broad conclusions. Firstly, the unforeseen growth of the Asian population has not been evenly distributed throughout ethnic space; pre-existing core areas in the inner and middle rings have gained disproportionately. As a consequence, life in a separate and encapsulated colony is becoming more, rather than less, of a norm for the average Asian in Blackburn. This inevitably has implications for the possibility of inter-ethnic contact. The converse of this point is that the better and newer areas of peripheral housing have gained fewer Asian inhabitants than predicted, even bearing in mind the very low level of anticipated dispersal. However, this increasing separation of suburbanized whites from central-city Asians is to a certain extent masked by a separate but parallel trend of rising Asian council housing occupancy. This trend has been discussed in detail elsewhere (Robinson, 1980b, 1982b) but it is important to note here that the movement has been a very selective one to certain highly-prized estates. This comes out clearly from Fig. 4 with peripheral inter-war estates and modern deck access and high rise estates enjoying a smaller growth in their Asian populations than even the minute amount expected. In contrast, the newer central estates of three and four bedroom houses show a greater growth than projected despite the fact that many of these were not fully occupied in 1977. The final and rather obvious point which comes out of a consideration of Fig. 4 is that there is a considerable mis-match between anticipated and actual numbers of Asians in clearance areas. Whilst this is to be expected it does, nevertheless, underline the major role that local authorities play in creating and shaping patterns of ethnic separation through their management of the housing stock.

Examples of each of these trends are seen in Fig. 5 which illustrates those discrepancies between expected and actual growth which exceed 50 Asian individuals or approximately 10 households. Brookhouse, Daisyfield and Queen's Park thus typify core areas where growth has exceeded expectations. Lower Audley exemplifies the popular inner area council estate which has experienced growth beyond anticipated levels, whilst Higher Audley is a clearance area where projections exceed the actual (minimal) remaining population. In a similar vein, the Montague

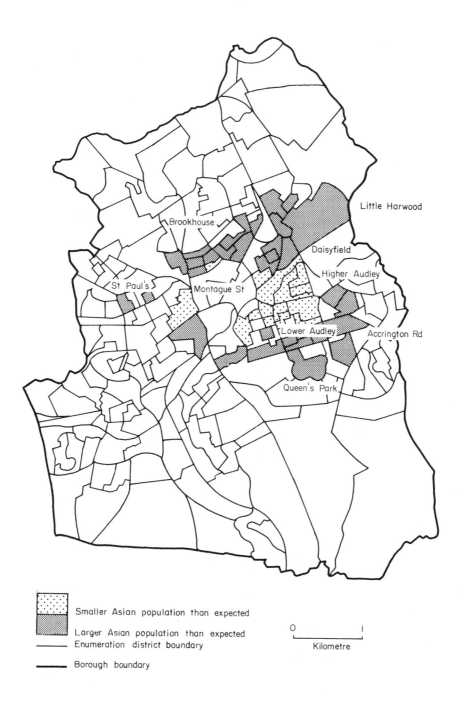

Figure 5. Major residuals between predicted and actual Asian populations.

Street area shows the way in which clearance, and the presence of flatted council accommodation combine to produce an area where growth has not fulfilled projections. However, Fig. 5 also brings out one further feature. That is the unexpected growth of new, less central, core areas in response to the growing forces of intra-community fission. The St Paul's Hindu area, the Accrington Road Sikh area, and the major growth zone of Little Harwood for Muslim East Africans all typifying the increasing level of intra-settlement residential polarization. This was not foreshadowed by the 1971 data.

The interaction of all these trends within Blackburn can be summarized by aggregate measures of residential segregation and more sophisticated measures of opportunities for interaction. In 1971, the ED level Index of Dissimilarity for the Asian and white populations was 71·3. The predicted figure for 1977 was also exactly 71·3 at this scale, thereby confirming the orientation of the simulation towards the status quo. In practice, as we have noted, a certain re-distribution of the Asian population did take place via council housing, but this was balanced by the withdrawal from clearance areas and the failure of the population to suburbanize. Consequently, the actual ID for the Asian and white populations at this scale in 1977 was 73·3, a small but not insignificant increase in residential dissimilarity from both the 1971 and anticipated 1977 levels. The increasing separation of the Asian and white populations is also demonstrated by the use of the P* index (see Robinson, 1980c) which measures the isolation of the average group member. In 1971, then, the average Asian lived in an ED where his minority formed approximately 28% of the total population. This was predicted to rise to 36% by 1977, but in fact rose to the point where the average Asian lived in an ED where over half the population was of Asian origin.

From the foregoing it is clear that use of a predictive simulation as a bench-mark has highlighted the fact that several important changes in patterns of residential segregation appear to have taken place in the period 1971–1977. However, whilst this model does build a stochastic element into more stages of its construction than previous attempts, one must still be cautious about conclusions derived from a single-run solution. Nevertheless, recorded changes were as follows: much of the Asian population has been redistributed as a result of housing clearance; several council estates have failed to attract Asian residents despite their apparent suitability; other council estates have proven to be considerably more popular than anticipated; the presence of early Asian pioneers in peripheral suburbia has failed to attract other Asians resident in the inner and middle rings; the central cores of Asian concentration have continued to gain a disproportionate share of minority expansion and have therefore grown at a rate greater than that anticipated; and the arrival of the East African Asians and the fission of the existing minority have ensured the growth of residential cores outside pre-existing ethnic space, occasionally in areas which would have been thought unsuitable in 1971. In total then, a greater percentage of the Asian minority in Blackburn remains locked in socially encapsulated ethnic space in 1977 than would have been predicted from an extrapolation of the conservative situation of 1971. For the proponents of policies aimed at residential dispersal and social integration, this must be disappointing.

Conclusion

The technique of Monte Carlo simulation modelling generated high hopes in the late 1960s and early 1970s. This promise was not fulfilled, however, largely because of the employment of the approach for inappropriate and unachievable goals. The technique was widely used in an effort to advance the social geographer's theoretical knowledge of the causes of residential segregation and ghetto growth. It was singularly unsuccessful in this role. However, the failure of the technique in this sphere, and its inherent methodological weaknesses when used in this way, tended to over-shadow the potential value of the approach when used as part of a simple monitoring system. Berry (1971) clearly demonstrated the utility of such studies in his work on Chicago but despite this early lead the technique was generally abandoned rather than re-orientated. This paper has argued for a resurrection of Monte Carlo simulation modelling along these lines, and has provided a case study to demonstrate the practical value of such work. It remains to extend this work into the future, where predictive simulation could be used as a key element in a process of policy-orientated annual monitoring of spatial and social change in Britain's larger multi-racial conurbations.

References

Allen, S. (1971). "New Minorities, Old Conflicts: Asian and West Indian Migrants in Britain". Random House, New York.

Anwar, M. (1979). "The Myth of Return: Pakistanis in Britain". Heinemann, London.

Bartholomew, D. J. (1967). "Stochastic Models for Social Processes". Wiley, London.

Berry, B. J. L. (1971). Monitoring trends, forecasting change and evaluating goal achievements: the ghetto vs. desegregation issue in Chicago as a case study. *In* "Regional Forecasting", (M. Chisholm, A. E. Frey, and P. Haggett, eds). Butterworths, London.

Bracken, I. (1978). Simulation: methodology for urban study. *Progress in Human Geography* **2**, 49-75.

Bunge, M. (1967). "The Search for System". Springer-Verlag, New York.

Bunge, W. (1962). "Theoretical Geography". Gleerup, Lund.

Cliff, A. D. and Ord, J. K. (1973). "Spatial Autocorrelation". Pion, London.

Cliff, A. D., Haggett, P., Ord, J. K., Bassett, K. A., and Davis, R. B., (1975). "Elements of Spatial Structure: A Quantitative Approach". Cambridge University Press.

Cressey, P. F. (1938). Population succession in Chicago 1898-1930. *American Journal of Sociology* **44**, 59-69.

Deakin, N. and Cohen, B. G. (1970). Dispersal and choice: towards a strategy for ethnic minorities in Britain. *Environment and Planning* **2**, 193-201.

Downs, A. (1968). The future of American ghettos. *Daedalus* **97**, 1331-1378.

Duncan, O. D. and Duncan, B. (1957). "The Negro Population of Chicago". Chicago University Press.

Ebdon, D. (1977). "Statistics in Geography: A Practical Approach". Blackwell, Oxford.

Guelke, L. (1971). Problems of scientific explanation in geography. *Canadian Geographer* **15**, 38-53.

Hägerstrand, T. (1967). "Innovation Diffusion as a Spatial Process". Chicago University Press.

Hägerstrand, T. (1971). Regional forecasting and social engineering. *In* "Regional Forecasting", (M. Chisholm, A. E. Frey, and P. Haggett, eds). Butterworth, London.

Hansell, C. R. and Clark, W. A. V. (1970). The expansion of the Negro ghetto in Milwaukee: a descriptive and simulation model. *Tijdschrift voor Economische en Sociale Geografie* **61**, 267-277.

Harvey, D. (1969). "Explanation in Geography". Arnold, London.

Johnston, R. J. (1979). "Geography and Geographers". Arnold, London.

Jones, E. (1956). Cause and effect in human geography. *Annals, Association of American Geographers* **46**, 369-377.

Krausz, E. (1974). "Ethnic Minorities in Britain". McGibbon and Kee, London.

Lindsay, I. and Barr, B. M. (1972). Two stochastic approaches to migration: a comparison of Monte Carlo simulation and Markov Chain models. *Geografiska Annaler* **54B**, 56-67.

Martin, A. F. (1951). The necessity for determinism. *Transactions, Institute of British Geographers* **17**, 1-12.

Montefiore, A. G., and Williams, W. M. (1955). Determinism and possibilism. *Geographical Studies* **2**, 1-11.

Moran, P. A. P. (1950). Notes on continuous stochastic phenomena. *Biometrika* **37**, 178-181.

Morrill, R. L. (1965a). "Migration and the Spread and Growth of Urban Settlement". Gleerup, Lund.

Morrill, R. L. (1965b). The Negro ghetto: problems and alternatives. *Geographical Review* **55**, 339-369.

Peach, C. and Winchester, S. W. C. (1974). Birthplace, ethnicity and the underenumeration of West Indians, Indians and Pakistanis in the Census of 1966 and 1971. *New Community* **3**, 386-393.

Rapkin, C. and Grigsby, W. G. (1960). "The Demand for Housing in Racially Mixed Areas". Commission on Race and Housing, Berkeley.

Robinson, V. (1980a). Correlates of Asian immigration 1959-74. *New Community* **8**, 115-123.

Robinson, V. (1980b). Asians and council housing. *Urban Studies* **17**, 323-331.

Robinson, V. (1980c). Lieberson's P* index: a case-study evaluation. *Area* **12**, 307-312.

Robinson, V. (1982a). Asians in Britain: a study in encapsulation and marginality. *In* "The Geography of Plural Societies", (C. Peach, C. G. Clarke, and D. Ley, eds). Allen and Unwin, London.

Robinson, V. (1982b). The development of Asian settlement in Britain and the myth of return. *In* "Ethnic Segregation in Cities", (C. Peach, V. Robinson and S. J. Smith, eds.). Croom Helm, London.

Rose, E. J. B. *et al.* (1969). "Colour and Citizenship: a Report on British Race Relations". Oxford University Press, London.

Rose, H. M. (1970). The development of an urban sub-system: the case of the Negro ghetto. *Annals, Association of American Geographers* **60**, 1-17.

Rose, H. M. (1972). The spatial development of black residential sub-systems. *Economic Geography* **48**, 43-66.

Sarre, P. (1978). The diffusion of Dutch Elm disease. *Area* **10**, 81-85.

Schaefer, F. K. (1953). Exceptionalism in geography: a methodological examination. *Annals, Association of American Geographers* **43**, 226-249.

Smith, D. M. (1973). "The Geography of Social Well-being in the United States". McGraw-Hill, New York.

Taylor, P. J. (1976). An interpretation of the quantification debate in British geography. *Transactions, Institute of British Geographers N.S.* **1.**, 129-142.

Thomas, C. J. (1970). Projections of the growth of the coloured immigrant population of England and Wales. *Journal of Biosocial Science* **2**, 265-81.

Warnz, W. (1959). Geography at mid-twentieth century. *World Politics* **11**, 442-454.

Waterhouse, J. A. H. and Brabban, D. H. (1964). Inquiry into the fertility of immigrants: preliminary report. *Eugenics Review* **56**, 7-18.

Woods, R. I. (1973). The role of simulation in the modelling of immigrant spatial sub-systems. Paper presented at the Institute of British Geographers Conference, Birmingham.

Woods, R. I. (1975). "The Stochastic Analysis of Immigrant Distributions". School of Geography Research Paper No. 11, Oxford.

Woods, R. I. (1980). Spatio-temporal models of ethnic segregation and their implications for housing policy. Paper presented at the symposium on Ethnic Segregation in Cities, St Antony's College, Oxford.

EIGHT

The impact of Asian estate agents on patterns of ethnic residence: a case study of Bradford ✓

JOHN CATER

Edge Hill College of Higher Education, Ormskirk, Lancs., UK

In the past decade a substantial ethnic dimension has emerged in British social geography with the publication of a wide range of predominantly empirical studies of West Indian and Asian residential segregation in several British cities. Examples from an increasingly voluminous literature include studies of London (Doherty, 1969; Lee, 1973; Baboolal, Ch.3), Birmingham (Jones, 1970, 1976), Coventry (Winchester, 1974), Leicester (Phillips, Ch.5), Glasgow (Kearsley and Srivastava, 1974; McEvoy, 1978) and Huddersfield (Jones and McEvoy, 1974). This trend has been followed more recently by attempts to place the readily identified pattern of considerable concentration into a choice/constraint framework (Simmons, Ch.4); to assess whether "the segregation patterns . . . are more a commentary upon white rather than Asian residential preferences" (Cater and Jones 1979; p.89) or are a result of choices exercised by the minority concerned (Dahya, 1974; Robinson, 1979).

In the same period studies of residential patterns within the city have undergone a change of focus. The long-established tenets of ecological theory, while still providing an important reference point for many empirical investigations, have been widely criticized as being "unable to say anything meaningful about the structure of the housing market, and consequently [the theory] has little explanation to offer for the patterns of residential differentiation it describes" (Bassett and Short, 1980; p.24). Similarly the neo-classical studies, though they may have succeeded in reproducing many of the internal characteristics of the city (Mills, 1972), have been roundly condemned for their failure to appreciate that household choices are severely restricted and moulded by the social structure and the systems of housing production and allocation (Bassett and Short, 1980; p.32). Such criticism has manifested itself in a series of studies of the overall political and economic framework within which the housing market operates, often adopting a neo-Marxist perspective. At the local level such work has often focused on the institutions involved in housing allocation, initially as quasi-autonomous units but increasingly in relation to the "political economy of urbanization" (Harvey, 1977). Within this framework 'urban managers' are seen to a greater or lesser extent to exert an independent influence on the allocation of scarce resources and facilities (Pahl, 1970). In the public sector this managerial influence is exercised by local authority housing officials (Rex and Moore, 1967; Gray, 1976), by planning officers (Gower Davies, 1972; Paris, 1974) and by local councillors (Muchnick, 1970). In the owner-occupier sector the respective roles of building society managers (Ford, 1975; Boddy, 1976, 1980; Williams, 1978a,b, surveyors (Lambert, 1976) and estate agents (Hatch, 1973; Williams, 1976) as 'urban gatekeepers' have all received detailed attention.

Although the role of the local authority in allocating housing to ethnic groups has been the focus of some recent research (Skellington, 1979; Robinson, 1980), studies linking the managerial institutions and ethnic residential patterns and processes have been limited, although Duncan's (1977) work on building society allocation policy and its impact on both the spatial distribution and the housing conditions of East Europeans and Asians in Huddersfield is an interesting exception. This chapter attempts to make some small contribution towards filling this empirical void by studying aspects of the ethnic housing market in Bradford, West Yorkshire, focusing primarily on the dominant owner-occupied sector. In particular the location of property sales undertaken by both Asian and white estate agents is analysed and an attempt is made to assess the effect of such exchanges on the pattern of ethnic residence. The findings are then briefly used in a limited evaluation of the managerial role of agencies dealing in the inner city, before relating the observed patterns to a discussion of choice and constraint factors in the ethnic housing market.

The study area

Following local government re-organization in 1974 the City of Bradford was ascribed Metropolitan District status, incorporating Ilkley, Keighley and considerable areas of Pennine moorland within its boundaries, with a combined total population of 467000 in 1977 (City of Bradford Metropolitan District Council, 1978). For the purposes of this paper however the boundaries of the old County Borough of Bradford are used. This pre-re-organization administrative unit accords well with the extent of the built-up area of the city and contained some 294000 residents in the 1971 census, a figure which has declined slightly in the past decade with the typical pattern of movement away from a decaying urban core. In 1971 9·1% of this population was of New Commonwealth origin or had been born in the UK to parents who were both New Commonwealth born (Lomas and Monck, 1975). Today the comparable figure has doubled, being estimated at 50900 in the Metropolitan District as a whole (City of Bradford Metropolitan District Council, 1980). With the exceptions of a Bangladeshi community in Keighley and a limited amount of overspill across the old Borough boundary into Shipley, this population is almost exclusively located in the County Borough which has an estimated current coloured population of some 47 000, 16·8% of the Borough total. This figure disguises considerable concentration. In 1977 10 452 of the 16 875 identified Asian electors (62·0%) were living in majority Asian environments when aggregated at the 250-metre grid square level, and just 92 of the 1744 squares covering the city contained five-sixths of the total Asian electorate (Cater and Jones, 1979; pp.93–94).

TABLE I

Projections of New Commonwealth
population and household increase, Bradford 1980-1990

Year	New Commonwealth population			NC households	
	MD*	CB†	CB Asians	No.	Av. size
1980	50 900	47 000	41 000	10 396	4·896
	(10·9)	(16·8)	(14·6)		
1982	56 800	52 400	45 800	12 359	4·596
	(12·0)	(18·9)	(16·5)		
1985	65 300	60 200	52 700	15 735	4·15
	(13·6)	(22·1)	(19·3)		
1990	78 200	72 000	63 100	19 550	4·00
	(16·3)	(27·1)	(23·7)		

*Metropolitan District.
†County Borough (pre- 1 April 1974 boundaries).
Figures in parentheses are the percentage of New Commonwealth or Asian residents of the appropriate row total.
Sources: City of Bradford Metropolitan District Council (1980); Housing Department, City of Bradford Metropolitan District Council, personal communication, 16 September 1980.

In the next decade this population is projected to grow to 63 100, some 23·7% of the total for the old Borough. Even this figure may prove to be an underestimate, being based on an increasing acceptance of Western conceptions of family size. If the recent fall in the ethnic birth rate does not continue a high estimate of 77 200 could be projected, 29·0% of the population total. Of particular significance is the potential increase in the number of households, linked to the possible demand from Asians to live in nuclear rather than extended family units. A rise of 88% in the total number of households between 1980 and 1990 means the anticipated addition of 9154 coloured families seeking dwelling units. Even with a static or marginally declining white population the competition for housing space, at present reasonably matched with the availability of units by number (if not type, size and location), is likely to become increasingly intense.

The survey

As part of a wider ranging study of ethnic residential segregation and the development and extent of the Asian sub-economy in Bradford, the existence of a small number of Asian estate agents was noted. The first report of ethnic activity in this aspect of the housing market can be found in evidence presented to the Select Committee on Race Relations in 1971, and it is apparent that several agencies prospered during the 1972-1973 property boom. With falling interest rates elsewhere the building societies received a rapid influx of funds which was translated into a flood of available mortgage capital, stimulating a 77% rise in average house prices in two years and an extremely buoyant property market (Boddy, 1980; p.99). With this sharp increase in assets society lending policies towards older property, inner city locations and lower status applicants were interpreted more flexibly, and it seems likely that the normally marginal ethnic housing market, usually starved of such support (Duncan, 1976a), may have received a limited amount of selective stimulation. The availability of mortgages further opened up the inner city housing market by helping to facilitate white movement out of the major areas of racial change, with the two wards containing the bulk of the Asian population, Manningham and University, both losing over one-tenth of their total population between 1971 and 1977, despite increases in the number of their New Commonwealth origin residents (City of Bradford Metropolitan District Council, 1978). The flood of building society lending also released an increased proportion of mortgage support from other sources on to the immigrant market. This applied particularly to local authority funding, but also included the clearing banks, Asian banking concerns and the fringe banks and finance houses.

By 1975, when the first field survey was undertaken, the house price boom was over, and two of the six Asian estate agents identified had diversified into travel, insurance and related services. By 1978, with mortgage funds in short supply and the housing market depressed, only two agencies were still in existence; one having changed ownership and the type of business and, of the two located in streets blighted by the prospect of eventual clearance, one had closed completely and the other had re-located half a kilometre east of its original site.

For each year from 1975 up to and including 1980 the property advertised by the Asian estate agencies has been monitored for one week in April. A total of 256 different and identifiable residential properties within the boundaries of the old Borough have been offered for sale. Using electoral registers it has been possible to ascertain a change of resident in 188 cases (73·4%), with no change in the registered voters named in a further 33 instances (12·9%) and no elector named, either because of a failure to register or because the property had fallen vacant in the remaining 35 cases (13·7%). Of the 188 completed transactions over three-quarters have been dealt with by the two Asian estate agents still in operation and, in view of this numerical dominance coupled with the added advantage of being able to interview agents currently in business, these two concerns are regarded as representative of the ethnic estate agents which have operated in the city. On the same basis five white agencies which deal regularly in property located in the central wards were monitored over the same time period. Initial records were made of all the property advertised by the white owned agencies, but for a detailed comparison with the ethnic sample both a price ceiling and a locational constraint were introduced. For each property advertised the following information was noted: full postal address, price when advertised, price adjusted to second quarter 1980 levels in accordance with the Nationwide Building Society's regional index of house prices, type of property, advertised condition, number and approximate size of bedrooms and attics, presence or absence of standard amenities, furnishings and fittings included, together with any other features of the property identified by the agents, whether positive or negative. In addition, the number and ethnicity of voters in the street (or the proportion of the street in the polling district) was noted for the appropriate year. The findings presented here focus primarily on location, property type and ethnic composition of the residences sold by Asian and white agents.

Findings

The location of property advertised

Of a total of 143 properties offered for sale by Asian estate agents in the survey period all but one were located in the inner wards of the city, which together had accounted for 98·5% of the enumerated Asian population in the 1971 census and 96·2% of the current Asian electorate in 1980. In comparison only 175 of the 570 properties advertised by white estate agents in the old Borough were in the same inner ten wards (30·7%). This is despite the fact that these wards accounted for 51·4% of the city's total population and 55·0% of the owner-occupied dwellings in 1971 (Office of Population Censuses and Surveys, 1974). The census breakdown of household and tenure types and of ethnic composition by ward is detailed in Table II.

The considerable under-representation by white estate agents in the inner area is even more evident at the level of the individual ward, and appears to bear no relationship to the proportion of owner occupied property; 61·2% of the property in the inner ten wards being owner occupied in 1971 in comparison with 54·4% in the outer wards, a figure exceeded in every inner ward except Little Horton. Similarly the rate of household movement and the turnover of residential property is apparently at least as high in the central wards as in the periphery. When account is taken of the properties advertised by Asian estate agents the balance is redressed somewhat, with the total dominance of the inner city as a location for Asian advertised property increasing the proportion to 317 of 713 (44·5%), still well below the anticipated share. Although all the estate agents claimed that they would deal with any property offered to them, this pattern may well reflect the greater rewards for selling more expensive property. In addition the generally lower prices and the frequent absence of formal mortgage funding in the inner area undoubtedly encourages more informal channels of house purchase. This may apply particularly to Asians, with the formal methods of exchange used in this paper underestimating the extent of ethnic dominance in the housing market in parts of the inner area.

At the ward level the differences between the location of property advertised by

TABLE II
Household tenure and ethnic population by ward, Bradford CB, 1971

Ward	Tenure types			Population character		
	Owner occupied	Local authority	Private rented	NC-born	Asian-born	Total
Allerton	3138	2670	388	114	52	18 230
	(50·6)	(43·0)	(6·3)	(0·6)	(0·3)	
Bolton*	3309	841	1096	326	214	14 753
	(63·1)	(16·0)	(20·9)	(2·2)	(1·5)	
Bowling*	2702	574	797	726	620	12 518
	(66·3)	(14·1)	(19·5)	(5·8)	(5·0)	
Bradford Moor*	3769	1002	632	2000	1796	16 044
	(69·7)	(18·5)	(11·7)	(12·5)	(11·2)	
Clayton	3057	780	888	74	23	14 337
	(64·6)	(16·5)	(18·8)	(0·5)	(0·2)	
Eccleshill	2332	2362	383	101	25	15 630
	(45·9)	(46·5)	(7·5)	(0·6)	(0·2)	
Great Horton*	3921	533	590	135	66	13 944
	(77·6)	(10·6)	(11·7)	(1·0)	(0·5)	
Heaton*	3810	143	1848	1436	1187	15 606
	(65·5)	(2·5)	(31·8)	(9·2)	(7·6)	
Idle	3320	1698	625	78	35	15 688
	(58·8)	(30·1)	(11·1)	(0·5)	(0·2)	
Laisterdyke*	2270	667	1139	1637	1417	11 868
	(55·5)	(16·3)	(27·8)	(13·8)	(11·9)	
Little Horton*	2184	3039	938	2344	1712	17 238
	(35·3)	(49·2)	(15·2)	(13·6)	(9·9)	
Manningham*	3957	813	1687	5828	4919	19 807
	(61·1)	(12·5)	(26·0)	(29·4)	(24·8)	
Odsal	3830	877	564	78	21	14 753
	(72·5)	(16·6)	(10·7)	(0·5)	(0·1)	
Thornton	2829	1312	482	68	27	13 357
	(61·2)	(28·4)	(10·4)	(0·5)	(0·1)	
Tong	1443	4067	412	181	34	18 889
	(24·4)	(68·7)	(7·0)	(1·0)	(0·2)	
University*	3147	349	1574	5045	4375	16 565
	(62·0)	(6·9)	(31·0)	(30·5)	(26·4)	
Undercliffe*	2925	781	773	435	353	12 987
	(59·9)	(16·0)	(15·8)	(3·3)	(2·7)	
Wibsey	3318	1454	322	111	26	15 256
	(65·1)	(28·5)	(6·3)	(0·7)	(0·2)	
Wyke	2949	2071	599	63	16	16 702
	(52·2)	(36·7)	(10·6)	(0·4)	(0·1)	
Total (all wards)	58 210	26 033	15 737	20 780	16 918	294 172
	(58·2)	(26·0)	(15·7)	(7·1)	(5·8)	
Inner ten wards (asterisked*)	31 994	8742	11 074	19 912	16 659	151 330
	(61·2)	(16·7)	(21·2)	(13·2)	(11·0)	

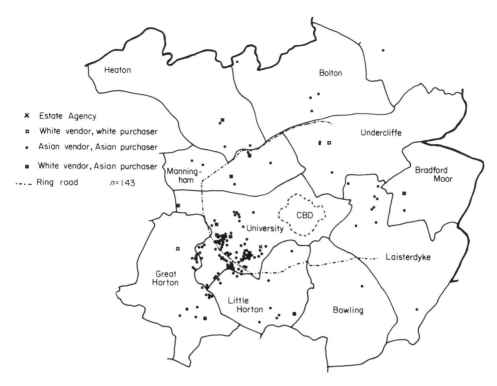

Figure 1. Location of all properties sold through Asian estate agents in the County Borough of Bradford (sample week in April, 1975–1980 inclusive).

white and Asian estate agents is again evident. This is illustrated in Fig. 1 and 2 which show the location of properties sold by the agencies in the inner ten wards of the city.

While the initial statistic that only one property advertised by an Asian estate agent was within the borough but outside the inner ten wards may be the most striking evidence of the limited market in which the Asian estate agent appears to operate, this pattern is emphasized by the location of sales by Asian estate agents in the inner ten wards, as is shown in Fig. 1. Of the properties sold almost three-fifths were located in University ward, while white agents offered only 5% of their inner ward properties in this area (and just 1·6% of their city total). This pattern only serves to emphasize the pile-up of Asian households in the ward which had a New Commonwealth born population in excess of 5000 in 1971 (30·5%), an electorate

Footnote to Table II opposite:

Figures in parentheses in columns one to three indicate the percentage of households in each tenure category; a small 'not stated' category is excluded from the tabulations.

Figures in parentheses in columns 4 and 5 are percentages of the population figure in column 6. These figures cover only those born in the New Commonwealth, thus excluding a substantial British born coloured population.

Source: Ward Library Statistics, Bradford CB 1971 census.

43·7% Asian in 1980 and, after taking account of the lower propensity of Asians to register to vote (Commission for Racial Equality, 1980) and the younger and far larger Asian household size (4·9 persons compared with 2·7 for non-Asian households), it appears that the ward is at least three-fifths Asian at present. In addition a large part of the white population are transients, students living in the larger multi-occupied Victorian terraces. In sum then, a substantial majority of the long term residents are of Asian origin, and the pattern of house purchase in the ward is perpetuating and extending this ethnic dominance.

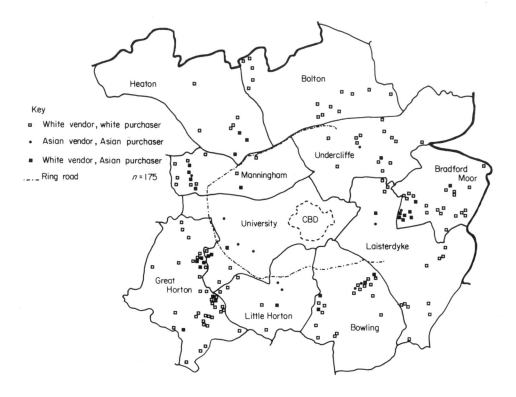

Figure 2. Location of properties sold by white estate agents in the inner ten wards of Bradford (sample week in April, 1975–1980 inclusive).

In contrast to the Asian advertised property, 395 of 570 dwellings offered for sale by white agents were in the outer zone (69·3%). As Fig. 2 shows, this differential pattern is repeated even after excluding the outer wards. While the property offered by white estate agents is more evenly distributed among the central wards, there is still a tendency for few sales to be in the main areas of ethnic concentration in Manningham and University. Within the wards the trend is for Asian estate agents to deal with property nearest the central area, generally corresponding with the oldest and least desirable housing environment for white residents, while white agents tend to sell, and white households tend to purchase, property in the more distant reaches of the inner wards (see Table III).

TABLE III

Proportion of property offered by estate agents
in each of the inner ten wards in Bradford CB area, sample week 1975-1980

Ward	Asian	White	Total
Bolton	2·8	8·0	5·7
Bowling	0·7	12·6	7·3
Bradford Moor	1·4	16·0	9·5
Great Horton	12·0	22·9	18·0
Heaton	2·8	4·6	3·8
Laisterdyke	6·3	8·6	7·6
Little Horton	7·7	4·6	6·0
Manningham	4·9	8·6	7·6
University	58·5	5·1	29·7
Undercliffe	2·8	8·6	6·0

Outer 9 wards — white agents 395 cases of a total of 570 (69·3%), Asian agents one case of 143 (0·7%). Figures in each column represent the percentage of properties offered by agents of the given ethnicity in each of the inner 10 wards.
Source: Personal fieldwork, Bradford CB 1975-1980.

TABLE IV

Mean direct line distance from an advertised property
to the Central Business District by race, inner ten wards, Bradford CB

Ward	White:white sales	Asian:Asian sales	White:Asian sales
Bolton (18)	2·52	2·47	—
Bowling (23)	1·81	1·51	1·45
Bradford Moor (29)	2·54	1·70	1·94
Great Horton (57)	2·62	2·23	2·31
Heaton (12)	2·47	1·90	1·94
Laisterdyke (25)	3·38	1·39	1·28
Little Horton (18)	1·92	1·56	1·70
Manningham (24)	2·04	1·94	1·92
University (92)	1·78	1·45	1·47
Undercliffe (19)	1·71	1·30	1·73
Inner 10 wards (317)	*2·19*	*1·60*	*1·81*
Outer 9 wards (396)	4·52	3·29	—
All CB areas (713)	*3·93*	*1·62*	*1·81*

Figures in parentheses indicate the sample size for each ward. Distances in kilometres.
Source: Personal fieldwork, Bradford CB 1975-1980.

As Table IV illustrates the mean distance of a white vendor to white purchaser transaction in the inner city was approximately 0·6 km further from the central business district than an Asian:Asian transaction, even after the white property had been constrained for price (under £14 000 in the second quarter of 1980, unless a terraced property). Over the entire County Borough this difference is more manifest, the mean variation being from 3·93 km for a white to white transaction to 1·62 km for Asian purchases from an Asian vendor. In the 50 instances in which a white vendor sold to an Asian purchaser the average distance from the central point was 1·81 km, marginally greater than the Asian to Asian figure, but hardly sufficient to suggest anything more than a slow creep outwards of the boundaries of the ethnic enclave. Further evidence to support an hypothesis suggesting that housing trans-actions among Bradford's Asians are locationally confined can be offered by noting the number of exchanges in varying distance bands from the centre. The innermost kilometre is characterized by central business district and associated 'fringe' activities, old industrial premises, warehouses and, where clearance has not occurred, predominantly low quality housing with a limited life expectancy. Within this area the white agencies offered no residential property for sale, and Asian-owned agencies sold just six houses. In the distance band between 1 and 1·5 km from the city centre Asian agents sold 62 properties, 43·4% of all Asian transactions, while white agents sold 17 premises (9·7%), of which 13 were to Asian clients. Similarly sales within all zones under 2 km from the city centre accounted for 114 of the properties sold by Asian estates agents to Asians (80·9%), but only 67 of the sales by white estate agents in the inner ten wards (38·3%); almost half of the 67 sales were to Asian purchasers.

The price of property advertised

The average price of a residential property advertised in Bradford during the survey period and adjusted to second quarter 1980 price levels using the Nationwide Building Society's index of regional house prices was £17 222, just under £1000 lower than the mean for the Yorkshire and Humberside region, which is in turn significantly below the national average. The survey of Asian estate agents identified just one detached, three semi-detached and one maisonette sold, along with 138 terraced or cottage properties; the white sample was thus restricted to terraced property and to houses offered for sale at under £14 000 at present price levels. Within this terraced category the mean price was considerably lower; £10 537 throughout the entire city, falling to £9 599 in the inner ten wards despite the inclusion of several large three storey Victorian terraces. The average price of sales by white agents to white purchasers within this restricted category was a little above the inner city average at £10 125, while sales by Asians to Asians averaged just £8685. This price variation appears to represent locational factors as much as the amenities of the dwelling *per se*, with several cases of comparable property being offered at two or three thousand pounds more when located away from the urban core. The most interesting category is that of Asians who have bought white-owned property which had been advertised by white agents. The group is small, 36 cases, but the average price of these transactions is just £7567 per unit, well below the mean sale prices for exchanges between white:white and Asian:Asian.

Profiles of property prices show that the variation in mean advertised price between transactions with both parties white and both parties Asian is almost totally accounted for by the propensity of Asians to buy property at the very bottom of the price range; 40% of Asian purchases were of property advertised at under £6000 at current prices, compared with 18% for the white sample. This in part reflects the differing level of demand for property in or on the fringes of the major immigrant areas, with the lowest price units in the worst areas of the inner city already relinquished by whites and unlikely to attract white households back in significant numbers. In part it may also reflect differing abilities to pay or to borrow capital. In contrast though, there is some evidence of Asians willing to pay a premium to be located on the fringes of the ethnic concentration without suffering the worst excesses of the residential environment. This is illustrated by the high prices paid for terraced property sold by Asian estate agents in the Hartington Terrace area on the fringes of University and Great Horton wards. In this area prices of £15 000–£19 000 are the norm, and appear to reflect some internal sorting within the enclave, being occupied by less deprived elements of the Gujarati community.

To summarize, although there is evidence of Asian purchasers paying prices well above the city norm, these cases are the exception rather than the rule at present. The overall picture presented by the sample is of Asians occupying and purchasing the lowest priced property even within the inner wards. Property purchased from white vendors through white estate agents proves the most interesting case, with the low prices suggesting that Asians dealing with white agents are buying that property least desirable to the host community.

The ethnic composition of 'receiving' streets

The ethnic composition of the street in which each property in the inner ten wards was sold was identified using the electoral register in force in the year of sale, and the ethnicity of the purchaser was noted; this information is presented in Table V. Although there were 17 844 Asian electors registered in the inner ten wards in 1980, 75 of the 131 property exchanges involving a white vendor and a white purchaser were in streets containing no Asian elector. A further 21 exchanges were in streets containing fewer than 10% Asian electors; together these two categories accounted for almost three-quarters of all white:white property exchanges. Similarly the mean percentage of Asians in all streets receiving a new white household was one-third of the inner area figure of 18%, and one-fifth of a proportional share of Asian residents for owner-occupier areas. In only 12 instances (9·2%) did a white household buy a property in a street more than 30% Asian in the appropriate electoral register, and this figure falls to just four (3·1%) in streets 40% or more Asian; in the sample none of the properties advertised by agents in streets over five-eighths Asian (58 cases) attracted a white buyer.

TABLE V

Property sold by estate agents in the inner ten wards of Bradford;
ethnicity of new occupier: ethnic composition of receiving street

% electors Asian*	White vendor: white purchaser	Asian vendor: Asian purchaser	White vendor: Asian purchaser
0–9·9	96 (73·3)	4 (3·0)	7 (13·7)
10–19·9	13 (9·9)	15 (11·1)	5 (9·8)
20–29·9	11 (8·4)	22 (16·3)	17 (33·3)
30–39·9	7 (5·3)	19 (14·1)	5 (9·8)
40–49·9	1 (0·8)	8 (5·9)	3 (5·9)
50–59·9	2 (1·5)	16 (11·9)	3 (5·9)
60–69·9	1 (0·8)	14 (10·4)	4 (7·8)
70–79·9	—	17 (12·6)	3 (5·9)
80–89·9	—	11 (8·1)	3 (5·9)
90–100·0	—	9 (6·7)	1 (2·0)
Totals	131	135	51

*Asian name electors as a percentage of all electors in the receiving street. Figures in parentheses are percentages of the appropriate column totals.
Source: Electoral Registers, Bradford Metropolitan District Council, 1975–1980. Personal fieldwork.

Inevitably exchanges between Asian households occurred much further along the white-to-Asian continuum, partly because of the obvious need for a prior Asian presence in the street to fulfil the role of vendor, but also because the exchange of property from Asian to Asian can be expected to be a second stage in the immigrant succession process, following some years after the initial Asian presence. For this reason only 3% of the Asian to Asian exchanges were in the streets in which three-quarters of white exchanges took place, while only 17 of the 84 exchanges which took place in streets over 50% Asian involved either a white vendor, or more exceptionally, a white purchaser (three cases). Comparatively few properties are exchanged in streets already 80% Asian or more, partially reflecting the poor quality of property in areas almost totally Asian, much of which would prove difficult to sell through formal channels; it can be reasonably assumed that informal methods of exchange play an important role at the bottom end of the housing market.

Exchanges from white to Asian display no consistent pattern, ranging from the first Asian household to buy into a street to the last white household to leave. With a small sample of just 51 moves it is impossible to offer anything other than tentative impressions, but one-third of the sales by white vendors to Asian buyers were in the range of 20·0–29·9%. This, coupled with the lack of white buyers in any street with more than a 30% Asian population, could perhaps give some very limited support to ideas of tipping points; a great deal more information at the micro-level and a much larger sample would be necessary to develop such an hypothesis. Interestingly there is a considerable variation between white and Asian estate agents selling property for white vendors to an Asian purchaser. White agents tend to sell low price, low amenity houses in areas perhaps one-quarter Asian, whereas in the eleven cases of white-owned property being sold through Asian estate agents the mean ethnic composition of the street was already 72·5% Asian.

Interpretation

Estate agents as urban managers

In his study of institutions operating in the Islington housing market Williams (1976) emphasized the active role of incoming estate agents in 'gentrifying' parts of the area. Such agents saw themselves as house salesmen, advertising beyond the traditional social and spatial catchment of Islington while increasing property turnover by actively soliciting properties for sale. This active role had proved a strong influence in enhancing the desirability of the area in which they operated, and had led to a strong temptation for agents to become involved in entrepreneurial activity, linked to companies buying, renovating and reselling property (Williams, 1976; pp.79–80). The extent of this role may, however, reflect the competitive nature of the London housing market. Inner Bradford, in contrast, represents an area near the other extreme, and it seems unlikely that any involvement in purchasing and re-selling property would prove sufficiently lucrative given the current state of the local housing market. The city's estate agents claimed to act solely in a referral capacity, fulfilling the role of 'shop windows' or dissemination points for information on all available property, whatever its location and price, on a simple commission basis. It may not be accurate to suggest, however, that the agencies were just 'passive intermediaries' (Lean, 1965, quoted in Williams, 1976). Sales to Asians by white agents reflect closely the current pattern of Asian settlement, with purchases almost invariably in streets with a significant Asian presence or, in the exceptional cases where this was not so, in streets fringing areas of ethnic settlement. The causal factors behind such a pattern are more difficult to isolate and could be interpreted as reflecting ethnic choice. If this is the key factor then the Asian purchaser is restricting himself to a narrow locational constraint from a very wide range of property offered for sale, and is buying property with a mean price a quarter below the inner city average and 12% below the mean advertised price for purchases by Asians from Asian agents. Such property has tended to be on offer for long periods of time and is in areas in which houses are 'rather difficult to sell'.

Asian estate agents claimed a similar referral role. Although 'blockbusting' has proven a lucrative practice for some black realtors in the USA (Berry, 1979) and may have occurred in some instances in British cities, particularly where Asian-owned and financed agencies have traded under English names and used white counter staff, there is little evidence of this in the study area. Both estate agents claimed that under no circumstances do they buy up property either within or on the fringes of ethnic areas, and just 11 properties (7·7%) offered for sale by Asian agents had white vendors. In these instances the agent concerned claimed that the property was usually referred to him by the executors or the family of a deceased former resident, or it reflected a realization by the departing white household that an Asian would be the most likely buyer and that he was the only agent operating in that particular locality. This is supported by the previously quoted figure for the ethnicity of the streets in question, seven-tenths of the resident electorate being Asian. However, the Asian estate agents do not have a completely passive function. Within the ethnic zone they were concerned to promote specific areas, often aiming their advertisements to status conscious ethnics by offering "an excellent opportunity to move to a best residential area" (Lidget Green on the northern fringes of University and Great Horton wards) or an opportunity to move into General Improvement Areas. This promotion of specific locations is reflected in prices well above the inner city norm for terraced houses of a similar standard and higher than prices asked by white agents in the same area.

In summary the managerial role of agents in the inner city may have an important influence on patterns of ethnic residence, but the effects are predominantly at the micro-level, with some possible directing of potential Asian purchasers by white agents. Asian property agents operate in a predominantly residual housing market selling dwellings for Asians to Asians and thus helping to reproduce the present pattern of ethnic residential segregation. The few instances in which Asian estate agents sold property previously occupied by white households served only to intensify the pile-up in areas of existing concentration.

Other institutions in the local housing market

When interviewed, Asian estate agents stressed the key role of the mortgage allocating institutions in deciding the nature and extent of activity in the inner city housing market. Although it is accepted that most major building societies are no longer engaged in a policy of explicit red-lining, both Asian estate agencies stressed that in practice it was impossible to obtain a mortgage on a property inside the ring road. This process was not noted in such specific terms by white agents, several of whom had access to a quota of building society funds through their subsidiary function as society agents. This undoubtedly reflects the differential importance of property inside the ring road; 50% of all transactions dealt with through Asian estate agents were located within this ring, compared with just 11 properties sold by white agents, just under 2% of their total sales in the Borough and only 6% of their sales in the inner ten wards. Like Duncan's 'blue zones' in Huddersfield (1976b) the areas of minimal society lending can easily be couched in racial terms. Even on purely status grounds there can be no doubt that Asian households suffer disproportionately; they are more likely to be unemployed or in unstable employment, they are predominantly in low status occupations without incremental salary scales and often depend on vulnerable overtime and shift payments to boost wages up towards the national norm.

Although nationally houses being bought with a mortgage allocated by sources other than a building society accounted for only 6·1% of the total housing stock in 1979 (Nationwide Building Society, 1980), this sector is extremely important in the inner city. The role of fringe or 'back street' sources was outlined in evidence submitted to the House of Commons Select Committee on Race Relations (1971), with some of the earliest estate agents buying up property and re-selling the premises with the promise of a high interest, short term loan. Such informal sources of funding are still important today, although the Asian estate agents interviewed claimed that they would never buy up properties themselves in the inner city housing market, possibly for commercial rather than ethical reasons, they were well able to direct people to finance house funding if so required. It was claimed, however, that such sources had declined in importance in recent years. The typical purchaser also sold his house through the same estate agent, buying a property for two or three thousand pounds more and still within the confines of the ethnic area, using personal savings for the balance due.

The only viable source of formal funding in the inner city for most prospective purchasers in recent years has been the local authority, and a substantial number of local authority mortgages has been allocated to Asian applicants in the past decade. There is no doubt, however, that the local authority, though it is willing to lend on much inner city property, has insufficient funds to provide a full substitute for the absence of building society support. To quote Duncan, "The credit provided by local authorities is not sufficient, however, to make much more than a gesture towards correcting the pattern of inverse-care maintained by building societies". (1976b; p.313). The result is long delays in allocating mortgages, particularly towards the end of every financial year, and sizeable waiting lists. In an attempt to alleviate the problem in the face of increasing cutbacks in central funding for local authority mortgage activity, Bradford has recently re-enforced the national agreement made between the government and the building societies whereby funds are ear-marked for suitable applicants referred to them by the local authority. Five national societies with offices in the city are co-operating, but the general impression is that the scheme has limited potential. Every applicant is subject to the normal building society status requirements and in competition with the societies' ordinary savers so, while the scheme may cream off a few of the most suitable applicants, its direct impact on the ethnic market is likely to be extremely restricted. The demand for local authority mortgages is likely to continue unabated and, faced with decreasing resources, the local authority is attempting to spread the jam more thinly. By preferring to allocate two mortgages of £4000 each rather than one of £8000, the local authority could be lessening the opportunity for its large number of Asian applicants to improve their residential environment in anything other than marginal steps.

One concomitant effect of this shortage of funds for ethnic housing in the inner city has been the rapidly increasing participation of Asians in the public housing sector, particularly from 1977 onwards. Today there are about 400 Asians living in council property, with the largest concentrations in low rise flats in Manchester Road and the inter-war Canterbury Avenue estate, both in Little Horton ward. The two main cells together account for approximately 37% of the total, and most other Asian households in local authority housing also live in the inner wards. In many instances this penetration is of unpopular estates, with a greater than average number of Asian households living in pre-war property, a situation which contrasts markedly with that identified by Robinson (1980) in Blackburn. Although every household has a free choice of area in which they wish to be offered a property, many Asians approach the local authority as a last resort and are prepared to accept a less popular estate in return for an early offer. This is reflected in the nature of the participating household; there is almost no demand for sheltered housing from well established families nor for rehousing following compulsory purchase orders. More typically participants are likely to be second generation Asians, recently married with no more than one or two very young children, poorly paid or unemployed, and from households in which family support to help finance house purchase is not available or is insufficient. In addition the small number of Asian men who have married a non-Asian woman are disproportionately evident.

This penetration of the local authority sector, despite its escalating importance, only involves 3·7% of the total number of Asian households at present. Similarly the rapid decline in the numbers in the private rented sector mean that approaching nine-tenths of the Asian households live in premises owned by themselves or their immediate kin. The realization of the restricted housing market within which they operate has led to an increasing amount of *in situ* improvement by Asian owner-occupiers. From the limited funds available 185 improvement grants were paid to Asian households in 1979, 23% of the city total. This figure increased to 48% of the 192 grants awarded in General Improvement Areas and to 72% of the 61 grants paid in Housing Action Areas; in contrast only 9% of grants in all remaining areas of the city were to Asian households.

Conclusion: the Asian housing market — a choice/constraint framework

The thesis that Asian households do not hold Western standards of housing provision and are content to occupy inner city property thorough choice has been forcefully propounded by Badr Dahya (1974) in his studies of the Asian communities of Bradford and Birmingham. Dahya is able to rationalize the occupation of low amenity ageing filtered dwellings by referring to the desire of the Asian community to utilize cheap shelter, principally to support remittances to the homeland and to facilitate non-participation in the morally lax, status-conscious, British society (Robinson, 1979; p.7). This accommodation is thus only inferior in terms of native white evaluations. Although writing in the early 1970s Dahya's fieldwork relates to a period from 1964 to 1966 and refers to a predominantly male population, who may well have had a very strong and *realistic* sojourner orientation. Dahya recognizes this, stating that, "the analysis offered above relates to the early stages of Pakistani settlement in England" (1974; p.114). He continues:

> It is likely that at a later stage, the immigrants may begin to re-evaluate their position *vis-à-vis* Britain/Pakistan and accordingly, adopt new values and aspirations and seek recognition in British society or, alternatively, modify their present perspectives and yet, given the external constraints as suggested by Rex and Moore (1967), may find their residential mobility blocked.
>
> Dahya (1974; p.114)

Dahya's thesis has received considerable support in the literature, most recently and most emphatically from Robinson working in Blackburn, whose findings "not only support Dahya's thesis of return migration, but also suggest that the Asian element neither sees itself as part of, nor is concerned with, the larger white society" (Robinson, 1979; p.38). Such findings cannot be reported for present day Bradford. In part this may be attributed to the differing value positions of differing authors, in part to differences between the two centres. In Bradford, the Asian population is predominantly Pakistani, is larger than the Blackburn Asian population in both absolute and percentage terms, and has been established in the city for longer. Indeed, in Blackburn 91·3% of the enumerated residents in the 1971 census had arrived in the town after 1960, the highest percentage for any of the fifty largest immigrant communities in Britain in 1971 (Jones, 1978; p.524).

In Bradford today many of the characteristics which Dahya identified as being important elements in producing the pattern of spatial cohesion are being eroded. The Asian banks which evolved largely to deal with remittances to the homeland are changing their focus, increasingly dealing in a wider spectrum of banking functions such as personal accounts, loans and mortgage finance. It is suggested that remittances are now of far less consequence, with most Asian families now complete (with the exception of the Bangladeshi community). Although many Asians still subscribe to the ideal of return to the homeland, there are few Asian households who have left the city in recent years and have not returned. The sojourner orientation, though outwardly expressed, is thus inwardly accepted by most as being unlikely to be fulfilled, and as time spent in this country increases the significance of this goal progressively decreases. This is particularly the case for the second generation, many of whom were born here or came to England at a very young age, particularly following the 1962 Commonwealth Immigration Act, and have no recollection of any other life than their British one. Educated in white schools their values and interests outside of the home environment are often similar to the host society, even though this outlook is usually restrained in family contacts.

Despite the development of an extensive Asian business sector, consisting of 660 retail and service outlets and 133 other establishments in 1980, most Asian income is earned in the host economy (Cater and Jones, 1978). If one uses the ratio of one family supported for each Asian business, an optimistic assumption when one views the marginality of many of the enterprises, over 92% of households are dependent on the white labour market. While socially-based models emphasizing internal differentiation within the Asian community are important, the significance of economically-based interpretations cannot be over-estimated. The sectors of the local economy within which the Asian community operates have been particularly affected; 60 000 textile jobs in the area have gone in the last two decades (City of Bradford Metropolitan District Council, 1980), and recent cuts in local transport services are having a disproportionate effect. With unemployment in the County Borough hitting 12 861 adult males in August 1980, over one-eighth of the workforce chasing 400 vacancies, there is no scope for being unduly sanguine. The Asian community has estimated unemployment rates in excess of 20%, a high level of disguised unemployment and under-employment and a substantial and rapidly increasing number of hard core unemployed, many of whom are school-leavers who have never had any work experience. It is within this framework that the operation of Asians in the local housing market can be most profitably studied.

Without doubt, Asian households currently occupy the kind of housing and environmental space rated by most whites as sub-standard. With few exceptions they occupy pre-First World War terraced property, and they are concentrated in some of the least desirable properties within this range; small terraces, side-sculleries and back-to-backs. With the increasing take-up of the limited number of local authority improvement grants the presence of indoor toilets, a bathroom and hot running water, though absent in many instances, is more common, but facilities such as central heating, gardens and garages are rarely found. In fact the most significant selling feature of much property is the presence of attics converted to bedrooms to accommodate Asian families averaging five per household and often much larger than this mean figure. The poor quality of much of this property is reflected in its price, a mean figure of £8685, just half the average house price in the region and 14% below white owned terraced property in the inner city. Similarly, two-fifths of all houses bought by Asians had advertised values of under £6000 at current prices, compared with less than one-fifth of the white sample. This property is also severely constrained by location, packed in a tight ring around much of the central area (Cater and Jones, 1979; p.91), broken only by non-residential functions. In the past four years the ward level dissimilarity index has fallen by one point each year from 61·1 in 1977 to 58·1 in 1980, which reflects some movement outwards along major roads into the city centre together with contiguous 'fringing' into relinquished space on the edge of the ethnic zone. Local trends suggest that this pattern is likely to be perpetuated. The extent of informal exchanges in the Asian housing market was estimated by one agent to be as high a 50% of all Asian to Asian transactions, particularly in the lowest price ranges and the least desirable environments. Similarly referrals to Asian estate agents were by Asian residents in 93% of cases, and were therefore in areas already penetrated by the immigrant community. Even purchases by Asians from white residents and through white agents were usually in streets with a substantial non-white presence, and were of the lowest price and the poorest quality. The scope for penetration of white areas is therefore limited by the restricted market within which Asian purchasers are operating and, while it may have been possible to attribute initial patterns of concentration to non-Western conceptions of housing need, there is little evidence of the potential to alter this pattern as needs and aspirations change. To some extent the managerial institutions operating in the Borough play a role, with minimal mortgage funding by formal sources to inner city residents and on inner city property. Similarly there are pointers to suggest the possible directing of Asian purchasers by some estate agencies. The principal factors, however, appear to operate at one stage removed. Part of the cohesiveness of the Asian population can be attributed to a conflict-evading function, a negative reaction to attitudes prevalent in the host society. Similarly the status of the Asian minority as a disadvantaged group within a rapidly declining urban economy militates against the prospect of receiving access to better quality housing resources.

Although there are considerable internal differences within the population, the prospect of economic parity for the vast majority of Bradford's Asians in the forseeable future is extremely remote. They have very little within-group control of the allocative mechanisms, in both the housing market and the wider economy which supplies the resources necessary to facilitate competition for a better residential environment. Although they may exercise some degree of choice, they do so within a severely constrained physical and financial framework. In the past the resulting patterns may have accorded with the desire of the Asian household to minimize expenditure on housing resources to facilitate remittances or savings. However, the decreasing significance of the homeland, linked with the rapid emergence of a second generation of residents, is progressively increasing the desire of Asian households to participate freely in a wider housing market. In the current economic and political climate this intent is liable only to be frustrated, and changes in the pattern of ethnic residential concentration are likely to be changes of degree rather than of kind.

References

Bassett, K. and Short, J. R. (1980). "Housing and Residential Structure: Alternative Approaches". Routledge and Kegan Paul, London.

Berry, B. J. L. (1979). "The Open Housing Question". Ballinger, Cambridge, Mass.

Boddy, M. J. (1976). The structure of mortgage finance: building societies and the British social formation. *Transactions, Institute of British Geographers N.S.* **1**, 58–71.

Boddy, M. J. (1980). "The Building Societies". Macmillan, London.

Cater, J. C. and Jones, T. P. (1978). Asians in Bradford. *New Society*, 13 April.

Cater, J. C. and Jones, T. P. (1979). Ethnic residential space: the case of Asians in Bradford. *Tijdschrift voor Economische en Sociale Geografie* **70**, 86–97.

City of Bradford Metropolitan District Council (1978). "District Trends 1978: Metplan". Corporate Planning Unit, Bradford MDC.

City of Bradford Metropolitan District Council (1980). "District Trends 1980". Policy Unit, Bradford MDC.

Commission for Racial Equality (1980). *New Equals*, 12 June.

Dahya, B. (1974). The nature of Pakistani ethnicity in industrial cities in Britain. *In* "Urban Ethnicity", (A. Cohen, ed.). Tavistock, London.

Doherty, J. (1969). The distribution and concentration of immigrants in London. *Race Today*, **1**, 227-233.

Duncan, S. S. (1976a). Research directions in social geography: housing opportunities and constraints. *Transactions, Institute of British Geographers N.S.* **1**, 10-19.

Duncan, S. S. (1976b). Self help: the allocation of mortgages and the formation of housing sub-markets. *Area* **8**, 307-316.

Duncan, S. S. (1977). "Housing Disadvantage and Residential Mobility: Immigrants and Institutions in a Northern Town". Faculty of Urban and Regional Studies Working Paper No. 5, University of Sussex.

Ford, J. (1975). The role of the building society manager in the urban stratification system: autonomy versus constraint. *Urban Studies* **12**, 295-302.

Gower Davies, J. (1972). *The evangelistic bureaucrat.* Tavistock, London.

Gray, F. G. (1976). Selection and allocation in council housing. *Transactions, Institute of British Geographers N.S.* **1**, 34-46.

Hatch, J. C. S. (1973). Estate agents as urban gatekeepers. Paper presented at the British Sociological Association Urban Sociology Group, University of Stirling.

Harvey, D. (1977). Government policies, financial institutions and neighbourhood change in United States cities. *In* "Captive Cities", (M. Harloe, ed.). Wiley, London.

House of Commons Select Committee on Race Relations (1971). "Housing, Minutes of Evidence, Bradford". HMSO, London.

Jones, P. N. (1970). Some aspects of the changing distribution of coloured immigrants in Birmingham, 1961-1966. *Transactions, Institute of British Geographers* **50**, 199-219.

Jones, P. N. (1976). Colored minorities in Birmingham, England. *Annals, Association of American Geographers* **66**, 89-103.

Jones, P. N. (1978). The distribution and diffusion of the coloured population in England and Wales, 1961-1971. *Transactions, Institute of British Geographers N.S.* **3**, 515-532.

Jones, T. P. and McEvoy, D. (1974). The residential segregation of Asians in Huddersfield. Paper presented at the Annual Conference of the Institute of British Geographers, Norwich.

Kearsley, G. W. and Srivastava, S. R. (1974). The spatial evolution of Glasgow's Asian community. *Scottish Geographical Magazine* **90**, 110-124.

Lambert, C. (1976). "Building Societies, Surveyors and the Older Urban Areas of Birmingham". Centre for Urban and Regional Studies Working Paper No. 38, University of Birmingham.

Lean, W. (1965). Some aspects of the real estate market. Unpublished MSc thesis, University of London.

Lee, T. R. (1973). Immigrants in London: trends in distribution and concentration 1961-1971. *New Community* **2**, 145-159.

Lomas, G. B. G. and Monck, E. M. (1975). "The Coloured Population of Great Britain: a Comparative Study of Coloured Households in Four County Boroughs". Runnymede Trust, London.

McEvoy, D. (1978). The segregation of Asian immigrants in Glasgow: a note. *Scottish Geographical Magazine* **94**, 180-183.

Mills, E. S. (1972). "Studies in the Structure of the Urban Economy". Johns Hopkins Press, Baltimore.

Muchnick, D. (1970). "Urban Renewal in Liverpool". LSE Occasional Paper in Social Administration No. 33. Bell, London.

Nationwide Building Society (1980). *Housing trends, 2nd quarter 1980.* Nationwide Building Society, London

Office of Population Censuses and Surveys (1974). "1971 Census, Ward Library Tabulations, Bradford County Borough." OPCS, Titchfield, Hants.

Pahl, R. E. (1970). "Whose City?" Longman, London.

Paris, C. (1974). Urban renewal in Birmingham, England: an institutional approach. *Antipode* **6**, 7-15.

Rex, J. and Moore, R. (1967). "Race, Community and Conflict: A Study of Sparkbrook". Oxford University Press for the Institute of Race Relations, London.

Robinson, V. (1979). "The Segregation of Asians within a British City: Theory and Practice". School of Geography Research Paper No. 22, Oxford.

Robinson, V. (1980). Asians and council housing. *Urban Studies* **17**, 323-332.

Skellington, R. (1979). "Council House Allocation in a Multi-racial Town". Faculty of Social Science, Urban Research Group Occasional Paper No. 2, Open University.

Williams, P. R. (1976). The role of institutions in the inner London housing market: the case of Islington. *Transactions, Institute of British Geographers N.S.* **1**, 72-82.

Williams, P. R. (1978a). Building societies and the inner city. *Transactions, Institute of British Geographers N.S.* **3**, 23-34.

Williams, P. R. (1978b). Urban managerialism: a concept of relevance? *Area* **10**, 236-240.

Winchester, S. W. C. (1974). Immigrant areas in Coventry in 1971. *New Community* **4**, 97-104.

NINE

Race, class and culture: towards a ✕
a theorization of the 'choice/constraint' concept

KEVIN BROWN

Centre for Urban and Regional Studies, University of Birmingham,
Birmingham, UK

Introduction

> The pattern is the net effect of two gross forces; the first is the positive self-ascriptive force which makes a group want to segregate itself; the second is the negative proscriptive force of outside society which prevents the segregated group from dispersing. From the pattern one can determine the net effect of both forces, but one cannot immediately distinguish the *relative* strengths of the positive and negative.
>
> Peach (1975a; pp.8-9)

This observation—the 'choice/constraint' concept—has emerged from R. E. Park's recognition of the relationship between social and spatial distance and has provided the dominant conceptual starting point for social geographical work within the field of ethnic social segregation. From empirical data, indices of (residential) segregation have been calculated but, as Peach notes above, the explanation(s) for the patterns created remains unresolved. This lack of a systematic theoretical framework within which to base the work, has resulted in 'choice' and 'constraint' being applied as loose, commonsense constructs. This paper contends that this is attributable to the transmitted assumptions inherent in the tradition of Robert Park and the 'Chicago School of Human Ecology'. The questions addressed are indeed central to social scientific/philosophical enquiry, i.e. to what extent do men and women exert control over their own destiny and to what extent are they controlled? However, in order to pose these questions in a form capable of resolution, the processes of abstraction and theorization are essential. When immersing themselves in empirical data, most geographers have turned debate away from attempts to provide broader societal analyses, in favour of the inward refinement of the tools of empiricism, for example, the recent debate centred upon the 'correct' level at which to measure segregation (Jones and McEvoy, 1978; Lee, 1978; Peach, 1979). In this way, British social geographers of ethnic social segregation have, in the last 25 years, re-created the problems of explanation that contributed to the decline in influence of the 'Chicago School' after the mid-1930s

185

—the city, and discrete areas within it, are treated as 'laboratories' from which 'social facts' may be gleaned through the process of observation.

This paper argues that the social segregation of a group or groups within a society is intimately related to the whole of that society, i.e. it cannot be segmented off and treated in isolation. Only when a societal analysis is undertaken which begins with a consideration of the economic basis of power relations, can the concept of 'choice/ constraint' come to have analytical power, and the fallacy of a 'sui generis race relations' (Fenton, 1980; p.164) be revealed.

The first section of this paper sets out to identify those ontological and epistemological assumptions, which the 'choice/constraint' concept is the symptomatic embodiment of, at the level of the text. These assumptions determine which types and forms of questions can be raised, and which must remain silent.* It is concluded that the empiricist tradition or problematic has structured the 'choice/constraint' concept and contains specific contradictions which result in the problems of explanation discussed above. These problems cannot, therefore, be resolved in terms internal to that problematic.

The second section represents an attempt to develop the concept within an alternative framework of Marxist analysis. This is not a process of outright rejection, but rather one of development through the incorporation, into the new framework, of those rational elements of the old. The aim is to raise those problems and questions previously unanswerable, excluded, or unstated, in a form which renders them amenable to solution.

The empiricist tradition:
Park, human ecology and the atomistic conception

Given the nature and the scope of this paper, a full analysis of the origins and development of human ecology in the USA, and later in Britain, is not possible.† What is necessary is to locate Park and the 'Chicago School' within the context of sociological and philosophical thought, to consider the conditions of the convergence of human ecology and urban geography and to examine the consequences that this 're-discovery' has had for the social geography of ethnic social segregation.

The intellectual debt owed to Park by social geographers concerned with ethnic social segregation is explicitly recognized by Peach, who states of Park's 1926 paper on 'The urban community as a spatial pattern and a moral order', "This paper is the fountainhead from which all else springs." (Peach, 1975a; pp.1-2).

---

*The form of critique employed in this paper is informed by the Althusserian notion of the 'problematic' defined as a theory's, "... *objective internal reference system of its particular* themes, the system of *questions* commanding the *answers* given . . ." (Althusser, 1969; p.67n). To extract the 'problematic' of a theory, a 'symptomatic reading' is employed. See especially Althusser and Balibar (1968; pp.25-28).

†For an account of the development of the 'Chicago School' of urban ecology, see Mellor (1977; Chs 4 and 5).

At the source of this 'fountainhead' is the conceptual relationship between social and spatial distance and the application of plant/animal ecology to the city. The particular conditions in which this arose were those of Chicago in the 1910s and 1920s. The rapid industrial growth of the city had required mass labour migration, and the already evident questions of social order and social control were brought into even sharper focus with the onset of the Depression. In this conjuncture, Park, Burgess, McKenzie and others sought to find explanations of the city in terms of a functioning unit, incorporating notions to account for ghettos and slums. This interest in the processes of urbanization drew upon a tradition reaching back to Comte (1858) and influenced particularly by Tönnies (1955), Durkheim (1964), Simmel (1971) and Weber (1968). The key area of enquiry was the effect upon social relations that the transition from a rural to an urban environment had had. Thus, Tönnies' *'Gemeinschaft/Gesellschaft'*, Durkheim's 'mechanical/organic solidarity', Simmel's concern with the change from emotional–affective relations to those based upon rational calculation, and Weber's conception of the city as the embodiment of bourgeois cultural and political society, were all centrally involved with questions relating to the dialetic of individual and community, and with social regulation. The influence of classical sociology upon Park was accompanied, and given particular direction by, the influence of social Darwinism developed by Spencer (1967) in England and Sumner (1906) in the USA. This application of the theory and techniques of plant/animal ecology to human communities fundamentally structured the framework of the 'Chicago School', and created within it specific contradictions arising from the ontological and epistemological assumptions. It is especially necessary, at this point, to indicate which texts are to be taken as the keys to the framework. This is largely because the 'Chicago School of human ecology' is not synonymous with a systematic theoretical framework (and it is argued below that this is a structural impossibility, given the starting assumptions). For the purposes of this paper, the key texts are taken to be Park (1916), Park and Burgess (1925) and Park (1926). These early works represent most clearly the effect of the pre-suppositions held, are concerned centrally with competition, invasion/succession and patterns of distribution, and it is to these texts that geographers of ethnic social segregation have most frequently turned (e.g. Peach, 1975a).

In order to discover the underlying propositions, the texts must be read for their lapses and silences, as much for what is unsaid as is said. These lapses and silences are symptomatic of the contradictions within the framework. Park's development of his major concept of 'natural' (i.e. unplanned) groups and areas, can be used to illustrate some of the major contradictions. He saw the city as possessing a physical organization based upon 'natural areas', and a moral organization based upon 'natural groups'. Physically, the city was regarded as an organism made up of an amalgamation of 'natural areas' created by the processes of competition. For example, land speculators are led to hold plots adjacent to the CBD in expectation of profit, resulting in the creation of 'twilight' zones. In this way, 'twilight' zones are 'natural areas', created in an 'unplanned' way and thus, ". . . industrial and residential suburbs . . . seem to find, in some natural and inevitable manner, their predetermined places" (Park, 1926; p.10).

When 'natural groups' inhabit their own particular 'natural areas', e.g. newly arrived migrants in the 'twilight' zone, then the city functions as a 'spatial pattern and a moral order'. What is left unstated is that 'unplanned' actually refers to the operation of land values in the specific conjuncture of *laissez-faire* capitalism represented by early twentieth century Chicago. This operation was taken by Park to be natural and given, i.e. to have an ontological status. Another quotation is indicative of his epistemological orientation: "All this emphasizes the importance of location, position and mobility as indexes for *measuring, describing, and eventually explaining,* social phenomena" (Park, 1926; p.12, my emphasis).

According to this epistemology, reality is immediately present in appearance i.e. on the surface of phenomena. Thus, an informed gaze can produce knowledge of the real in a relatively unmediated way. This in turn springs from the philosophical notion of totality deriving from Descartes which sees the whole as the sum of simple facts—the atomistic conception. The functionalism that results from this, evident in the 'natural groups/areas' concept, is linked to a consensual view of society. The operation of capitalism was seen by Park to be natural, universal and timeless, regulating a society regarded as the sum of its individual parts. Thus, individual or group conflicts are always subordinated to the movement of the social totality towards a position of equilibrium comparable to the biotic balance in plant life. Whilst unchecked migration to a city might cause conflict and upset the metabolism of the city as a whole, the tendency towards the balanced 'natural order' of capitalism would tend to counteract it. Park was later to develop a specific theory around race—the 'race relations cycle', which characterized his framework,

> The race relations cycle which takes the form, to state it abstractly, of contacts, competition, accommodation and eventual assimilation, is apparently progressive and irreversible . . . . Races and cultures die—it has always been so—but civilization lives on.
>
> Park (1950; p.151)

Hence, the invasion-succession studies which resulted were set firmly within a host-immigrant framework, e.g. Burgess (1925), Cressey (1938), McKenzie (1929). What remained silent were structural questions relating to the economic base of, and the power relations in, society. Within such an empiricist framework, systematic theoretical formulations are subsumed under the unswerving drive towards description.

The 're-discovery' of human ecology by urban geography will now be considered with particular reference to the development of a British social geography of ethnic social segregation. The intent is to point to the ways in which the contradictory structure of the empiricist tradition has been perpetuated.

Human ecology and urban geography

During the 1920s and 1930s, human ecology began to lose its influential position in American sociology in the face of the rise of a 'scientific' systematic sociology.* This emphasized human ecology's own lack of theoretical systematization, and the 'Chicago School's' reliance upon using only one city as a research laboratory. Human ecology progressively abandoned any theoretical basis that it may have gained from the early work of Park in favour of purely descriptive works. This resulted in a series of small-scale descriptive empirical studies of communities in Chicago, e.g. Wirth (1928), and the growth of social area analysis and factorial ecology. What this move represented was a retreat from the problems which accompanied moves towards theorization and which were symptomatic of the contradictions within the framework. The basic structures remained the same however, for the assumption that reality is present in appearance was fundamental to such descriptive mapping and correlation. In Peach's categorization of the progress of 'spatial sociology', defined as, ". . . that part of sociology which employs spatial analysis to elucidate social structures" (Peach 1975a; p.5), he identifies the Duncans as belonging to a fourth approach (after human ecology, factorial ecology and social area analysis) which he terms the 'dissimilarists' and which grew out of the tenets of 'classical' human ecology. In their 1955 paper, Duncan and Duncan set out their connection with Park by quoting from his seminal paper thus, ". . . it is only as social and psychical facts can be reduced to, or correlated with, spatial facts *that they can be measured at all*" (Duncan and Duncan, 1955; p.493, my emphasis).

The effect was a renewed interest in the relationship between social and spatial distance in a systematic way. This was achieved by means of mathematical abstraction (indices of segregation etc.) which provided an aggregate, city-wide view of spatial mix, as opposed to a simple linear measurement of distance. This 'mathematicization' of the social totality taken from Park and the 'Chicago School' cannot be regarded as being a mere taking up of a methodology. A methodology stands in front of those assumptions from which it has been created—in this case, the empiricist tradition. So despite the differences between this approach and that of the other three (above), e.g. that the 'dissimilarists' are concerned with 'space' rather than 'place', all approaches are fundamentally structured by the empiricist tradition and because of this, all remain silent on the question of explanation. Lieberson and the Taeubers (see Peach, 1975a) continued to apply mathematical indices and when, in 1951, the first census data comparable to the USA block statistics became available in Britain, similar work was taken up by British geographers. This coincided with the decade of the highest migration to Britain of black Commonwealth

---

*It is not within the scope of this paper to provide a detailed account of the developments in American sociology required for a more closely argued analysis of the human ecology tradition, its assumptions and developments. Such an account would be concerned with the developments at Chicago of a 'general scientific' orientation, begun by A. Small and W. I. Thomas and clearly seen in the appointment of W. F. Ogburn in 1929 from Columbia. The increasing intervention of theoretical systematizing started by P. Sorokin at Harvard and carried on by T. Parsons, the move towards structural functionalism (Parsons and Bales, 1956), and the subsequent methodological refinements characterized by the work of Lazersfeld and Rosenburg (1962), are obviously central. In particular, the development of 'social behaviourism' under Mead (1934) and symbolic interactionism under Blumer (1969), which displaced human ecology at Chicago, is crucial.

workers, although the first major work was a socio-spatial study of Belfast by Jones.* He concluded the study in this way,

> This paper does nothing more than state the problem and suggest that spatial relations are one essential in explaining social phenomena. But it should be a starting point only of a sociological study of the total social situation in which the human relationships which have been dealt with above exist and develop.

> Jones (1956; p.188)

Yet, what has subsequently happened has been that geographers have refined their techniques of measurement to produce descriptions of segregation which have found an uneasy explanatory resting place in the 'choice/constraint' concept. Attempts to 'fit' explanations onto these patterns have been the result (for example, Jones, 1967, 1970, 1976; Lee, 1973, 1977). However, even if British geography had attempted the 'bridge building' at the 'interface' between geography and sociology called for by Harvey (1973; Ch.1), the dominant British sociological tradition of 'race/ethnic relations' has not provided the analytical tools necessary to enable a "study of the total social situation . . ." called for by Jones.

The domination of the consensual based social administration/problem area approach, has gradually given way to a culturalist/pluralist emphasis upon conflict/stratification.† Perhaps the most important theoretical intervention in this tradition, and probably the most widely reported to geographers, has been the work of Rex (1967, 1970, 1979). His notion of 'housing classes' within a conflict based Weberian framework has challenged the ethnocentrism and cultural pluralism of the tradition. However, Rex's conceptualization of 'class' and 'class struggle', involves the actions of conflicting groups over differential access to the 'scarce resources' of housing, jobs and so on. In this way, there can theoretically be as many 'classes' as there are market situations. As Gilroy points out,

> Their Weberian method provides Rex and Tomlinson with a view of the social formation as a system of market structures which relegates classes to the distributive sphere, rather than as a structured system — an ensemble of modes of production.

> Gilroy (1980; p.51)

Within such a conception of society, power lies in access to political bargaining within the welfare state — something that black groups in Britain have not yet achieved. What does not appear in this analysis is a developed notion of the state which is capable of addressing such questions as, ". . . how the underclass came about? Why is it black/colonial? What is the connection between it being black/colonial and its position as an underclass?" (Bourne, 1980; p.349).

In the main then, sociology has not provided a strong enough critique to challenge the dominance of the ethnocentric host/immigrant framework typical of most

---

*The term 'black' in this paper refers to those members of the British working class, of Afro-Caribbean, Indian, Pakistani, Bangladeshi, or Sri Lankan descent.

†For example, Brooks and Singh (1979), Jeffery (1976), Khan (1977) and Watson (1977). For an analysis of the sociological contribution to race relations in Britain see Bourne (1980) and also Gilroy (1980).

geographic work in ethnic social segregation. The result is a body of work which lacks theoretical rigour. Thus, without a developed notion of power relations, the 'choice/constraint' concept operates as a sliding scale with various positions being adopted on it according to particular pieces of empirical evidence. For those who would stress 'choice' (e.g. Dahya, 1974; Kearsley and Srivastava, 1974; Peach, 1975b; Robinson, 1979; Phillips, Ch.5), the tendency is towards a pluralistic conception, thus Peach (1979; p.83) talks of 'ethnic villages'. What this does not account for, of course, is that power in society is not distributed on a pluralistic basis. On the opposite side of the scale, the 'constraints' of outside society have been stressed (Gray, 1975, 1976; Pahl, 1975). However, by attributing the causal mechanism of black disadvantage to *individual* attitudes and/or small group prejudice/exclusion (racialism), the fundamental role of institutionalized racism is missed. This limited focus can only discover one form of racial oppression, i.e. prejudice. It cannot detect racism in actions, sentiments and systematic practices usually thought of as non-racist (see Blauner, 1972; Ch. 1 and Wellman, 1977; Ch. 1). Thus, managerialist studies tend to focus upon the racialism of actors and gatekeepers rather than the ways in which racism is mediated through them (Duncan, 1977; Williams, 1978, 1979). The research reveals once again, only the outcome of processes and not the processes themselves. Peach's (1968) work shows well the connection between black (West Indian) migration to Britain and the requirements of British capital, but stopped short of a class analysis which could have revealed the systematic process of exploitation.

As is the case with the differing approaches of 'spatial sociology' above, Peach's analysis of the four main stages in the geographical contribution to the spatial analysis—'macro-scale', 'descriptive', 'dissimilarist' and 'predictive models'—are all firmly structured by the empiricist framework. A point made by Harvey in 1972 still remains valid.

> We have enough information already and it is a waste of energy and resources to spend our time on such work. In fact mapping even more evidence of man's patent inhumanity to man is counter-revolutionary in the sense that it allows the bleeding-heart liberal to pretend that he is contributing to a solution when in fact he is not.
>
> Harvey (1972; p.10)

By ignoring the economic basis of society and by treating 'race relations' as a discrete 'area' of the social totality capable of being studied in isolation, the social geography of ethnic social segregation has both re-created the textual problems symptomatic of the structural contradictions within the empiricist tradition, and contributed to a 'tradition' of 'race relations' which mystifies the real conditions of existence. An alternative framework is needed in which the unresolved and unstated questions discussed above, can be raised in forms capable of resolution.

The Marxist tradition:
humanism, structuralism and the problem of determination

The alternative framework considered in this paper is based upon a Marxist analysis. Against the atomistic conception of totality, Marxism holds that the whole is the structured interdependence of its parts, "Society is not merely an aggregate of individuals; it is the sum of relations in which individuals stand to one another" (Marx, 1973; p.265). Men and women are not born as 'individuals' but are cast into pre-constituted, antagonistic class relations, and "The history of all hitherto existing society is the history of class struggles" (Marx and Engels, 1977; p.38).

History is motored by the contradictions created by the mode of production—in capitalism, the basic contradiction is that between the forces and relations of production. It is through the transitions and phases of development of the mode of production (MOP), that classes come to be economically constituted. However, the proposition that the economic is reflected in the superstructure in a systematic way, leads to a reductionism which cannot explain the development of capitalism since Marx. Central to this debate upon determination are the notions of 'contradiction' and 'dialectic'. In his essay, *Contradiction and over-determination*, Althusser (1969) argues that although the contradiction between the forces and relations of production provides the determinacy in the last instance, it is not possible to 'think' the capitalist MOP as if the capital/labour contradiction is reflected simply and in an unmediated way, in each part of the superstructure. Rather, the levels of the social formation must be thought of as relatively autonomous, i.e. with their own specificity and internal history. Thus, the economic determines the complex unity of instances in the social totality in the last instance, but their relative autonomy ensures that contradictions are both determined *and* determining. This is the basis of Althusser's notion of 'overdetermination' which stands firmly in opposition to any form of economic reductionism (see Althusser, 1969; p.206).

It has been noted above that the question of men and women's control or lack of control over their own destiny, is central to philosophy. In Marxism this debate centres on the question of the determination of the economic base upon the superstructure of society. It is the contention of this paper that the 'choice/constraint' concept represents a partial, contradictory and unsatisfactory attempt to address the question of determination. This is directly attributable to the empiricist framework from which it has resulted. The primary task of the theorization of the concept, therefore, lies in its incorporation within the Marxist framework and centrally, within the debate upon determination.

Structuralism and humanism are two approaches to this problem which stand in opposition to one another.* The humanist position, seen in the work of E. P. Thompson, stresses the role played by human agency in the process of history. Thompson argues that it is through 'experience' that men and women convert objective determinations into subjective initiatives. Formal theory is distrusted as being too static—concepts should be viewed as expectations rather than as rules.

---

*It is important to point out that both structuralism and humanism oppose the economism of 'manifesto' or 'vulgar' Marxism. This opposition is characterized by Althusser's notion of 'over-determination' and Thompson's use of the category of 'experience' (Thompson, 1978; p.362). For a discussion of these three approaches, see Johnson (1979) and Anderson (1980).

Structuralism however, emphasizes the part played by ideology in structuring thought and consciousness. In the work of Althusser, 'experience' is regarded as an illusion—men and women are instead the prisoners of ideology.* Therefore, knowledge of the real can be produced only through theory, i.e. in thought. In the context of this paper, the two positions may be seen to represent theoretical conceptualizations of 'choice' (the humanist stress upon 'experience') and 'constraint' (the structuralist conception of determination).

The main strength of humanism may be seen in the focus on the specificity of historical 'moments' and on concrete class experience. In his preface to his 1963 work, Thompson states,

> 'I am seeking to rescue the poor stockinger . . . from the enormous condescension of posterity . . . They lived through these times of acute social disturbance and we did not. Their aspirations were valid in terms of their own experience . . .'
>
> Thompson (1963; pp.12-13)

The danger in this approach lies in the drift towards empiricism and lack of adequate theorization. Thompson (1978; p.387) has recommended the use of Hexter's 'reality rule'—knowledge of the real is that which seems the most reasonable explanation according to the evidence. In so doing, Thompson moves away from the central tenets of Marx's method—the need for abstraction, and the realization that social relations necessarily appear in a mystified form. The strength of Althusserianism therefore lies in the recognition that the form in which the capitalist mode of production is manifested, conceals the real conditions of existence. This is not simply illusion—the process of concealment is a necessary part of the mode of production which could not operate without it. However, the high and sustained level of generalization, which results from Althusser's epistemology (that the production of knowledge must take place entirely within thought), means that the theoretical task is wholly separated from actual situations. No form of verification external to the thought process can break the circularity of his epistemology. As a result of this, the contested process of reproduction is presented in a relatively unproblematic way. This tendency towards the suppression of actual forms of class struggle leads to charges of rationalism and functionalism.†

In the following discussion which attempts to develop ways of 'thinking' of 'choice' and 'constraint' in relation to the social segregation of Blacks in advanced Western capitalist societies, the move towards 'common ground' between humanism and structuralism is attempted.‡ Given that the social totality is, above all, complex, a case can be made for a lower level of generalization to complement the structural analysis. Cues for this may come from humanism's treatment of concrete class experience, the recognition (following Gramsci) of the 'heterogeneity

---

*Represented by the notion of history as ". . . the process without a subject" (Althusser, 1970a; pp.182-183).

†For example, in his essay "Ideology and ideological state apparatuses" (Althusser, 1970b), the *sites* of ideology, e.g. schools, churches, etc., are presented *as ideology*, i.e. as if the process is uncontested.

‡This movement towards a 'common ground' between structuralism and humanism has been informed by Johnson (1979).

of cultures' and the dialectic between ideology and culture situated within the hegemonic struggle (Gramsci, 1971; p.333). Structural determination may then be seen to 'set the limits' ('constraint'), within which, culturally mediated and negotiated actions can occur in the continuous struggle over the process of reproduction ('choice').

Structural determination

A Marxist analysis starts from the economic position of black people in Britain (Berger and Mohr, 1975; Castles and Kosack, 1973; Sivanandan, 1976, 1978, 1980). In the economic boom of the immediate post-war years, British capital needed labour. The resulting migration of West Indian, Indian and Pakistani workers therefore reflected the economic relationship between labour and capital and the specific historical relationship of British colonialism which had left the ex-colonies with large, but unproductive labour forces. These economic ties which had systematically drawn back surplus-value to Britain during the period of imperialism, had now drawn the physical presence of part of that labour power. The immigrant workers acted as replacement labour, taking the unskilled low status jobs that the indigenous working class were increasingly coming to reject. This insertion of black migrant workers into the class structure of Britain calls for an examination, not only of the ensuing relationship between race and class, but also of the specific ways in which racism during this period, has developed and worked, and how these elements have articulated with one another within this conjuncture.

An influential Marxist view has held that racial oppression should be seen as a form of class exploitation and that racism is therefore a variant of class discriminatory practices and ideologies (Cox, 1959; Harris, 1964; Nikolinakos, 1973; Wolpe, 1972). In short, this view subsumes race to class. However, this rather mechanistic interpretation of racism as flowing from, and serving the economic needs of, capital, is not adequately able to explain the post-war British experience. The profits taken from the black migrant workers in their position as an 'underclass' or 'sub-proletariat' below the indigenous working class, had to be balanced against the potential for social disruption engendered by racism and highlighted by the race riots of 1958 in Notting Hill and Nottingham. By the late 1950s, black people in Britain were concentrated at the focal points of the contradiction between profit maximization and social policy, for example in the provision of housing. Lea (1980) argues that the problem for capital—that of retaining a cheap labour force, while at the same time seeking to integrate Blacks into white society to a minimum level at which the needs of social control would be satisfied—explains the contradictory nature of race relations legislation in Britain since 1960, i.e. separate structures for integration (Race Relations Acts) and for control (Immigration Acts). The location of immigrant workers in the class structure of advanced Western capitalist societies is discussed in Castles and Kosack (1973; pp.476–477) and Castells (1975) who rejects the deterministic view,

While uneven development explains why people emigrate, it does not explain why capital is ready to provide jobs for migrant workers in the advanced countries occasionally even in conditions of unemployment. Neither does it explain why the dominant classes introduce a social and political element (immigrant labour) whose presence contradicts their ideology and necessitates more complex mechanisms of social control.

Castells (1975; p.44)

Faced with such complexities and contradictions, a move away from a crude economic determinism must be made by considering that while white racism in advanced capitalist societies principally performs an economic role, this role is played out against a back-drop of specific cultural forms in which non-economic factors have played their parts. The sort of Marxist functionalism which sees ideologies as 'mere artefacts' of the economy (Gabriel and Ben-Tovim, 1976; p.139), fails to grasp the specificity of racial oppression in which race, as a non-economic factor, has a relative autonomy. Racial oppression and class exploitation are therefore different, not only in quantitative but also in qualitative ways, i.e. racial oppression takes place beyond the point of production. So while retaining the fundamental assumption—that racism is a structural relationship by which one racial group subordinates another—it may be more fruitful to consider that although the material basis of existence creates space within the relations of production in which racism can originate, the effect is far from being uni-linear, for once created racism can act back against and change that basis from which it arose (see Genovese, 1971). Racism is not therefore, the inevitable product of the capitalist MOP, but a specific and dynamic ideological form which enables Whites systematically to gain advantages in social, economic and other relationships at the expense of Blacks. This operation is situated in, and helps to re-create, the stratified and discriminatory social totality necessary for the perpetuation of the capitalist MOP (see Henderson, 1978).

Racism is manifested ideologically, but also institutionally, and as personal prejudice. It is through these sets of ideological and cultural practices that consciousness is structured in a profoundly *unconscious* way. Specific 'world views' may then appear to be natural, timeless and obvious, i.e. as 'commonsense'. Whites are thus able to distance themselves from the subordination of Blacks by deflecting blame onto black people themselves. This process is rooted in the real material conditions of existence and is above all *dynamic*, particular forms of racism arising from historically specific conditions. In this way, the deflection of blame onto Blacks has variously been achieved through biological, psychological and cultural arguments in particular societies and conjunctures.

Finally, racism must be seen in the context of the wider struggle for legitimation in which hegemony is sought to be exerted by a provisional alliance of groups/ classes holding the monopoly of power in society, over other groups/classes, so that the legitimacy of the ruling classes appears to be normal. The structuring of consciousness has already been discussed above as a way in which Whites can think of their superordinate position over Blacks as being 'natural'. However, it is also through this structuring process that other non-racial contradictions, manifested at the level of the state, may be in particular circumstances, deflected on to and articulated through race (see Hall *et al.*, 1978; Ch.10).

> The ideas of the ruling class are in every epoch the ruling ideas . . . The class which has the means of material production at its disposal, has control at the same time over the means of mental production . . . The ruling ideas are nothing more than the ideal expression of the dominant material relationships grasped as ideas.
>
> Marx (1970; p.64)

In the class struggle over ideology, hegemony is sought to be exerted so that the legitimacy of the ruling classes appears to be normal. The site of this struggle is the superstructural institutions of the state and civil society. It is through the regulation of the subordinate classes by the State institutions that the reproduction and re-creation of the existing relations of production is achieved. Hegemony has to be won — it is a 'moving equilibrium' (Gramsci, 1971). Racism is therefore one structure within the 'moving equilibrium', a specific form of ideology with its own history(ies). Above all, racism interpellates the lives of men and women and gives their subordination a 'lived reality'.

> . . . racism is not a set of false pleas which swim around in the head. They are not a set of mistaken perceptions. They have their basis in the real material conditions of existence . . . Racism represents the attempt ideologically to construct those conditions, contradictions and problems in such a way that they can be dealt with and deflected in the same moment.
>
> Hall (1978; p.35)

Racism, institutionalized in the education system, the housing market, the law, and so on, represents the systematic structural determinant which sets the limits upon the social actions of black people. To what extent these limits can be pushed back and hegemony overthrown, depends upon the particular relation of forces within the 'moving equilibrium' at any one time. Thus, the ways in which black groups experience their subordination, and the solutions adopted within the limits set ('choice') take place against the background of class struggle.

The experience and consciousness of structured subordination

Within the limits set by the structural operation of racism, there is space in which specific cultural forms can arise. "Culture is the way, the forms, in which groups 'handle' the raw material of their social and material existence" (Hall and Jefferson, 1975; p.10). A culture provides a symbolic ordering of social life which is objectivated in the structures of social organization,

> A social individual, born into a particular set of institutions and relations, is at the same moment born into a peculiar configuration of meanings, which give her access to and locate her within 'a culture'.
>
> Hall and Jefferson (1975; p.11)

It is in this way that the institutions, systems of belief, mores and customs of, for example, Mirpuris in Britain, not only differ from those of West Indian groups, but also other Asian groups. There exists a 'heterogeneity of cultures' (Gramsci, 1971).

However, the spaces inhabited by these cultures do not exist in a vacuum; they are undercut and crucially 'shot through' by the wider system of the social relations of capitalism. ". . . cultures are differentially ranked, and stand in opposition to one another, in relations of domination and subordination along a scale of 'cultural power' " (Hall and Jefferson, 1975; p.11). Under these conditions, forms of actions which arise are *negotiated*-created under conditions of subordination. Race is the form through which the black working class, ". . . 'live', experience, make sense of and thus come to a consciousness of their structural subordination" (Hall *et al.*, 1978; p.347). Because of this, the forms of resistance/opposition/compliance, are primarily expressed *through* race. The subordinated culture comes to experience itself in the terms laid down by the dominant culture, and the ideas of the ruling class become the basis of ideology. Cultural domination therefore seeks to negate the oppressed person's or group's self-definitions and replace them with alternatives framed from the culture of the oppressor. Racism's tendency is to destroy culture and ethnicity, but in so doing the contradiction becomes apparent whereby, in response to racism, resistance is primarily expressed *culturally*, e.g. Ras Tafari (see Campbell, 1980). It should be reiterated that it is these cultural/ethnic values which adapt and transform those 'objective' sources of black cultural forms in Britain, namely, relative poverty and lower-class position. As Blauner notes, ". . . Racial oppression provides the basis for a more elaborate and more ethnic cultural response than does class exploitation" (Blauner, 1972; p.133).

Black working class cultural forms are therefore distinct from one another, forming as they do, part of the overall heterogeneity of working class culture. The particular forms of negotiated actions vary according to the possibilities within each group's existing cultural patterns. The process is dynamic, it is a progressing and a lived experience, but the fundamental point is that a culture can never 'handle' raw materials wholly of its own making. Asian 'migrant' culture which experienced racial oppression through overseas colonization is therefore the result of processes very different from those of the Afro-Caribbean experience—a more complete cultural domination through transportation and slavery. The extent to which a black consciousness may develop in Britain through the common experience of racial oppression must depend upon it being the product of organized theoretical/practical action by Blacks (Sivanandan, 1977). These will be acts of self-definition which must exclude Whites.

Geographers of ethnic social segregation have to a large extent, focused their attention on the roles played by black cultures in Britain, in the perpetuation of (residential) segregation (Dahya, 1974, Kearsley and Srivastava, 1974, Phillips, Ch.5; Robinson, 1979; and others). Thus, Robinson's socio-spatial study of Asian groups in Blackburn shows the heterogeneity of cultural groupings and the importance of place and locality in the formation of these groups.

However, by not fully considering the structural nature of subordination and the way in which this is lived out and experienced in the space won, the crucial aspect of the *negotiation* of those cultural forms is missed. Thus, 'return migration orientation' can be seen as a negotiated solution to the migrant workers' position in a racist society—as a support for day to day living drawing upon their 'cultural framework'. In these ways, the formation of 'ethnic/cultural colonies' by the migrant workers was partly a reflection of defensive strategy. But it also represented the winning of cultural space to provide a concrete [*sic*] base in which negotiated cultural strategies could develop. What I want to stress, is that the processes involved in 'ethnic' residential segregation cannot be viewed as if they take place in a vacuum. Black cultural forms in Britain do not involve an unproblematic 'importation' of established norms or 'ways of life'—rather, they are the results of *dynamic* negotiated processes. To argue that Asian groups have rejected British society purely on the basis of their cultural forms alone, is to miss the point that in British society, racism is institutionalized—an ideological form with its basis in the real material conditions of existence. Assimilation, and to a large extent, integration, are therefore not, and never have been, avenues open, "As a collective solution, the option of assimilation has not only been officially closed by white society, but blacks have actively closed the door on it themselves, from the inside, and turned the key" (Hall *et al.*, 1978; p.355). So while it is necessary to stress the centrality of place and locality to black cultural groups, it is vital to see that the notion of place is equally central to racial domination which ultimately depends upon the restriction and control of oppressed groups.

Conclusion

The value of socio-spatial studies lies in their identification of the multitude of differences between the forms of working class culture which have historically arisen, and particularly so in the case of black cultural forms in Britain. In the face of this heterogeneity, the view that economic position determines class cultural forms, in a direct and unmediated way, is shown to be untenable. However, only through the process of abstraction can this complexity be seen as the result, not of non-determination, but overdetermination. Capital must continually strive to reproduce labour in forms which enable it to perpetuate itself (i.e. by the concealment of the extraction of surplus value). It is through this base process, that the complex and contradictory forms of working class culture arise. Attention must be turned around to this process, to the ways in which the state has attempted to create and to maintain the conditions for continued capital accumulation, the particular contradictions which have arisen, and the responses which have been developed. Moves towards such a focus on the state in geography serve to place an ever larger question mark against the tradition of race research in the discipline.* White academics with an interest in race must relinquish their self-appointed role as the 'translators' of black cultures, in favour of analyses of white society, i.e. of racism. The task of academic research connected directly to Blacks in terms of action and consciousness can only be attempted by black workers involved in particular

*Particularly by Harvey (1973), also Bunge (1971) and Pahl (1970), and recently by Johnston (1980, Ch. 10).

struggles in which the dialectical relationship between theory and practice can be fully explored.

In the present crisis of British capitalism, structural unemployment has created a 'reserve army' of black youth. In order that capital may be re-structured, the social relations of production must also be re-structured. The state, through its regulatory institutions, must therefore seek to shape the social relations required for reproduction within the new conjuncture. The creation of the Manpower Services Commission and its 'Youth Opportunities Programme', therefore represent direct State interventions into the process of reproduction. It is against this background that such a rapid rise in youth training and work induction must be seen (see Finn and Markall, 1981). Structurally, black youth in Britain face a similar position to that of their migrant worker parents. Their experience of life in Britain differs in important ways however. Not only have they grown up in 'colonies' where the myths of assimilation and integration are daily exposed, but they have also been inserted into the key institution of the education system. In its coercive and ideological attempts to 'manage' black youth in conditions of structural unemployment, the state must face the contradictions which arise when these attempts take place within the constraints of a racist society. This is not an uncontested process and the state must also face therefore, the potential for growing opposition from groups of black youth (the heterogeneity of black youth should again be stressed) against an acceptance of an unemployed/casual labour future.*

Through the attempt to theorize the 'choice/constraint' concept within a Marxist framework, this paper has tried to suggest ways in which a fuller understanding of race, class and culture might be achieved. Cues provided by this may offer the possibility of the development of a more rigorous theoretical approach. Above all, the study of race must be set within a societal analysis in which the role and nature of the state, the articulation of race and class, the centrality and dynamics of racism, and the forms of cultural/political resistance and/or accommodation, are set within their specific historical and structural settings.

Acknowledgement

I am grateful to Jeff Henderson for his comments on earlier drafts of this paper and to the SSRC whose grant has funded the first year of my research, of which this paper is a reflection.

*The condition of being unemployable holds out the possibility of a rejection of the work ethic, what Hall terms ". . . negative consciousness around the condition of being unemployed" (Hall *et al.*, 1978; p356). For a fuller description of the forms of cultural resistance to habituation, see Henderson and Cohen (1979) and Hall *et al.* (1978; Ch. 10). Whether or not such forms can become the basis for a *class* strategy is a crucial question.

References

Althusser, L. (1969). "For Marx". Penguin, Harmondsworth.

Althusser, L. (1970a). Marx's relation to Hegel. *In* "Politics and History", (L. Althusser, ed. 1972). New Left Books, London.

Althusser, L. (1970b). Ideology and ideological state apparatuses. *In* "Lenin and Philosophy and Other Essays", (L. Althusser, ed., 1971). New Left Books, London.

Althusser, L. and Balibar, E. (1968). "Reading Capital". New Left Books, London.

Anderson, P. (1980). "Arguments within English Marxism". New Left Books, London.

Berger, J. and Mohr, J. (1975). "A Seventh Man". Penguin, Harmondsworth.

Blauner, R. (1972). "Racial Oppression in America". Harper and Row, New York.

Blumer, H. (1969). "Symbolic Interactionism". Prentice Hall, Englewood Cliffs.

Bourne, J. (1980). Cheerleaders and ombudsmen: the sociology of race relations in Britain. *Race and Class* **21**, 331-352.

Brooks, D. and Singh, K. (1979). Pivots and presents. *In* "Ethnicity at Work", (S. Wallman, ed.). Macmillan, London.

Bunge, W. (1971). "Fitzgerald: Geography of a Revolution". Schenkman, Cambridge.

Burgess, E. W. (1925). The growth of the city: an introduction to a research project. *In* "The City", (R. E. Park and E. W. Burgess, eds). University of Chicago Press.

Campbell, H. (1980). Rastafari: culture of resistance. *Race and Class* **22**, 1-22.

Castells, M. (1975). Immigrant workers and class struggles in advanced capitalism: the western European tradition. *Politics and Society* **5**, 33-66.

Castles, S. and Kosack, G. (1973). "Immigrant Workers and Class Struggle in Western Europe". Oxford University Press for the Institute of Race Relations, London.

Comte, A. (1858). "The Positive Philosophy of Auguste Comte". 2 volumes. Chapman and Hall, London.

Cox, O. C. (1959). "Caste, Class and Race". Monthly Review Press, New York.

Cressey, P. F. (1938). Population succession in Chicago 1898-1930. *American Journal of Sociology* **44**, 59-69.

Dahya, B. (1974). The nature of Pakistani ethnicity in industrial cities in Britain. *In* "Urban Ethnicity", (A. Cohen, ed.). Tavistock, London.

Duncan, O. D. and Duncan, B. (1955). Residential distribution and occupational stratification. *American Journal of Sociology* **60**, 493-503.

Duncan, S. (1977). "Alienation and Explanation in Human Geography". Discussion Paper No. 63, Department of Geography, London School of Economics.

Durkheim, E. (1964). "The Division of Labor in Society". Free Press, New York.

Fenton, S. (1980). 'Race realtions' in the sociological enterprise (a review article). *New Community* **8**, 162-168.

Finn, D. and Markall, G. (1981). 'There's work to be done'?—the Manpower Services Commission and Youth Unemployment. *In* "Working for Capital", (J. Henderson, ed.). Routledge and Kegan Paul, London.

Gabriel, J. and Ben-Tovim, G. (1978). Marxism and the concept of racism. *Economy and Society* **7**, 118-154.

Genovese, E. (1971). "In Red and Black: Marxian explorations in Southern and Afro-American History". Pantheon, New York.

Gilroy, P. (1980). Managing the 'underclass', a further note on the sociology of race relations in Britain. *Race and Class* **22**, 47-62.

Gramsci, A. (1971). "Selections from the Prison Notebooks". Lawrence and Wishart, London.

Gray, F. (1975). Non-explanation in urban geography. *Area* **7**, 228-235.

Gray, F. (1976). Selection and allocation in council housing. *Transactions, Institute of British Geographers N.S.* **1**, 34-46.

Hall, S. (1978). Racism and reaction. *In* "Five Views of Multi-racial Britain". Commission for Racial Equality, London.

Hall, S. and Jefferson, T., eds. (1975). "Resistance through Rituals". Hutchinson, London.

Hall, S., Critcher, C., Jefferson, T., Clarke, J. and Roberts, B. (1978). Policing the Crisis: Mugging, the State, and Law and Order. Macmillan, London.

Harris, M. (1964). "Patterns of Race in the Americas". Walker, New York.

Harvey, D. (1972). Revolutionary and counter-revolutionary theory in geography and the problem of ghetto formation. *Antipode* **4**, 1-13.

Harvey, D. (1973). "Social Justice and the City". Arnold, London.

Henderson, J. (1978). Philip Randolph and the dilemmas of socialism and black nationalism in the United States, 1917-1941. *Race and Class* **20**, 143-160.

Henderson, J. and Cohen, R. (1979). "Work, Culture and the Dialectics of Proletarian Habituation". Papers in Urban and Regional Studies No. 3, University of Birmingham, Centre for Urban and Regional Studies.

Jeffery, P. (1976). "Migrants and Refugees". Cambridge University Press.

Johnson, R. (1979). Three problematics: elements of a theory of working-class culture. *In* "Working Class Culture", (J. Clarke, C. Critcher and J. Johnson, eds). Hutchinson, London.

Johnston, R. J. (1980). "City and Society: an Outline for Urban Geography". Penguin, Harmondsworth.

Jones, E. (1956). The distribution and segregation of Roman Catholics in Belfast. *Sociological Review N.S.* **4**, 167-189.

Jones, P. N. (1967). "The Segregation of Immigrant Communities in Birmingham, 1961." Occasional Papers in Geography No. 7, University of Hull.

Jones, P. N. (1970). Some aspects of the changing distribution of coloured immigrants in Birmingham 1961-1966. *Transactions, Institute of British Geographers* **50**, 199-219.

Jones, P. N. (1976). Colored minorities in Birmingham, England. *Annals, Association of American Geographers* **66**, 89-103.

Jones, T. P. and McEvoy, D. (1978). Race and space in cloud-cuckoo land. *Area* **10**, 162-166.

Khan, V. S. (1977). The Pakistanis: Mirpuri villagers at home and in Bradford. *In* "Between Two Cultures", (J. Watson, ed.). Blackwell, Oxford.

Kearsley, G. W. and Srivastava, S. R. (1974). The spatial evolution of Glasgow's Asian community. *Scottish Geographical Magazine* **90**, 110-124.

Lazersfeld, P. and Rosenburg, M. eds (1962). "The Language of Social Research". Free Press, New York.

Lea, J. (1980). The contradictions of the sixties race relations legislation. *In* "Permissiveness and Control", (National Deviancy Conference, ed.). Macmillan, London.

Lee, T. R. (1973). Immigrants in London: trends in distribution and concentration 1961-1971. *New Community* **2**, 145-159.

Lee, T. R. (1977). "Race and Residence: the Concentration and Dispersal of Immigrants in London". Oxford University Press.

Lee, T. R. (1978). Race, space and scale. *Area* **10**, 365-367.

McKenzie, R. D. (1929). Ecological succession in the Puget Sound region. *Publications of the American Sociological Society* **23**, 60-80.

Marx, K. (1970). "The German Ideology". Lawrence and Wishart, London.

Marx, K. (1973). "Grundrisse". Penguin, Harmondsworth.

Marx, K. and Engels, F. (1977). "Manifesto of the Communist Party" 15th ed. Progress Press, Moscow.

Mead, G. H. (1934). "Mind, Self and Society". University of Chicago Press.

Mellor, R. (1977). "Urban Sociology in an Urbanised Society". Routledge and Kegan Paul, London.

Nikolinakos, M. (1973). Notes on an economic theory of racism. *Race* **14**, 365-381.

Pahl, R. E. (1970). Poverty and the urban system. *In* "Spatial Policy Problems of the British Economy", (M. Chisholm and G. Manners, eds). Cambridge University Press.

Pahl, R. E. (1975). "Whose City?" 2nd edn. Penguin, London.

Park, R. E. (1916). The city: suggestions for the investigation of human behavior in the urban environment. *In* "The City", (R. E. Park and E. W. Burgess, eds, 1925). University of Chicago Press.

Park, R. E. (1926). The urban community as a spatial pattern and a moral order. *In* "The Urban Community", (E. W. Burgess, ed.). University of Chicago Press.

Park, R. E. (1950). "Race and Culture". Free Press, New York.

Park, R. E. and Burgess, E. W. (eds) (1925). "The City". University of Chicago Press.

Parsons, T. and Bales, R. (1956). "Family, Socialization and the Interaction Process". Routledge and Kegan Paul, London.

Peach, C. (1968). "West Indian Migration to Britain: A Social Geography". Oxford University Press for the Institute of Race Relations, London.

Peach, C. (ed.) (1975a). "Urban Social Segregation". Longman, London.

Peach, C. (1975b). Immigrants in the inner city. *Geographical Journal* **141**, 372-379.

Peach, C. (1979). Comment on race in cloud-cuckoo land. *Area* **11**, 82-84.

Rex, J. (1970). The concept of race in sociological theory. *In* "Race and Racialism", (S. Zubaida, ed.). Tavistock, London.

Rex, J. and Moore, R. (1967). "Race, Community and Conflict' A Study of Sparkbrook". Oxford University Press for the Institute of Race Relations, London.

Rex, J. and Tomlinson, S. (1979). "Colonial Immigrants in a British City". Routledge and Kegan Paul, London.

Robinson, V. (1979). "The Segregation of Asians within a British City: Theory and practice". Geography Research Paper No. 22, Oxford.

Simmel, G. (1971). The metropolis and mental life. *In* "Georg Simmel on Individuality and Social Forms", (D. N. Levine, ed.). University of Chicago Press.

Sivanandan, A. (1976). "Race, Class and the State: The Black Experience in Britain". Institute of Race Relations, London.

Sivanandan, A. (1977). The liberation of the black intellectual *Race and Class* **19**, 329-343.

Sivanandan, A. (1978). "From Immigration Control to 'Induced Repatriation'". Institute of Race Relations, London.

Sivanandan, A. (1980). "Imperialism in the Silicon Age". Institute of Race Relations, London.

Spencer, H. (1967). "Principles of Sociology". 2 volumes. University of Chicago Press.

Sumner, W. G. (1906). "Folkways". Ginn, Boston.

Thompson, E. P. (1963). "The Making of the English Working Class". Penguin, Harmondsworth.

Thompson, E. P. (1978). "The Poverty of Theory and Other Essays". Merlin Press, London.

Tönnies, F. M. A. (1955). "Community and Association". Routledge and Kegan Paul, London.

Watson, J. L. (ed.) (1977). "Between Two Cultures". Blackwell, Oxford.

Weber, M. (1968). "Economy and Society" 3 volumes. Bedminster Press, New York.

Wellman, D. (1977). "Portraits of White Racism". Cambridge University Press.

Williams, P. (1978). Urban managerialism: a concept of relevance? *Area* **10**, 236-240.

Williams, P. (1979). Urban managerialism: an overview with special reference to housing. Paper presented to the SSRC seminar series on Social Geography and the City.

Wirth, L. (1928). "The Ghetto". University of Chicago Press.

Wolpe, H. (1972). Industrialism and race in South Africa. *In* "Race and Racialism", (S. Zubaida, ed.). Tavistock, London.

TEN

The state and the study of social geography

R. J. JOHNSTON

Department of Geography, University of Sheffield, UK

Social geographers prefer to avoid placing any clearly-defined boundaries around their sphere of influence. Thus Jones introduced his *Readings in Social Geography* by stating that "A subject dealing with so wide a topic as the spatial component of human behaviour is not easy to define" (Jones, 1975; p.1), and implicitly agreeing with Buttimer (1969) that social geography has "neither a unified concept nor even an agreed content". However, he provides a definition that "social geography involves the understanding of the patterns which arise from the use social groups make of space as they see it, and of the processes involved in making and changing such patterns" (Jones, 1975; p.7), and this is maintained in a later book (Jones and Eyles, 1977; p.6), whose co-author provides an alternative focus—"the analysis of the social patterns and processes arising from the distribution of, and access to, scarce resources" (Eyles, 1974; p.29). Their joint work considers four themes: the meanings that social groups attach to space; the identification of order in the social use of space, especially within urban areas; the understanding of the processes which bring about this spatial order; and the identification of the spatial aspects of social problems, along with suggestions for their amelioration (see also Jones, 1980).

In order to discuss the state in the context of social geography some definition of subject matter is needed. That employed here separates human geography into economic and social geography. Economic geography, it is contended, is the study of *production* and *distribution* whereas social geography is the study of *consumption*, whether by individuals or by groups. That this distinction is as artificial as any other is immediately recognized. The allocation of distribution to economic geography is not entirely satisfactory, since although some aspects of distribution—via the wholesale and retail sectors, for example—are clearly economic (within a capitalist society, which is the only type considered here), others, such as the provision of public welfare services, are not. This criticism is not crucial, however. Much more fundamental as a criticism is the implicit separation of consumption from production/ distribution in a capitalist society where the three are so strongly interdependent. Consumption, according to certain holistic approaches, comprises two components: that which is necessary for the reproduction of the working class and that which reflects the appropriation and personal use of surplus value by the capitalist class.

Some presentations of the content of social geography (such as Jones, 1975, 1980) include elements of what is widely termed cultural geography, especially in the USA. This includes not only work on the inter-relationships between social groups and their physical environments—with its roots in the Berkeley School under Carl Sauer—but also more recent excursions into phenomenology, existentialism, and idealism. Such work is excluded from the discussion here, in part for lack of space and in part because the links between such humanistic orientations and the more holistic approaches of the radical/structural/Marxist schools are not clear. Ley (1978) has argued that the latter treat man as an automaton. Others would counter that this is not so, but rather that the beliefs and values of men and social groups (including their religions) are manipulated by the current social formation. The state is central to such manipulation, because of its ideological importance (Abercrombie *et al.*, 1980), and its relationship to this aspect of social geography clearly requires detailed study elsewhere.

The contents of a geography of consumption

Having provided a general definition of social geography it is necessary to outline the topical investigations which the field incorporates. A survey of the contents of social geography texts—including the relevant parts of books on 'welfare geography', which has clear connections with the definition provided here (Smith, 1977)—indicates a concern with four main topics: the consumption of housing, the consumption of social services, the consumption of other services (in leisure, for example), and the distribution of social problems which presumably reflects under-consumption (relative to some, usually undefined, level of needs). Neither this list nor the tentative definition provided by Jones (1975, 1980) covers all of the subject matter variously identified as social geography. Indeed, some of the work discussed elsewhere in this book on social interaction within and between defined ethnic groups fits very uneasily into those categorizations. However, as Brown argues (Ch. 9), such social processes are constrained by spatial patterns, notably those relating to the operations of the housing market and the creation of group identities.

The present section outlines a classification of consumption goods which incorporates the role of the state in their provision, and which provides a foundation for studying social geography. There seems little need to stress here the importance of the state to any geographical study, whether economic or social. At the empirical level there have been several recent demonstrations of the size and growth of the public sector in capitalist societies (e.g. Johnston, 1979a) and these have been the focus of much public debate in recent years. The influence of the public sector is widespread and significant in most aspects of modern economy and society.

The classification employs a very wide definition of the term goods, to encompass not only goods and services but also state controls. It comprises the following three elements:

(1) *Goods provided solely by the private sector.* Foremost in this, at least in some countries (notably the USA among capitalist nations), is private sector housing. Nevertheless, in nearly all countries the public sector in some ways influences aspects of the provision of such goods—its price, its type, its standards, and its location. Indeed, because of controls on location (even in the USA, only one large city—Houston—has no zoning scheme) it is difficult to identify many goods which fall entirely into this class. The provision of primary medical care by physicians in the USA is perhaps a clear example (although the standard of care is overseen by state bodies), but the case made previously concerning the widespread role of the state is supported by the difficulties encountered in identifying goods provided solely by the private sector.

(2) *Goods provided entirely by the public sector.* In contrast to the previous class, these ought to be more easily identified. Certainly there are goods which are provided exclusively by the state: national defence (excluding mercenary armies) and the administration of justice (except by vigilante groups and organizations such as the Ku Klux Klan) are prime examples. But many of the goods provided by the state are also, often to a small extent and for a limited population only, available in the private sector. Protection of individuals and property is provided by private security agencies as well as by police forces; there are private as well as public ambulance and fire services, pension schemes, hospitals and so on. Thus although the influence of the state extends into most aspects of its citizens' consumption, it monopolizes relatively few.

(3) *Goods provided jointly by the private and public sectors.* The discussion of the previous two classes suggests that this last must be by far the largest. It ranges from goods in which the joint provision involves equal partnership to those in which one of the sectors is a small minority provider only. It also includes those goods provided by the private sector, within constraints defined by the public sector: the main example of such constraints is the planning system, with its basis in zoning, but there are many others, such as that used by the British National Health Service to encourage general practitioners to move to 'under-doctored areas'.

The classification of goods into public, private, and mixed in terms of their origin must be supplemented by a second, based on their availability. Three main classes are involved:

(A) *Pure goods.* These are those which are equally provided for all of the members of the relevant society (within some territorial boundary). The most frequently cited example comes from the public sector—national defence. Others include public broadcasting systems, which are accessible to all people wherever they live; private sector broadcasting systems are in many cases pure goods too.

(B) *Impure goods.* These cannot be provided equally to all individuals since their provision is locationally specific and some people are more accessible to the chosen locations than are others. In the public sector, facilities such as hospitals, parks, and fire stations are often presented as examples of impure public goods: those living close to fire stations have, it is assumed, higher levels of protection (since the fire service can respond more rapidly to calls for assistance, with consequent higher

TABLE I

Classification of goods and services considered in social geography

		Mode of provision		
		Public	Joint	Private
Availability	Pure	National defence Public broadcasting Local government		Private broadcasting
	Impure	Public facilities (e.g. hospitals)	Residential area characteristics	Health (e.g. physicians in USA)
	Impurely distributed	Police services Welfare state payments	'Public' transport services	Funds for house purchase

probabilities of success in containing a fire) than do those living further away. In the private sector, proximity to desirable neighbours is presented—implicitly at least—as an impure good, as is distance from undesirables; much of the existing theory of urban residential patterns is based on the inter- and intra-class conflict over such desiderata (Johnston, 1980a).

(C) *Impurely distributed goods*. These fall between the first two classes. They comprise goods which are, theoretically at least, generally available to all but are not provided equally for all because of territorial discrimination: unlike impure goods, they are not locationally fixed and their unequal provision reflects distributional policies, which may be based on political considerations in the public sector (Johnston, 1979b). Most of the examples come from that sector: they include different densities of provision, as with policing services, and equal provision (in unemployment benefit levels, for example) where unequal provision is needed because of other factors (such as variations in the cost of living between places).

Both of these classifications are characterized by some fuzziness at the edges, and it is not altogether clear where some aspects of social geography should be placed. (The pure public goods cited—national defence and public broadcasting systems—may be pure goods within the territory for which they are intended, for example, but outside that territory spillover effects may make them impure goods—neither public nor private but provided by a third party—in adjacent societies.) The classifications (Table I) are sufficient, however, to provide a basis for the discussion here.

The state in capitalist society

Social scientists are now focusing considerable attention on the role and actions of the state in capitalist societies and are seeking viable theories relating to those topics. Among geographers, this has led to a broadening of the range of topics generally considered under the head 'government influences', which has commonly meant regional development policies. (For some reason, town and country planning is rarely presented in the same way.) Much of the theoretical work in other social sciences has a strong structuralist/Marxist flavour, and most attempts by geographers to operate in this area have been pitched at relatively abstract levels (as in the papers by Scott and Roweis (1977) on the nature of town planning and by Dear and Clark (1978) on the state); there are, indeed, considerable difficulties in relating some of the theories to concrete realizations (Johnston, 1980b).

Four views of the state

The volume of work on the state in recent years has produced a plethora of competing theoretical orientations, and it is neither practicable nor sensible to attempt a full review of them here. A brief outline of the major theoretical orientations (much of which is based on Saunders, 1980) provides sufficient background for the remainder of this essay. Four main theoretical orientations are reviewed.

The instrumentalist position: the state as an arm of the capitalist class
This, perhaps the 'crudest' of the theories to be reviewed, presents the State as separate from the two main classes (capitalist and working) in capitalist society but to all intents and purposes as an element in the capitalist manipulation of the working class: Marx and Engels provide support for this in their statement in *The Communist Manifesto* that "The executive of the modern state is but a committee for managing the common affairs of the whole bourgeoisie". Thus the state is an arm of the capitalist class and its actions are undertaken to bolster that class's power.

This theoretical position does not claim that the state apparatus is necessarily a puppet of the ruling capitalist class. Nor does it claim that every state action is pro-capitalist class and anti-working class; in order to protect the long-term interests of the former it may be necessary to make short-term concessions to the latter (see Piven and Cloward, 1972). Instead the case is made (notably by Miliband, 1969) that the composition of the state sector—both the elected representatives who form the governments and the permanent bureaucrats who operate the system—is dominated by recruits either from the capitalist class itself or from those members of the non-capitalist class (mainly the managers and professionals of the upper-middle-class in Weberian terms) who are strongly orientated towards capitalist objectives and maintenance of the status quo. (Some would argue that the loyalty and support of the managerial and professional classes to the capitalist cause is 'bought', both explicitly through incomes and implicitly through privileges—such as control of entry to their ranks.) Thus there are close links—both at a personal and at a group level—between the capitalist class and the operators of the state which allows the former, usually discreetly and often only implicitly—because of a shared consciousness—to manipulate the state to its own ends.

The pluralist position: the state as mediator and arbiter
This position presents the state as an independent sector of capitalist society which reacts to the many demands made on it for support (of various kinds) from the wide range and great number of separate interest groups: these bring either specific demands or requests for assistance in settling disputes. Central to the position are the contentions that each class is divided into several sectional interest groups, and that no one interest group dominates the state mechanism for long periods of time, so that the state is neutral with regards to the various claims made on and of it. (The electoral process is considered as a guarantor of that neutrality—the neutrality of the bureaucracy is presumed to follow from its subservience to the elected representatives.)

This pluralist position has two components. The first relates to the operation of the state itself. This is controlled by the group(s) or party(ies) that win elections and thereby earn the right to define state policy and action. The second concerns the groups and individuals who are outside the state and trade with it for privileges. In both, some elements within society are better able to compete than are others, and so have greater access to the state and its power. Although this almost inevitably means rule by elites, the pluralist position denies the existence of any consistent class bias.

The managerialist position: the state as independent bureaucracy

According to this position, the machinery of state—both the elected component and the bureaucracy—is operated by a 'class' which is independent of either the capitalist or the working class. The political forces which lead to one group in society capturing the elected component may be based on class interests (in the Marxist sense) but they may not—as with the two main political parties in the USA. Once in control, the holders of power in the state have the autonomy to manage its affairs as they see fit, according to their parituclar value judgements and belief systems.

The structuralist position: the state as economic and political regulator of capitalism

According to this, the state reflects the current system of class relations in society as a whole, and serves to maintain the hegemony of the ruling class, thereby providing the conditions for the continued success of capitalism. It presents itself as representing and serving the interests of the entire society; it fosters disunity among the exploited class, to prevent it challenging the hegemony of the dominant class; and it protects the interests of the latter as a whole by guaranteeing conditions that are favourable to the goal of capital accumulation.

Rapprochement?

These cartoons of four competing theoretical positions do them scant justice; they present the bare outlines of the arguments only. For the current purpose this is sufficient, since the aim here is not to develop one of the theories nor to suggest a major rapprochement between two or more; rather the aim is to evaluate the positions in terms of their relevance to social geography.

Of the four positions, the instrumentalist and the managerialist are insufficient alone to provide a working theory that is valuable to the study of social geography. The instrumentalist position fails for two reasons: first, although it is true that, except in 'revolutionary' situations, the state exists to aid capitalist accumulation, the deterministic argument does not allow any independence for the government and bureaucracy which form the state; and secondly, as the structuralist position indicates, the capitalist class cannot be considered as a homogeneous unit all members of which are seeking identical goals. Capitalism is built on competition and conflict, within the capitalist class as well as between it and the working class; any viable theory of the state must recognize this and must locate the state's role within such conflicts. The managerialist position goes to the other extreme. The state and its managers are not autonomous decision-makers any more than they are automatons; they operate within externally-defined degrees of freedom.

A middle ground is needed, it seems. The pluralist position does not fill it completely, since it suggests that all interest groups have opportunities to get their wishes granted and that power is not inevitably centralized. Casual observation indicates that this is an incorrect representation of capitalist society. This leaves the structuralist position as the most attractive: the state is that body which acts to maintain the present mode of production and social formation by ensuring their legitimation and providing the necessary conditions for their successful operations.

But this is insufficient. As already argued, the capitalist class is not homogeneous. It comprises a series of vested interest groups whose demands, if met, will mean greater success for some capitals than others. Some capitals may always succeed whereas others will invariably fail, thus suggesting a modified instrumentalist position. This is clearly impossible, however—unless monopoly capitalism is to proceed to its logically ultimate conclusion. Different capitals must win at different times, suggesting a modified pluralist position; the determination of who wins, and when, indicates the need to incorporate the managerialist position too, if the aim is to understand particular decisions and patterns.

The arguments of the last paragraph are crucial to social geography if it is accepted that the human geographer's basic philosophical position is that of the naive realist (Johnston, 1980b). Within the social sciences, the role of the geographer is that of accounting for the patterns on the ground, the actual realizations of the processes being modelled by the various theories of capital and the state (in the capitalist world). For the social geographer, this means describing and accounting for observed geographies of consumption. Part of any account which involves consideration of the role of the state will be provided by the structuralist position. But, as pointed out elsewhere (Johnston, 1980b), although this position accepts that the processes which it describes will lead to spatial patterns, it cannot 'explain' the particular pattern that emerges. For this, the instrumentalist, managerialist and pluralist approaches are necessary, to provide accounts of why particular decisions are made at particular times and places, within the constraints as defined by the structuralist position. The nature of those accounts will vary from study to study: in some, idealism or phenomenology may be used; in others, the methodology of logical positivism can be employed as a descriptive device with no intention—despite the claims of critics (e.g. Gregory, 1980; Sayer, 1979)—of providing either generalizations of universal applicability in space and time or a technology for social control.

There is considerable spatial variability in state activity (Johnston, 1979b). To account for its detailed morphology (as well as its general existence) requires a theory of the state that can tackle both capitalist processes and their concrete realizations. The sructuralist position provides the former; some combination of the pluralist, managerialist and instrumentalist is needed for the latter.

The local state
The preceding discussion in this section has been based entirely on an implicit assumption that the state is conterminous with a national territory: each capitalist country is an independent unit. This is an over-simplification. Above the national territory is a web of inter-national and super-national organizations, some of which

share characteristics with the national state as described here, and indeed are reactions to ongoing trends in the capitalist mode of production. (The European Economic Community is a major example of such organizations.) And within the national territory is a range of subsidiary territories, making up what is often termed the local state. This is of particular relevance to social geography for, although there is no clear-cut division, whereas the national state is primarily responsible for issues relating to production and distribution much of the responsibility for matters concerning consumption is devolved to the local state—albeit in most cases within carefully-designed constraints set nationally (for, as argued by the Thatcher government in Britain, expenditure on consumption, especially the collective consumption controlled by the local state is dependent on activity in the sphere of production). For the social geographer, therefore, there is need not only for a theory of the state in general but also for a theory of the local state in particular.

All four of the positions presented earlier can be applied to the local state. Thus the instrumentalist position (favoured by Cockburn, 1977) views the local state as that arm of capitalism which controls the reproduction of the labour force. The pluralist position has been much favoured by American political scientists, notably in their analyses of 'who rules?' cities there (see, for example, the classic study by Dahl, 1961); the managerialist approach has been propagated in Britain especially, notably by Pahl (e.g. Pahl, 1979) who has stressed the importance of professionals such as local authority housing managers in the allocation of resources for both collective and individual consumption. The structuralist position, favoured by Dear (1981), portrays the local state as part of the mechanism by which the interests of the capitalist class are supported locally through the reproduction of the social formation, the legitimation of the capitalist mode of production, and the obfuscation of class conflict through intra-class manipulations.

Theoretical analyses of the local state are relatively few. Those available, plus the wealth of empirical studies, suggest the need to incorporate the instrumentalist, managerialist and pluralist positions within an approach guided by the structuralist view, in order to meet the needs of the social geographer to account for particular spatial patterns. The arguments for this are basically the same as those presented above.

One of the major criticisms of some approaches to a theory of the state is that they are ahistorical; as Marx made clear, we are all very much constrained by our past. This criticism is particularly valid for approaches to the local state, especially with respect to investigations of an individual country only. National states vary considerably in the powers and autonomy which they grant to the local state, and which they retain the right to remove; the UK government exercises a great deal of central control over local authorities, for example, whereas in the USA there are strict constitutional limits both on the amount of control the federal government can exercise over the constituent States and on the relative autonomy of local governments within States. (The latter are defined by State constitutions.) To appreciate these variations requires a theory of central-local state relations as well as separate (though far from independent) theories of each component of those relations.

The state and the social geography of black–white relations in the USA

A wide range of topics could be used to illustrate both the classification of goods introduced in Table I and the three sub-theories of the state (and the local state) outlined above. No encyclopaedic attempt is made here to cover such a range. Rather a single topic relevant to the general theme of this book is considered and the various approaches to understanding state action are illustrated as relevant to study of that topic.

Instrumentalist and managerialist reactions after the Civil War

The social and spatial segregation of the black and white populations of the USA is a widely-remarked-on element in that country's social geography. The Blacks were brought to the country as slaves, to meet the labour requirements of the southern plantation economy. In the 1860s, the Civil War was fought between the Republic and Confederacy over the slavery issue, and the victory of the northern States led to the passing of the Thirteenth, Fourteenth and Fifteenth Amendments to the US Constitution. Legally, the slaves were emancipated, but more than a century later their achievement of social and economic equality with the white population still seems many decades distant.

Many barriers to the full integration of Blacks into white American society have been employed. In the South, after the armies of occupation had been removed the Whites rapidly asserted their political dominance via the Democratic party. Measures were introduced in the State legislatures to prevent Blacks becoming enfranchised and thus operating the pluralist model to win economic and social gains. These measures were not directed against Blacks *per se*, but against other groups such as illiterates (the basis of the franchise in many States was passing a literacy test), thus bypassing the constitutional requirement that no individual be denied the vote on the basis of race. Thus the local state—both the State governments and the subsidiary local governments—was captured by one group in society, providing an illustration of the value of an instrumentalist approach to studying certain aspects of the problem. At the same time, the local state managers designed an education system which would keep the two races apart: this was the 'separate but equal' system, by which each education authority provided two school systems, one for Blacks and the other for Whites.

For as long as the Blacks remained in the southern States, therefore, it was unlikely that they would achieve full equality with the Whites and complete integration (if not assimilation) into American society. For more than a century, their pluralist participation in local democracy was hindered, and white instrumentalist superiority was maintained. The managers of the local state reflected this superiority in, for example, their operation of the various social security programmes introduced under the New Deal in the 1930s. The structure of these programmes reflected the inability of the federal government to operate social welfare schemes (because of constitutional limitations). Thus the State governments were encouraged to operate such schemes by the offer of matching federal grants to meet part of the costs. State and local governments were given flexibility in how much they paid out in, for example, unemployment benefits and payments to single parents with dependent children. Those in the South chose to be much less generous than their contemporaries elsewhere in the country, thus helping relatively few families to escape from poverty (Wohlenberg, 1976a,b,c); indeed some programmes, such as Medicaid, were not even operated in several southern States. (For a fuller discussion, see Johnston, 1979b.) That such policy decisions by the local state were a clear illustration of managerial racist attitudes is illustrated by Cowart (1969); Piven and Cloward (1972) have suggested that pluralist attempts to rectify this through protest movements have had little lasting success.

Urbanization and spatial segregation

During the twentieth century, large numbers of Blacks have moved from the depressed economic and social conditions of the South to the urban areas, especially to the cities of the nation's manufacturing belt. There, the operation of the housing market—aided and abetted by the local state—has herded them into ghettos and denied them access to many residential areas.

The managerial actions of state bureaucracies have been closely involved in this ghetto creation and maintenance. In some cities, for example, separate black and white residential areas were included in the zoning map of the town plan (Vose, 1959). Thus spatial segregation was imposed via the legal system as well as through the economic operation of the housing market. Similarly, social contact between Blacks and Whites in schools was prevented by the gerrymandering of catchment areas, so that almost all black children attended all-black schools and nearly every white child attended an all-white school. And in many places, the urban managers discriminated against the black residential areas in the provision of public services (Keech, 1968; Salih, 1972; Lineberry, 1977).

As the black populations increased in the metropolitan areas, so their threat to the entrenched white power base grew. Both elements of the pluralist model were open to them—participation in the electoral system and protest against the policies of elected bodies and their managers. One reaction to this threat of potential defeat by Blacks—at least among the more wealthy whites—has been to desert the central cities of US metropolitan areas, leaving them to black majorities. (A considerable number now have elected black mayors, for example Karnig (1976); Welch and Karnig (1979).) The Whites have moved to the suburbs.

Suburbanization is used by many geographers to describe the outward expansion of urban areas and the movement of people and jobs to the urban periphery: the inner boundary of the suburbs is rarely a precise one. But in most parts of the USA that boundary is very clear, for almost all metropolitan areas are clearly demarcated, in their provision of local government, between the central city and the suburbs. The former is a large, single, multi-functional territorial authority; the latter is a zone comprising a large number of separate municipal authorities—some very small, some with populations exceeding 100 000—of which there are more than 100 in some of the largest metropolitan areas. The suburban municipalities are also overlaid by a mosaic of *ad hoc* special purpose districts providing single services only: the most important are the school districts, which are independent in most States. The central cities have many fewer such special districts, and indeed the city government may provide most of the services—such as education—which in the suburbs are provided by *ad hoc* territorial authorities.

In most States, suburban municipalities can be incorporated, according to rules laid down either in the State constitution or by State legislation, at the request of local residents and with the approval of a majority of voters in the prescribed territory. Formation of the municipality involves establishing a separate government to replace that of the county which formerly administered the area.

The reasons for incorporating a suburban municipality are several, but most relate to the independence of its government with regard to certain functions. The most important concern the control of land use and budget. The municipality is the zoning authority with few, if any, constraints imposed by either superior govern- ments (county or State) or *ad hoc* encompassing territorial authorities (regional planning boards). Much of the finance for operating the municipalities—and also the school districts—comes from the property tax, based on the value of local homes and land.

The incorporation of suburban municipalities, the small size of many, and their relatively large number, represents a desire to escape from the pluralist base of political activity in the central cities and to prevent those cities annexing the newly- developing areas. One of the problems with pluralist politics is that you and your particular interest group may lose—in certain conflicts if not in every one. The losses may affect the quality of your life, either directly, through the nature of development around your home, or indirectly, through the demands on your finances made by the property tax. But both can be avoided if you join with your interest group in a separate residential area—perhaps with necessary commercial and other services—and incorporate yourselves as a separate municipality. As a consumption class, this gives you control over the local land use—not only its arrangement but what is allowed and what is not; the property taxes that you pay relate only to the services which you want to provide for yourselves and are not used in part to subsidize provision for other consumption classes; and you can decide the form and nature of your local government. (Many American suburbs are governed by small elected commissions and an appointed manager, rather than by a mayor supported by a council whose members represent separate ward interests and therefore are involved in pluralist politicking; the suburban commissions are usually elected 'at large' rather than as ward representatives, and inter-party contests for the seats are forbidden.)

The small suburban municipality in the USA is comprised, therefore, of the members of a consumption class—usually a relatively high-income one—who have created a separate local government unit in order to gain complete control over their environment; they have replaced the pluralist situation of large territorial units containing a range of consumption classes by the equivalent of an instrumentalist situation in which their local state is an arm of the ruling class in the area. They exercise their instrumentalist aims through policies designed to maintain the exclusive character of their suburb. The zoning scheme is the mechanism used. A high-income suburb can maintain its socio-economic milieu by ensuring that lower-income households, and therefore Blacks, cannot afford to live there. Several ploys are used. Most common are maximum densities and minimum lot sizes—Müller (1976) reports that 64% of the as-yet unbuilt-on land in suburban Philadelphia in 1971 was zoned for a minimum lot size of one acre (33% had a minimum size of two acres)—along with regulations relating to the distance between dwellings and lot boundaries, to dwelling height, and to the proportion of the lot that can be covered by buildings. In addition, many municipalities allow no apartment buildings (38% of all suburban municipalities in Philadelphia), and of those that do many restrict the number of bedrooms (42% in Philadelphia); such restrictions are based on the belief (erroneous, it seems; James and Windsor, 1976) that low-income apartment dwellers, especially those with large families, will make substantial demands on the property taxes paid by other residents. The entire practice is known as exclusionary zoning (Danielson, 1976).

The flexibility of the local government system in most American States has thus enabled high-income consumption classes to create suburban fastnesses for themselves. Others have similarly used this ease of incorporating municipalities, plus the 'home rule' privileges which it brings, to provide instrumentalist strong-holds not for consumption classes but for segments of the capitalist class. Indeed, Gordon suggests that economic interests first indicated the benefits of separate incorporation relative to the costs of annexation into an expanding central city: "After industrialists joined the movement against central city extension, political fragmentation was the natural consequence" (Gordon, 1977; p.77). Thus in many suburban rings there are independent municipalities dominated by non-residential land uses, in which a segment of the capitalist class has established an instrumentalist position and avoids paying taxes to subsidize the services provided in the rest of the metropolitan area. Most of these are dominated by manufacturing industries (e.g. Nelson, 1952), but there are examples of municipalities zoned almost entirely for dairy farming (Fielding, 1962), for cemeteries, and for pleasure parks.

Not all suburban municipalities in the USA are dominated by a single consumption class or by a single segment of the capitalist class. Not all practice exclusionary zoning. Those which are and do are examples of how a political system can be manipulated by class groups (and how the society as a whole, as represented by the State governments, has been unprepared to counter that manipulation) to place themselves in an instrumentalist position, albeit only with respect to the functions of the local state—two of which, the quality of the local residential environment and the nature of local schools—are of fundamental interest to certain consumption classes (Johnston, 1982). They do not produce land use and socio-economic segregation in American metropolitan areas. This would undoubtedly occur whether or not local instrumentalism was possible (as in other capitalist countries and within the American central cities), but suburban political separatism undoubtedly allows the desires for segregation to be pursued.

This use of the local instrumentalism option through the system of local government in most States has allowed the Whites, especially the relatively affluent whites, to escape potential contact with the black population. Use of the zoning power to exclude the poor effectively excludes almost all Blacks, whilst the separate and independent existence of suburban school districts is an excellent 'gerrymandering' of catchment boundaries to ensure that white children do not have to share their classrooms with Blacks. (There is some black suburbanization, of course, but in general the central city/suburban municipality divide has been a major barrier to inter-racial contact in metropolitan areas.)

Pluralist attempts to desegregate: the role of judges as managers

Most analyses of the local state portray the managers as the bureaucrats involved in the day-to-day operations of local government, in many cases obeying the dictates of their political masters. Thus the protest element in the pluralist model involves groups pleading their causes with managers and politicians, both of whom are involved in the issues concerned: they are required to act as judges of their own policies, and to alter them if the case of the protesters is upheld.

In the USA, pluralist protesters have access—in certain situations—to another set of managers. These are the judges of the country's court systems; the most important are the nine members of the federal Supreme Court, who form the ultimate board of appeal against actions by other managers which involve legal and constitutional issues (Hodder-Williams, 1980). The courts have been widely used throughout American history, and the decisions of the nine judges have been crucial determinants of many details in the evolution of the country's economy, society and polity. In recent years, they have been asked to adjudicate on issues relating to the residential and educational segregation of Blacks.

Most of the cases brought through the courts, and eventually reaching the Supreme Court, have involved interpretations of the clause of the Fourteenth Amendment guaranteeing all citizens "equal protection under the laws". Thus protagonists for the black population (notably the National Association for the Advancement of Colored People, whose chief advocate for several years—Thurgood Marshall—became a Supreme Court justice) have claimed that the various educational and zoning policies described above are unconstitutional.

These arguments won initial support and sympathy from the judges. The racial ghettos of city plans were deemed unconstitutional in 1919, for example. Undoubtedly the major victories concerned segregation in schools. The "separate but equal" system operated in the South was found unconstitutional in a classic decision in 1954—*Brown v. Board of Education*—although the integration that the judges insisted on was not introduced rapidly. Many ploys were used by local state managers and instrumentalist politicians to try and avoid introducing integrated schools, and it is unlikely that the judges' decisions would have led to major change without the later support of Congress and the Executive. (Local education authorities were denied federal grants if they did not comply with the integration requirements, for example.) A later decision extended the requirement to integrate schools to northern cities, wherever the gerrymandering of catchment boundaries on a racial basis could be proven.

These successes suggested that the managerial role of the Supreme Court judges was developing into a crucial element in the achievement of desegregation in the USA. More recently, however, the Supreme Court has been much less sympathetic to discrimination cases brought to it under the Fourteenth Amendment. A full account of their decisions cannot be provided here (for a fuller discussion see Anon., 1978; Johnston, 1981). In summary, however, the Court has upheld the zoning policies of suburban municipalities whose intent has been to exclude the poor and whose effect has been to exclude the Blacks. (Perhaps to be more accurate, the Court has not upheld exclusionary zoning but rather it has found no grounds to over-rule it.) Similarly, it has ruled that suburban and central city school districts should not be combined for busing plans, which would produce integration on a metropolitan scale rather than merely within each individual school district. Thus black attempts to 'open-up' the suburbs as residential areas and to prevent white families avoiding school integration by fleeing to all-white suburban school districts have been thwarted.

That the initial gains of the protagonists for an integrated society have not led to further victories in the Supreme Court reflects on the changing nature of that body. Supreme Court justices are appointed by the President—usually "in his own image"—and confirmed by the Senate. They are appointed for life, or at least until they either retire or, very rarely, are impeached. In the late 1960s and early 1970s, a number of seats fell vacant, and the nominees of Richard Nixon occupied them. These new judges are largely conservative in their orientation, and are less disposed to interpret the Fourteenth Amendment sympathetically towards the black population than were their predecessors who formed a majority of the nine in the decade or so surrounding 1970. Thus the attitudes of this group of managers reflects the political opinion of those who appoint them. Because who will get the chance to appoint the managers, and how many, is unknown, it is difficult to estimate whether challenging segregation through the Courts is likely to succeed in the 1980s. Of course, success in the Courts may be outflanked by other actions of the dominant group—the Whites: the Supreme Court cannot change a basic aspect of USA society, only influence the means by which racist desires are put into operation and —perhaps—slowly bring about a change in attitudes.

Conclusions

The study of most topics in social geography is likely to be incomplete if it fails to take account of the role of the state as a regulating influence on the geography of consumption. Such an account must be theoretically informed, and several theories of the state are currently competing to offer the necessary guide. The discussion here has suggested that the structuralist approach offers most for the general interpretation of the state's role as a bulwark of the capitalist mode of production, but that it is insufficient to explain particular spatial patterns. The structuralist approach allows certain degrees of freedom of action—to capital and to state. To understand how these degrees of freedom are manipulated, it is argued, the other three approaches—instrumentalist, managerialist, and pluralist—are needed, in particular situations, to provide a full geographical explanation.

The field of social geography is much broader than can be illustrated in a short chapter, and the illustration presented here provides only a general treatment of the role of the state as an influence on social segregation and integration in the USA. The state itself is divided into many components, some of which have more independence than others, and almost all are influential on the detailed geography of consumption (see, for example, Harvey, 1975, and Checkaway, 1980, on the influence of the national state on suburbanization in the USA). The need for more theoretical work and relevant empirical testing is clear. The time is past when 'government influence' can be considered a residual variable causing deviations from free market forces. The state is central to both economic and social geography —in all parts of the world. Realization of this fact and its incorporation into the main body of geographical work will strengthen the latter accordingly.

Acknowledgement

A grant for a pilot study on which this chapter is based was provided by the Nuffield Foundation, and is gratefully acknowledged.

References

Abercrombie, N., Hill, S. and Turner, B.S. (1980). "The Dominant Ideology Thesis". George Allen and Unwin, London.

Anon. (1978). Developments in the law—zoning. *Harvard Law Review* **91**, 1427-1708.

Buttimer, A. (1969). Social space in interdisciplinary perspective. *Geographical Review* **59**, 417-426.

Checkaway, B. (1980). Large builders, federal housing programmes, and postwar suburbanization. *International Journal of Urban and Regional Research* **4**, 21-45.

Cockburn, C. (1977). "The Local State". Pluto Press, London.

Cowart, A. T. (1969). Anti-poverty expenditures in the American States: a comparative analysis. *Midwest Journal of Political Science* **13**, 219-236.

Dahl, R. E. (1961). "*Who governs?*" Yale University Press, New Haven.

Danielson, M. N. (1976). "The Politics of Exclusion". Columbia University Press, New York.

Dear, M. (1981). A theory of the local state. *In* "Political Studies from Spatial Perspectives", (A. D. Burnett and P. J. Taylor, eds). Wiley, London.

Dear, M. and Clark, G. L. (1978). The state and geographic process: a critical review. *Environment and Planning A* **10**, 173-184.

Eyles, J. (1974). Social theory and social geography. *Progress in Geography* **6**, 22-87.

Fielding, G. J. (1962). Dairying in cities designed to keep people out. *Professional Geographer* **14**, 12-17.

Gordon, D. M. (1977). Class struggles and the stages of American urban development. *In* "The Rise of the Sunbelt Cities", (D. C. Perry and A. J. Watkins, eds). Sage Publications, Beverly Hills.

Gregory, D. (1980). The ideology of control: systems theory and geography. *Tijdschrift voor Economische en Sociale Geografie* **71**, 327-342.

Harvey, D. (1975). The political economy of urbanization in advanced capitalist societies. *In* "The Social Economy of Cities", (G. Gappert and H. M. Rose, eds). Sage Publications, Beverly Hills.

Hodder-Williams, R. (1980). "The Politics of the U.S. Supreme Court". George Allen and Unwin, London.

James, F. J. and Windsor, O. D. (1976). Fiscal zoning, fiscal reforms and exclusionary landuse controls. *Journal, American Institute of Planners* **42**, 130-141.

Johnston, R. J. (1979a). Governmental influences in the human geography of 'developed' countries. *Geography* **64**, 1-11.

Johnston, R. J. (1979b) "Political, Electoral and Spatial Systems". Oxford University Press.

Johnston, R. J. (1980a). "City and Society: An Outline for Urban Geography". Penguin, Harmondsworth.

Johnston, R. J. (1980b). Observations on explanation in human geography. *Transactions, Institute of British Geographers N.S.* **5**, 402-412.

Johnston, R. J. (1981). Conflict, voice, the courts and externalities in American residential areas. *In* "Conflict, Politics and the Urban Scene", (K. R. Cox and R. J. Johnston, eds). Longman, London.

Johnston, R. J. (1982). "The American Urban System: A New Perspective". St Martin's Press, New York.

Jones, E. (1975). Introduction. *In* "Readings in Social Geography", (E. Jones, ed.). Oxford University Press.

Jones, E. (1980). Social geography. *In* "Geography Yesterday and Tomorrow", (E. H. Brown, ed.). Oxford University Press.

Jones, E. and Eyles, J. (1977). "An Introduction to Social Geography". Oxford University Press.

Karnig, A. K. (1976). Black representation on city councils. *Urban Affairs Quarterly* **12**, 223-242.

Keech, W. R. (1968). "The Impact of Negro Voting: the Role of the Vote in the Quest for Equality". Rand McNally, Chicago.

Ley, D. (1978). Social geography and social action. *In* "Humanistic Geography: Prospects and Problems", (D. Ley and M. S. Samuels, eds). Maaroufa, Chicago.

Lineberry, R. L. (1977). "Equity and Urban Policy". Sage Publications, Beverly Hills.

Miliband, R. (1969). "The State in Capitalist Society". Quartet Books, London.

Müller, P. O. (1976). "The Outer City". Resource Paper 75-2. Association of American Geographers Commission on College Geography, Washington, DC.

Nelson, II. J. (1952). The Vernon area, California: a study of the political factor in urban geography. *Annals, Association of American Geographers* **42**, 177-191.

Pahl, R. E. (1979). Socio-political factors in resource allocation. *In* "Social Problems and the City", (D. T. Herbert and D. M. Smith, eds). Oxford University Press.

Piven, F. F. and Cloward, R. A. (1972). "Poor People's Movements". Pantheon Press, New York.

Salih, K. (1972). "Judicial Relief and Differential Provision of Public Goods: A Case Analysis and Certain Prescriptions". Research on Conflict in Locational Decisions Discussion Paper No. 20. Department of Regional Sciences, University of Pennsylvania, Philadelphia.

Saunders, P. (1980). "Urban Politics: A Sociological Approach". Penguin, Harmondsworth.

Sayer, R. A. (1979). Epistemology and conceptions of people and nature in geography. *Geoforum* **10**, 10-44.

Scott, A. J. and Roweis, S. (1977). Urban planning in theory and practice: a re-appraisal. *Environment and Planning A* **9**, 1097-1120.

Smith, D. M. (1977). "Human Geography: A Welfare Approach". Arnold, London.

Vose, C. E. (1959). "Caucasians Only". University of California Press, Berkeley.

Welch, S. and Karnig, A. K. (1979). The impact of black elected officials on urban expenditures and intergovernmental revenue. *In* "Urban Policy Making", (D. R. Marshall, ed.). Sage Publications, Beverly Hills.

Wohlenberg, E. H. (1976a). Interstate variations in A.F.D.C. programs. *Economic Geography* **52**, 254-266.

Wohlenberg, E. H. (1976b). Public assistance effectiveness by states. *Annals, Association of American Geographers* **66**, 440-450.

Wohlenberg, E. H. (1976c). An index of eligibility standards for welfare benefits. *Professional Geographer* **28**, 381-384.

INDEX

Italics refer to citations in References;
numbers followed by 'n' refer to citations in footnotes.

I

J